The Sierra Club Guide to

SKETCHING IN NATURE

NEW EDITION

BOOKS BY CATHY JOHNSON

New Edition

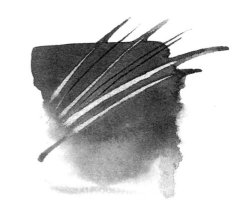

The Sierra Club Guide to
SKETCHING IN NATURE

BY CATHY JOHNSON

SIERRA CLUB BOOKS·SAN FRANCISCO

The Sierra Club, founded in 1892 by John Muir, has devoted itself
to the study and protection of the Earth's scenic and ecological
resources—mountains, wetlands, woodlands, wild shores and
rivers, deserts and plains. The publishing program of the Sierra Club
offers books to the public as a nonprofit educational service in the
hope that they may enlarge the public's understanding of the Club's
basic concerns. The point of view expressed in each book, however,
does not necessarily represent that of the Club. The Sierra Club has
some sixty chapters coast to coast, in Canada, Hawaii, and Alaska.
For information about how you may participate in its programs to
preserve wilderness and the quality of life, please address inquiries
to Sierra Club, 85 Second Street, San Francisco, CA 94105.

www.sierraclub.org/books

Published by Sierra Club Books.

Produced and distributed by The University of California Press
Berkeley · Los Angeles · London
www.ucpress.edu

SIERRA CLUB, SIERRA CLUB BOOKS, and Sierra Club design logos are registered
trademarks of the Sierra Club.

Production by Janet Vail
Book and cover design by Paula Schlosser
Illustrations by Cathy Johnson

Library of Congress Cataloging-in-Publication Data
Johnson, Cathy (Cathy A.)
The Sierra Club guide to sketching in nature / by Cathy Johnson.
Includes bibliographical references and index.
1. Landscape drawing—technique. 2. Artists' tools. I. Title.
NC795.J64   1991
743'.83—dc20   90-45266

ISBN 0-87156-932-9

10 9 8 7 6 5 4

To Harris, who is always there

CONTENTS

Acknowledgments

No book is the effort of one person; there are too many facets. In the early stages, there are those who help to form the book, shape it in imagination, before it ever gets to the manuscript stage. Later, friends help by reading chapters for clarity and sense. Still later, the book is sculpted and polished, designed and typeset and packaged.

I thank my editor, Jim Cohee, who has functioned in overlapping stages throughout; *no* book worth its salt makes it to this stage without the ministrations of a good editor, and this book had one of the best.

Ann Zwinger has been an inspiration from the first; I became acquainted with her work twenty years ago and with Ann herself in the early eighties. She is, quite simply, the finest artist/naturalist I know. Factor in her writing and she is unbeatable.

Clare Walker Leslie was also an inspiration; this book was in the formative stages when her first book, *Nature Drawing: A Tool for Learning*, arrived in my mail. Our relationship became a valuable one to me in the intervening years, and she deserves my deepest thanks.

Patti DeLano—friend, fellow writer, reader—helped me in the sculpting stages (and in the panic stages that followed).

My husband, Harris, keeps me from going off the deep end while working under pressure—and a book *is* pressure, no matter how pleasurable its subject matter. He's a brick.

And, finally, thanks to my students and the readers of my other books for their input, feedback, and intelligent questions. This book tries to answer them.

INTRODUCTION

Think of sketching and you may imagine the preliminary steps an artist goes through before beginning to paint—a planning stage before getting down to business. It *is* that, and much more.

Sketching is also a tool, a visual aid—not only for artists but for *anyone* who wishes to learn from nature, a way to preserve what you've seen, like a fly in amber. Botanists, birdwatchers, biologists; teachers and students; hikers and bikers and backpackers; family campers, mountain climbers, naturalists—anyone can learn to sketch in the field, to capture the moment. It's a kind of observational note taking, a visual shorthand.

Your sketches can track the sequence of sprout and leaf and flower or the life cycle of a moth. An unfamiliar bird's field marks, the behavioral rituals of a mountain cougar at mating, the distinctively patterned wings of a specific butterfly—these can be sketched quickly in the field for later verification, comparison, or study. You can use your sketches to check ID in a field guide, to cross-reference earlier sketches, or to provide information for an expert you may have contacted to learn more about your subject. My field-journal sketches are a very personal and immediate record of my own observations. I remember them as if time travel were, indeed, possible.

Subject to the vagaries of memory and attention, the explanation I may glean from a published field guide or text may be all too fleeting. Lawrence Kilham, author of *On Watching Birds*, says, "Reading is a poor way to start oneself on a research project. Go out into the field, build up some unprejudiced observations, make good notes, and you then have a *live* interest in something." (My italics.) I can only add a heartfelt *amen* and add that sketching is what helps bring us to life, as well. The lessons I learn from my *own* visual aids, made over a period of intense on-the-spot observation, are mine forever.

My field sketches are more than study notes or ways to learn the facts of nature. Nor are they just research for later paintings, simple studies in composition or value. They're a means of opening a door to a different way of seeing.

When I sketch and annotate those quick drawings with observation, I distill the moment. It's a tool for artists, sure, but also for anyone who enjoys nature and wants to experience it fully—and to recall it as if it were this morning. It's a tool accessible to anyone who will pick up a pencil.

There's another advantage to sketching in nature, for me. These quick drawings or more carefully observed studies of the things I find in my rambles are sheer pleasure. They *may* be used as study or research—they may not. There is no preconceived purpose in the doing, no agenda, no rules— just delight in the simple coordination of hand and eye and mind and the magic of nature appearing suddenly from blank paper. It *is* magic, a bit— no one who draws hasn't felt at least once "did *I* do that?" But yes, we did. The magic is in us, and in the world we respond to.

Chapters build on one another in this book: ideas are repeated and expanded in new contexts as they appear. The concept of values to depict lights and darks, for instance, appears in the chapters on learning to see like an artist, on putting the basics to work, and on capturing the illusion of light.

If you are an old hand at this drawing business, use the first chapters as review, as a kind of artistic calisthenics, or skip them altogether. If you are new to the attempt, give the suggested exercises a try; you'll teach *yourself* in the doing.

This book is intended to share with you the ins and outs of sketching in nature, the tools and techniques—and the sheer joy of it. That's the best reason for going out to sketch—to be there.

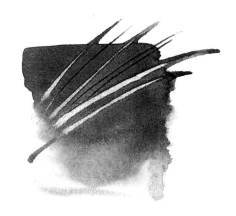

ONE

Tools and Equipment

SKETCHING IN NATURE can be as complex or as simple as you want to make it—after all, early naturalist-artists made do just fine with only scraps of paper and a quill pen. (Or with charred sticks of wood and the colors gleaned from the earth, if you are counting from still earlier artistic forebears like the cave painters at Lascaux or the Anasazi in the Southwest.)

If you are like most of us, you're always on the lookout for the perfect tool, the one that will make just that mark you see with your mind's eye, just that perfect line that distills the essence of your subject. It would be so simple if you could just find the right tool. You're sure that one day you'll find a smooth, well-balanced pencil with a wonderfully broad value range, one that holds a razor point but still is capable of bold effects, depending on your mood. Surely you'll find a brush with a fine, responsive point that will limn the most delicate of calligraphic twigs, then turn generous enough to splash the immense escarpment you've sketched with rich light and shadow. Or a tube of color that perfectly captures the cool reflection on the underside of a cloud. You fill drawers and bins and backpacks with this and that—sketch pens, pencils, brushes, and tubes and sticks and pans of color.

But it's never that simple. The key is in you, not in any tool.

You may develop your favorites; I have. I depend on a certain brush because I know I can make it do what I want it to—if I've been living right. I use a particular palette because it meets my need for plenty of color-mixing space. I buy a specific brand of watercolor because I know how it handles and just how much water to mix in to make a graded wash. And the reason I know these things is because I've taken the time to get to know my tools, to become familiar with them, to explore their possibilities—*there's* the magic. In practice. The alchemy is in the application; it's work. (Too bad all work isn't as much fun as this!)

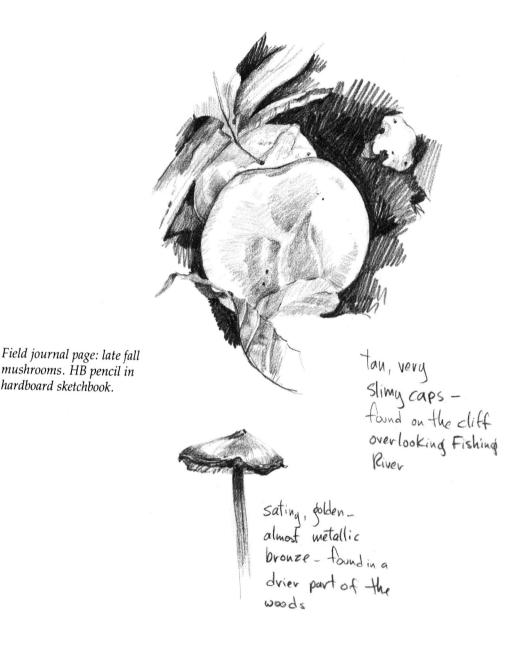

Field journal page: late fall mushrooms. HB pencil in hardboard sketchbook.

tan, very slimy caps — found on the cliff overlooking Fishing River

satiny, golden — almost metallic bronze — found in a drier part of the woods

I can't presume to pick your tools for you. What works for me may not for you. But I can share my own experience, and a few of the things I've found that have worked. This chapter is intended to familiarize you with some of the choices, to give you an idea of what's out there and how it functions; then, when you hit the art supply store the array of possibilities won't seem so daunting (or so tempting!). You can make an informed decision before you buy an unfamiliar tool.

PENCILS

Since 1795, when the first clay and graphite sticks came out of the kiln, pencils have been the simplest of ephemeral drawing tools—ephemeral because the marks they make can be erased. You can change a line in an instant if you don't like what you see.

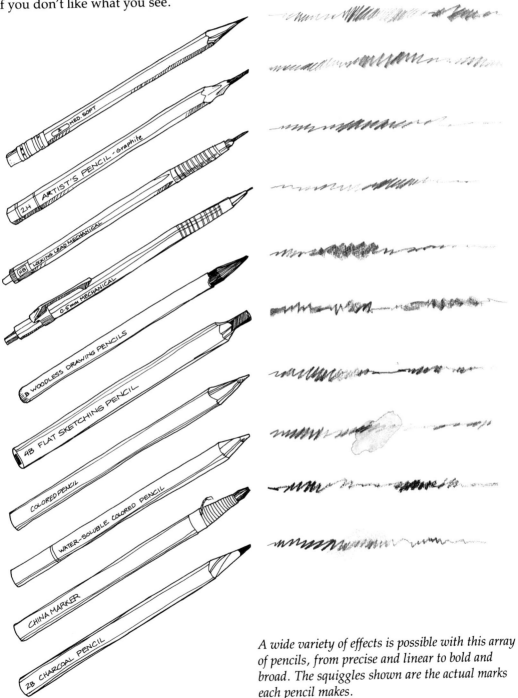

A wide variety of effects is possible with this array of pencils, from precise and linear to bold and broad. The squiggles shown are the actual marks each pencil makes.

Pencils are portable, practical, and wonderfully flexible drawing tools. They fit Thoreau's dictum—"Simplify, simplify"—to a T; maybe that's why I like them so much. Near the end of the nineteenth century, techniques were perfected to encase the graphite stick in a wooden shaft—these pencils have been the mainstay of the sketcher's art ever since. A mid-range HB drawing pencil is capable of the most delicate of silvery grays when used with a light touch, or a rich, thunderous dark when applied with firm strokes. An inexpensive No. 2 office pencil is a fine substitute if that's what's available to you; happily, to paraphrase Gertrude Stein, a pencil is a pencil is a pencil.

Graphite is the most common form of drawing pencil, though carbon and other "leads" are available in pencil form. "Lead" is a misnomer here. There is no lead in a pencil; just as well, or we'd all have lead poisoning.

The proportion of clay to graphite is what gives a pencil its relative hardness; the range in general is from 9H (hard) through all the interim grades to HB (middle range) and on up to 7B (soft). Faber Castell and Turquoise both make wonderful drawing pencils.

Office pencils often come only in No. 1, very soft; No. 2, the medium range; F for firm; No. 3, hard; or No. 4, a very hard pencil that is rather like trying to draw with a shard of glass. Don't count these office supply tools out, though; I've done some of my best sketches with a good old No. 2 school pencil.

For convenience, I carry a fine-lead mechanical pencil (0.5 or 0.7 mm) loaded with HB leads; the point never needs sharpening, and if it breaks or runs out, I simply advance the lead down the minuscule barrel. Even with this small lead, I can achieve a wide range of values over large shaded areas by using a heavier pressure, repeated hatching, or closely placed strokes. (And if I need it, there is even a small eraser hidden under the cap.) You can buy your favorite lead, from hard to quite soft, to fit this relatively inexpensive tool, but the softest ones are prone to break at this small size. With care, a mechanical pencil itself can last for years; just reload with new leads.

A locking-lead mechanical is an older-style pencil; it does require a sharpener of some sort, but it is still quite handy—sturdy, too. Long a tool

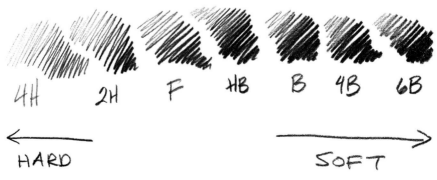

The proportion of clay to graphite determines the relative hardness of the lead; 9H is hardest, F, H, and HB are the middle range, and 7B is quite soft. In general, the harder the lead, the lighter and finer the line.

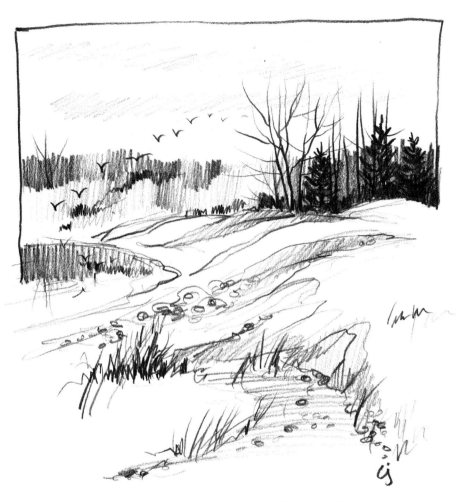

A wide variety of effects is possible with a simple office-style No. 2 pencil.

of choice for draftspeople and architects, this pencil also takes a variety of lead refills.

For a very versatile sketching tool, try a flat sketching or carpenter's pencil. Kohinoor makes a good one for artists, but you may find a similar carpenter's pencil at your hardware store. I laid in a nice supply when I built my cabin studio; they were free from the lumberyard. The lead within the somewhat oval wood shaft is a flattened rectangle; like other graphite pencils, these come in various hardnesses. You can sharpen it to a wedge for a wide variety of effects: the corner will produce a fine line much like a regular pencil point; the edge will give you a variable line from thin to thick; the entire width of the lead can be used to quickly cover broad areas. Some artists even carve nicks or wedges into the flat edge to produce crosshatch effects.

The new woodless drawing pencils from Progresso are just that—all "lead" and no wood. A column of graphite is coated with enamel to keep your fingers from getting smudged—other than that, the entire pencil is a

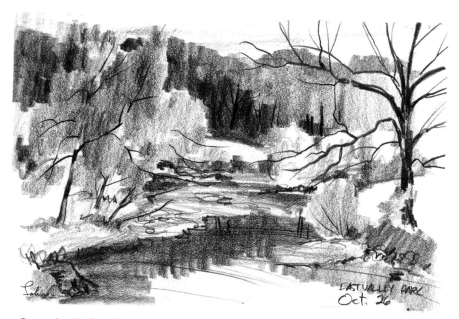

General's 2B sketching pencil with a broad, flat lead was used to quickly lay in the values in this sketch.

drawing tool. You can use only the tip, as you might with any pencil, or the entire width of the lead, for extremely broad effects and ease of shading. These come only in HB, 2B, 4B, and 6B, the softer range.

A new drawing tool on the market is the Derwent water-soluble *graphite* sketching pencil. Like the watercolor pencils you may have tried, such pencils make marks that dissolve when brushed with clear water, giving lovely, broad areas of value (grays) instead of color. There are only three grades here, one to make a light wash when wet, one a medium, and one dark. They look darker when wet; you may want to add a bit more pencil work when your sketch is thoroughly dry.

Carbon and charcoal pencils both produce very rich, dark lines, from a true black to pale gray as you decrease pressure on the lead; you can buy them in a range of hardnesses as well. Like the new water-soluble graphites, carbon pencils may also be wet with clear water to make washy halftone effects.

All these pencil lines are subject to smudging; use a spray fixative such as Krylon to preserve them.

A dust-free, crayonlike mark in a good dark black can be gained from a china marker or litho pencil. You "sharpen" these paper-wrapped pencils by pulling a string on the side to tear one layer of the paper wrapping, which you then pull away in one long curl to expose more lead. The tip may then be shaped with a sharp blade. I like their bold marks on textured paper, and although they are not intended primarily for sketching, they make a wonderfully fresh, bold mark. They are excellent for working large; less so for detail work.

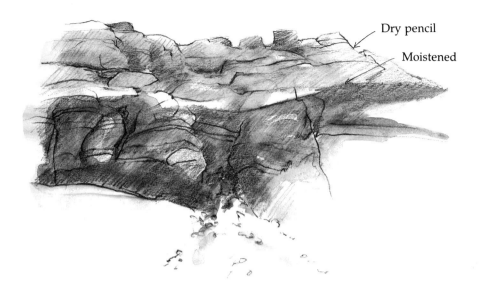

Dry pencil

Moistened

Water-soluble graphite sketching pencils come in only three grades; this is the softest lead. I moistened it with clear water in places while leaving others dry to show the difference in effect.

Colored pencils are experiencing a renaissance in the last few years, not only as sketching tools but for fine art applications. For my purposes, their portability and color range make them perfect for the trail or backpack.

Most colored pencils have a wax and pigment base; the leads will break if handled too roughly, and they must be sharpened with care to avoid breaking the tip. You may want to use the exposed side of the lead for bolder effects and save the point for details. There's a wide range of colors available, or create your own nuances by layering strokes of one color over another.

I often work on a toned or colored background with these pencils for an even richer effect. Berol Prismacolor and Eberhard Faber's Colorama pencils are two of the best-known brands of colored pencil; you can buy these individually or in sets of up to seventy-two pencils. Heavy applications of color may "bloom" or become coated with a pale dustlike layer over a period of time; this bloom can be wiped away with a soft cloth or prevented by spraying with fixative.

For a limited palette—and if you're just going for a bit of color—there are neat mechanical pencils that have several colors in one barrel. Leads can be changed in an instant; just twist for a new hue. They are not as richly pigmented as the larger wood-encased pencils, and the leads are of necessity quite small, but they are portable to the extreme.

Richer by far are the sets of woodless wax/oil colored pencils like those from Caran D'Ache. A starter set of some 15 Neocolor pencils will cost under $15 from most suppliers. Derwent makes a similar 24-pencil set. You'll find it in the Daniel Smith catalog. See "Where to Buy Art Supplies," p. 223.

For watercolor effects from a colored pencil, try one of the *water-soluble* sketching tools like Caran d'Ache or Derwent. I have a forty-pencil set of the Swiss-made Caran d'Ache in a metal carrying case; it's a versatile sketching tool. Don't worry about toting a heavy container of water along to activate the watercolor effect; clear water can be brushed on later, at your convenience. But be advised: some of these pencils change color rather radically when you wet them. Make a chart with bars of each color to show how the pencils look both dry and wet—then you'll know which pencil to choose to achieve just the color you're after.

It's often inconvenient to use a pencil that has become too short—they're hard to hold or sharpen. A pencil extender, available at office or art supply stores, will extend almost any pencil to a comfortable working length. That way, too, you get the full use—no need to throw away a stub.

Before long you'll develop a favorite pencil—graphite, charcoal, whatever—and you may find that your sketching needs can be met with only a few carefully chosen tools. You'll develop your own working style, a kind of personal shorthand. Once at that point, you can cut a lot of weight from your pack—and deadwood from your life; my own "absolute necessities" have been narrowed to a single mechanical pencil and a warm, dark gray colored pencil for a wide variety of effects. From there I can branch out as much as I like.

PENS

At one time pens were the *only* game in town for sketching—except for chunks of charcoal. They weren't the most convenient sketching tools in the world, requiring a bottle of liquid ink and a knife for trimming the goose quill nib. Today we're blessed with a range of pens that are practical, portable, and capable of beautiful, expressive lines. Many carry their ink supply with them as cartridges or refillable reservoirs.

You can still buy a variety of sizes and styles of dip pens, metal nibs to fit wooden or plastic holders, and a rainbow of inks. The choice of nib configurations is astonishing—your creativity is limited only by need and imagination. The crow quill pen is popular with artists and illustrators for great delicacy and expressiveness of line, but do try a hawk quill as well. Experiment with lettering nibs, ovals or rounds.

For sketching outdoors—unless I am exploring what it must have been like to be an early naturalist-artist—I use the more modern, portable sketching tools that don't require an open bottle of ink. There are fountain-type sketch pens with flexible nibs, capable of delicate, seismic lines or bold slashes. Most fountain pens designed for writing rather than sketching produce a more uniform line, but the effects can still be very pleasing to the eye; some pens can be filled with ink cartridges in a variety of colors. I like to sketch with a soft, sepia brown to capture the subtleties of nature—bad for reproduction in print, great for mood. I can buy a cartridge in just that shade—or red, blue, green, or purple in addition to black.

Try a technical pen for a uniform, clean black line. Even for sketching, these pens are capable of great expressiveness within the limitations of a

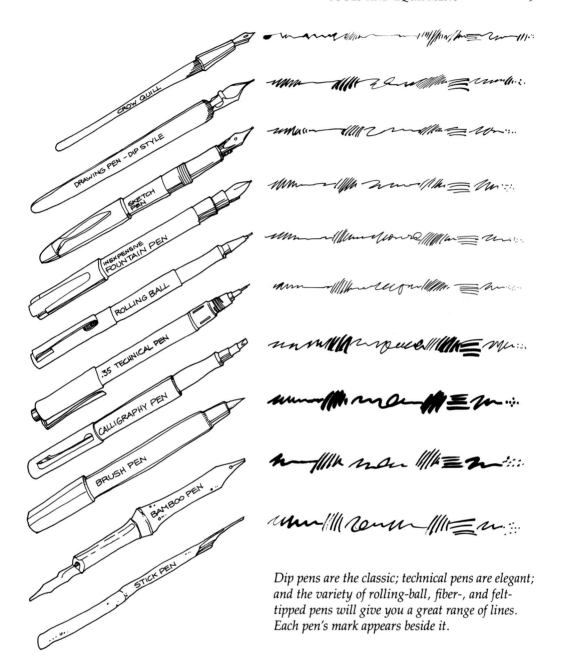

CROW QUILL

DRAWING PEN - DIP STYLE

SKETCH PEN

INEXPENSIVE FOUNTAIN PEN

ROLLING BALL

.35 TECHNICAL PEN

CALLIGRAPHY PEN

BRUSH PEN

BAMBOO PEN

STICK PEN

Dip pens are the classic; technical pens are elegant; and the variety of rolling-ball, fiber-, and felt-tipped pens will give you a great range of lines. Each pen's mark appears beside it.

line of consistent width. Used with a quick, light stroke (especially on paper with a bit of "tooth"), the pen will produce a broken line that suggests texture or the effects of light. A more controlled, contemplative handling will give you a drawing of elegance and style. I use a Rotring Rapidograph pen set, from a very fine 0.25 to a bold 0.70; these are an advance over the earlier technical pens that clogged easily and required the care of a brain surgeon to prepare them for use; you may have found another brand that works as well.

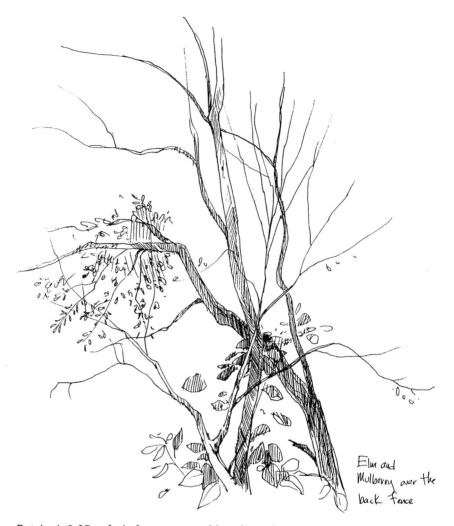

Elm and
Mulberry over the
back fence

Rotring's 0.35 technical pen was used loosely to sketch this pair of trees in my backyard.

Try sketching with a pen intended for calligraphy—one with a flat, square-ended nib—for more dramatic effects. Experiment with thick and thin strokes, using the edge of the nib for narrower lines and the whole width for bolder ones. You can buy these as separate nibs to fit interchangeably in a holder, as cartridge-loaded fountain pens, or as fiber-tipped pens—all worth a try.

And speaking of fiber-tipped pens, these are a revolution for drawing as well as writing. Use a medium point for a bolder line, a fine tip for delicacy and detail. Lightweight, inexpensive, available in a range of colors, these are wonderful drawing tools. With my unfortunate habit of losing my tools in the field, I especially appreciate their affordability.

If you have chosen a nonpermanent ink, you can even modify the line with clear water as you can with water-soluble pencils, though you may find your black line has become rather blued with the addition of water. Sketch-

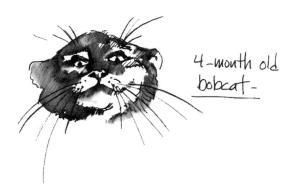

4-month old
bobcat-

*I drew this young bobcat with
an extra-fine fiber-tipped pen,
then moistened the line with
my finger to give me a halftone effect. Using my finger
rather than a brush loaded
with water let me control the
amount of wetness; too much,
and the pen line nearly
washes away.*

ing in the air over New England, I wet the pen lines with saliva for soft,
cloudlike halftones. Broad value ranges and fresh watercolor effects are possible with this technique, though you do sacrifice some clarity of line. I often
restate lines once everything is dry.

A rolling-ball pen is also usable for sketching; inexpensive, easy to find
in any store that sells writing instruments, and no great loss if you mislay it
while hiking.

And if you're interested in working in color, look for a set of fiber-tipped
pens; you may find them in an art supply store—or even your local discount
store. These may not be entirely lightfast, so they're not suitable for fine arts
applications—but they're lovely for sketching. They can be quite expensive
if they're of high quality; my own are discount store buys, a set of twenty-
four for under five dollars.

Shop carefully when buying any of the fiber-tipped pens for serious
sketching. Some start smoothly with a good, clean line while others seem
to stutter a bit first, making a spiky, uncertain line or an unexpected blob of
ink.

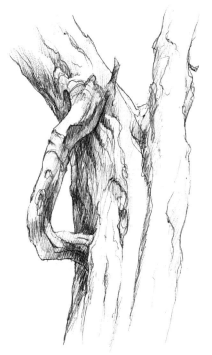

*I used a delicate, silvery ball-
point pen to sketch my favorite tree; some orchardist must
have had fun with this one
years ago. The limb comes
out, then re-enters the trunk
about 18 inches away; it's like
a Zen koan.*

That's a flaw these newer pens share with ballpoints. I like the great subtlety of a ballpoint pen line, but some pens are prone to blobbing when you first touch them to paper—a *very* frustrating occurrence, especially if you smear the blob of ink back over your drawing as your hand moves across the paper. Again, shop carefully, even if you are buying a ballpoint intended expressly for drawing and sold in an art supply store. Try before you buy. Some will blob, some won't. It may be a good idea to keep a tissue handy before you begin a stroke—take a quick swipe with your pen point, *then* draw.

Look for a good black or brown ink for drawing, and be advised—ballpoint ink may not be lightfast. That is, your black lines may fade with time and *become* a soft brown—nice if you are expecting it, frustrating if you're not.

A new sketching tool on the market is the brush pen. You may find these as fountain-style pens with an actual brush on the end—an older concept—or as a specialized fiber-tipped pen shaped like a brush. You can even buy these in color to "paint" your sketches with. I like the expressive line and broad range of effects possible. It really is more like painting.

For special linear effects, try an Oriental bamboo pen. With the pronounced cellular structure of bamboo, you'd expect that they would outperform a metal nib; they don't. They simply don't hold as much ink. But their effect is so lively that I forgive them much. They *do* require a supply of liquid ink, but the Oriental masters ground their own on the spot with an inkstone and solid ink that they mixed with water. You can do likewise for a sense of what it might have been like to work from nature in ancient Japan or China.

A similar effect can be had from a very simple and accessible tool; break a twig or dowel rod to dip into your ink—a lively line indeed, unpredictable and fresh. If you've forgotten to pack your pen, here is your answer. (Use berry juice or earth and water for ink; our ancestors did.)

ART STICKS

Try the art sticks (for lack of a better name) for a bolder handling. You won't be able to get fine lines as easily as with a pencil or pen, but many art sticks *can* be sharpened; they'll hold a point for a reasonable period. Some have sharp corners that stand in for points; others are round. Ample, expressive effects are possible using the side of the stick.

Square or rectangular graphite sticks will give you a taste of what sketching was like before wood-clad pencils were available—these are nice for covering broad areas quickly, but you can also achieve finer, more linear effects by using only a corner of the graphite block. Like pencils, these come in various hardnesses. A sandpaper block can be used to shape the corner or edge of the stick for controlled effects.

Hard (square stick) and soft (round) pastels are becoming more popular as field materials; these chalklike color sticks come in virtually any hue or shade you might wish. They can be blended softly or left as distinct and separate marks for fresh, immediate effects. A mixture of pigment, binder,

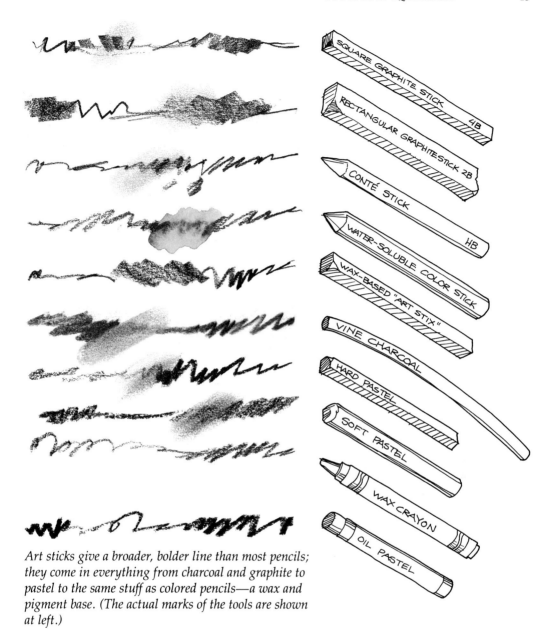

Art sticks give a broader, bolder line than most pencils; they come in everything from charcoal and graphite to pastel to the same stuff as colored pencils—a wax and pigment base. (The actual marks of the tools are shown at left.)

and inert clay, they are somewhat delicate. Your finished sketches will need to be sprayed with fixative to protect them from smearing.

Conté crayons have been used by such masters as Degas and Picasso; you may find them to your liking. Pastel-like sketch sticks have a wonderful working consistency and a kaolin base. These come in black, gray, sanguine (red-brown), white, medicis, and bistre, and can be blended for subtle shading. If you like Conté crayons' handling properties but prefer more vibrant colors, they now make sets of from twelve to forty-eight sticks, or buy open stock to get just those colors you prefer.

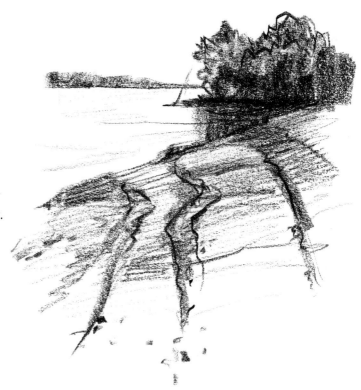

Berol Prismacolor Art Stix come in many colors; this sketch of the Missouri River near the old German town of Hermann uses only the black.

Oil pastel is a wonderful sketching tool. Just as it sounds, this is pigment with an oil binder in stick form; the finished work can be quite rich, more like an oil painting than a sketch unless your technique is quite spare and linear.

A newer sketch stick is made of the same material found in colored pencil leads—a wax and pigment base that works delightfully in the field. These can make broad or fine lines and come in the same range of hues as colored pencils, and like these tools, they can be layered for subtlety. They can't be blended as pastels or Conté crayons can, but they *are* neater to take along for field work. No dust.

Hot on the heels of this innovation is a water-soluble color stick. Draw with it like any art stick, then wet with clear water for splashy watercolor effects.

And of course, don't forget a set of kid's crayons. Find a good brand that still uses a wax base rather than plastic, and you'll get brilliant colors along with good portability—and a very inexpensive set of sketching tools. Crayons get a bad rap, and it's undeserved. I've seen wonderful landscape drawings, true fine art, done with a set of crayons. This might be a good way to get started to see if you like working in color—you can buy as few as eight or a set of at least sixty-four.

The great-granddaddy of all art sticks is a piece of vine charcoal, a fine, delicate tool actually made from kiln-burned vine. These do break easily; you'll probably want to invest in a holder made especially for the stick.

When you sketch with vine charcoal, you are as close as possible to our artistic ancestors.

And if you find yourself out with your field journal and nothing to sketch with, look to the remains of the campfire. I was once in a similar position and rather than give up on the idea of recording the day, I sketched with a chunk of charcoal from a night fisherman's fire. The sketch is one of my favorites.

ERASERS

We all make mistakes. Most, in sketching, can be incorporated into your final drawing or left to stand as an interesting vibration beside your restated line; it's a different kind of perfection. But if you really need to erase, there are a number of tools available to do it with.

The old artgum eraser is easily available—but that's about all it has to recommend it, as far as I'm concerned. It crumbs like day-old bread.

A kneaded eraser can be a handy tool, but really more as a drawing aid than an eraser. It will pick up areas of tone from a pencil or charcoal drawing, reclaiming highlights like nothing else; used for straight erasing, it may redeposit the gunk from your *last* erasure and rub it indelibly into your drawing.

The new white vinyl erasers are efficient and kindest to your paper while they're at it. They remove almost any pencil mark without scuffing your paper's surface; I even use them on fine watercolor paper with no ill effects to later washes.

There is also a mechanical pencil-style vinyl eraser that can be used in tight spots. Advance the column of eraser as you need it.

Ink erasers are gritty and hard on your paper, but you may need them to lift stubborn ink lines. You won't be able to re-ink or lay a watercolor wash smoothly over such an erasure.

You may prefer an electric eraser—a bit of an expense, but worth it if your sketches must look pristine. (I use my electric model for commercial work, for the most part.) With an eraser shield, with its wide array of masked shapes, I can get into the most crucial areas. I use a pink eraser refill rather than an abrasive ink-style eraser; it takes a bit longer but is easier on paper surfaces.

BRUSHES

If you plan to sketch with watercolor, choose brushes as carefully as you might a good sleeping bag; this is an emotional investment as well as a monetary one—you need to be comfortable with your tools. Buy the best you can afford. A red sable brush is optimum; Kolinsky is the finest. Sable holds a good point and a lot of water, and will last a long time if properly cared for. I'm still using a twenty-year-old brush; I'll admit its point has become a bit round with the years, but then it's covered a lot of territory.

When painting with watercolor, I use the biggest brush I can as *long* as I can, to avoid getting too tight and niggling my work to death. (For painting

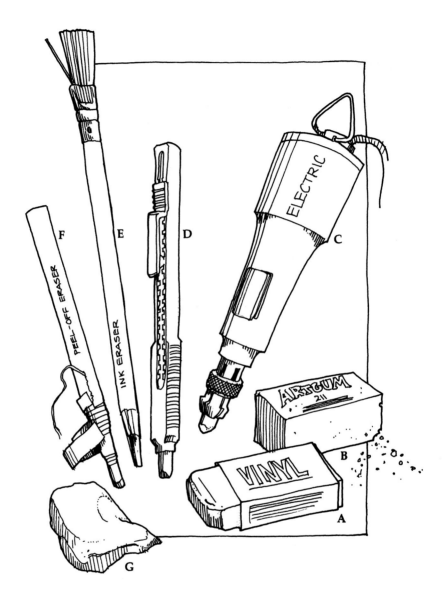

*Choose the proper eraser for the job; my favorite is the white vinyl eraser (**A**)—it's kind to my paper's surface and leaves fewer crumbs. An artgum eraser (**B**) is an old workhorse, but leaves too many bits of itself for my taste. I use an electric eraser (**C**) at home when my sketches must be pristine. In the field or at home, the white vinyl mechanical-style eraser (**D**) gets into tight spots and works as well as (**A**). Tough spots call for an ink eraser (**E**); the brush end makes getting rid of the crumbs easier. Peel-off erasers (**F**) come in a pink, a medium-grain, an ink style, or a slightly more harsh vinyl. A kneaded eraser (**G**) is a fine tool for gently lifting or picking out highlights; not so fine for day-to-day erasing.*

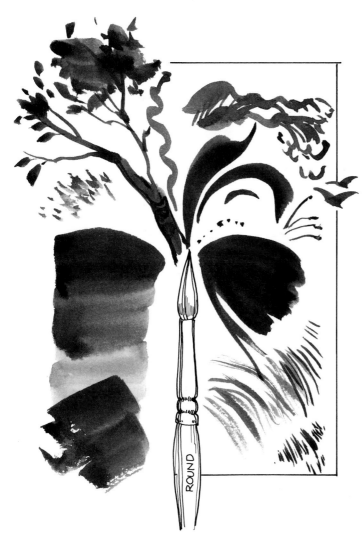

A round watercolor brush is essential; it's the old classic, and no wonder—it's capable of almost anything you ask of it. The marks here were made with a No. 10 Kolinsky sable.

a full-sized work, that means at least a No. 12 round and a 1-inch flat; for sketching, my brushes are somewhat smaller. Ounces add up on the trail; a No. 6 round and a ½-inch flat will usually do it.)

A sable-and-synthetic blend is a good compromise between quality and economy, especially for field work. I can relax with these; even if I should lose my brush I'm not out the Denver mint. (I *never* take my No. 12 Kolinsky round out of the studio!)

I use a round brush with a fine point for washes, detail work, and linear effects, and a flat or square-ended brush for broad areas. I can also use the edge or the corner of the flat for details almost as fine as the round. With a bit of attention to brush handling and some experimenting to find all the things these two are capable of, that's all you need, if you're opting for simplicity—and a lightweight pack.

My flat brush has an aquarelle tip, an angled, plastic handle that has a myriad uses: scraping, incising the paper for dark lines, pushing damp pig-

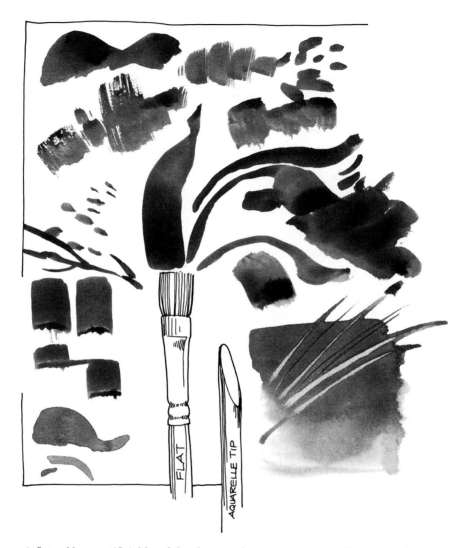

A flat sable or artificial brush has become the new essential; with practice, it is as versatile as the round. All the marks here were made with a ½-inch sable brush; the aquarelle tip let me scrape back through a damp wash to create lighter lines, lower right.

ment around to regain lighter areas. This angled tip works well to suggest tall grasses, light-struck limbs, or jagged cracks in rocks when scratched into wet or just-drying pigment—try it.

I've broken off the end of my old round field brushes to give me an additional painting or scraping tool; the exposed wood works well for a variety of effects, including the types of lines possible with the broken stick or dowel mentioned in the last section.

I could do with just these two, if I had to. But, of course, the variety of brushes available and the scope of their possibilities tempt me to expand my supply list. A rigger or liner brush, as its name suggests, makes fine, lively lines. These brushes have extra-long hairs that hold a lot of liquid; a full

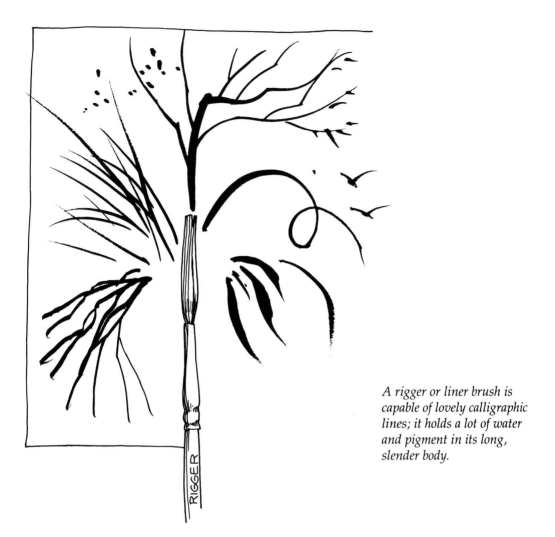

A rigger or liner brush is capable of lovely calligraphic lines; it holds a lot of water and pigment in its long, slender body.

charge of pigment goes a long way. The length of the hairs makes them fun to use; they dance calligraphically across the paper, making lovely twigs and branches, rough weeds, or even the rigging on ships (that's where they got their more archaic name).

A fan brush is used most often in oil painting, for blending colors smoothly, but I use mine with watercolor. Look for a stiff boar-bristle brush, not a soft sable one, and trim it a bit raggedly with a razor or small scissors. You can use this to suggest grasses and weeds, foliage, wood grain—you're limited only by your own imagination. Use the stiff bristles and clear water to loosen dried pigment to lighten an area, if you wish.

An inexpensive stencil brush is great for spattering, or aiming small droplets of color at your paper to suggest texture. Clear water produces lighter spots when they hit a wet watercolor wash; drops of darker pigment can be spattered into wet or dry areas for a variety of textures. Run your thumb or finger over the bristles to direct the spray. (Some artists use an old toothbrush for this, but I find a stencil brush easier to control.) The fan brush will also double as a spattering tool.

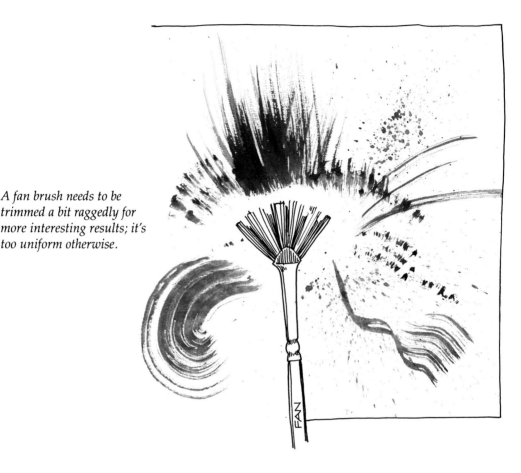

A fan brush needs to be trimmed a bit raggedly for more interesting results; it's too uniform otherwise.

You can even paint with your stencil brush if you like, for unexpected results. Practice a bit to see what it can do.

When I'm really going light, I take along my traveling watercolor brushes. These fold to only a few inches long and weigh almost nothing. Some have handles that fit protectively over the bristles, then screw onto the end of the brush to extend it to a comfortable working length. You can buy the screw-on type in sable or synthetics from Daniel Smith, Inc., in a variety of sizes up to a No. 10.

PAPERS

Unless you're going in for cave painting—or graffiti—you'll need to choose a paper to work on. If you're just getting started or if your sketches are only intended to be an adjunct to your field notes, a spiral notebook is fine, or an inexpensive sketchbook. Many artists and naturalists like to work on a good bond paper (typing paper) with a clipboard to support their paper; this can be 100 percent rag with a neutral pH, which means it's acid free and won't crack or yellow with age. These loose sheets can be collected in a binder, later, for protection, and organized however you like—by subject, by season, or chronologically, as you complete them.

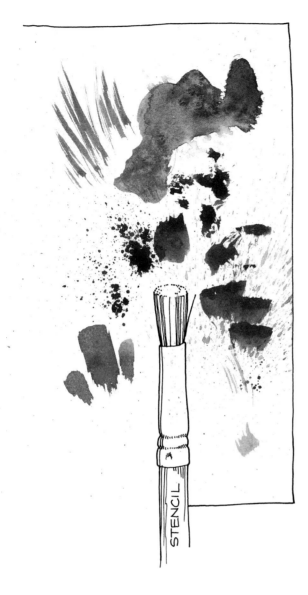

An inexpensive stencil brush is great for spattering, but it can even be used to paint with.

Years ago, choosing a neutral pH paper wasn't so much of a concern, because all paper (except newsprint) was of reasonable quality—I have an eighty-year-old notebook of my grandmother's that looks like new. On the other hand, I have a cheap sketchbook of my own from fifteen years ago that's already begun to yellow and crack at the edges. Unless you specify good paper, this cheaper stuff is probably what you'll get; if your sketches are only to be practice pieces that you don't intend to keep, that's fine. But if your field sketches are to be like a diary to you, an end in themselves, you'll want to make sure you have paper that will last.

That said, I'll admit that some of my favorite sketches were done on the spur of the moment, on whatever paper I could lay hands on quickly: the back of an envelope, a paper napkin, the border of a newspaper. The important thing is to *get it down*. If you're prepared, and have the proper tools,

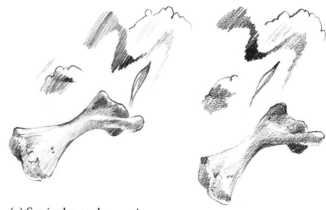

The paper's "tooth" or surface helps determine finished results. A smooth paper allows much finer details with a more linear style. You can create almost seamless tones on this paper as well, with careful rendering. A vellum or rougher paper gives nice, open sketchy effects, as your drawing tool tends to skip over the minute valleys in the surface.

(a) Squiggles and snapping-turtle bone on smooth paper   (b) On vellum surface paper

so much the better. If not—sketch anyway. You can always transfer your sketch to good paper later, if need be.

Papers come in a variety of surface textures; this factor will most affect the outcome of your sketches. What medium you plan to use on it (pencil, watercolor, charcoal) will make a difference in which surface you choose and how much texture it will have; a paper intended for one use may behave badly if used for another.

A drawing paper might be very smooth (plate surface) to use with ink or pencil, or have a vellum surface—that is, a bit of tooth or texture. Pastels are often done on a more textured surface—sometimes, so textured that fine sand is embedded in the surface.

To keep things simple, I often choose a spiral-bound drawing pad with a little tooth and medium-weight paper, for the broadest range of applications. That way, if I want to add a watercolor wash or use one of the water-soluble pencils or sticks, the paper won't buckle too much as it dries, especially if I use only the minimum amount of water.

For sketching in nature, *most* often I use a hardbound sketchbook with neutral pH drawing paper. This provides a good surface to work on while it protects my field sketches—and sometimes they need protecting. Once I tossed my book to safety on the bank as I sunk to my backside in quicksand; another time I dropped it over a cliff with only minor scuffing to the book's cover and no damage to my work inside at all. (And obviously I lived to tell the tale.)

These books come in a variety of sizes and shapes: my favorites are a tiny 4- × 6-inch size that fits in a pocket or purse; a 5- × 8-inch size that acts as my field journal as well as a sketchbook, and a great 8- × 11-inch size bound along the short dimension—it's a good landscape sketchbook. It's also big enough for a whole page of sketches if I find an interesting enough subject—and that's not hard to do. I filled this page with elk studies while watching a nature special on television. Working in a hardbound sketchbook keeps my year all together under one cover; it provides a kind of chronology.

If you plan to paint in the field—sketches or finished works—you may want to explore watercolor blocks. These are good-quality paper bound to a cardboard backing on all four sides, with a small access slot to allow you to remove the sheets as you use them. A block provides a number of sheets of paper and a firm working surface all at the same time and keeps you from having to lug loose sheets of watercolor paper, extra supports, tape, or fasteners into the field. I use a 9- × 12-inch Fabriano cold-press block for much of my outdoor work, and find it fits perfectly into my daypack with my water containers, paints, brushes—and lunch. Blocks come as small as 5 × 7 inches or as large as 18 × 24 inches.

It's perfectly possible to work on a full-sized painting (22 × 30 inches or larger) in the field, of course; I often do, and simply carry along a Masonite support, masking tape to fasten my paper down so it won't buckle or blow in the wind, and a supply of watercolor paper—plus larger brushes and a bigger palette. But that's hardly what you could call sketching—that's major business, and requires the planning of an assault on Mount Everest!

If you prefer loose sheets, there are many brands of watercolor paper in a variety of weights and surfaces. Seventy-pound (the weight of a ream of 22- × 30-inch paper) is light and thin and tends to buckle wildly when wet, unless prepared beforehand by stretching. I prefer a 140-pound paper; taping it to a board with masking or drafting tape prevents most buckling. As the paper dries, the hills and valleys flatten back out. Three-hundred-pound paper needs no stretching or taping; it's like painting on pre-stretched paper—or cardboard. It's elegant, but expensive per sheet. Cut watercolor paper to any size you like; I often cut a stack of 9- × 12-inch pieces to tuck into my pack.

Choose your paper's *surface* according to personal preference and how you plan to work. If you are using mixed media, you may need to take this into account. Hot-press paper is very smooth, and watercolor tends to make hard-edged puddles on the surface—which I happen to like. You can get very fine details with this paper, as it has no texture of its own to dictate the final results. It will take pencil or pen and ink beautifully.

Cold press (medium surface) is my favorite; I can create my own texture or use the paper's inherent tooth for a variety of effects. It's versatile enough to allow mixed media handling and takes a pencil or ink line quite nicely.

Rough paper can be very rough indeed, and dictates textural possibilities. It is very popular with watercolorists. Ironically, it is easiest to get smooth, flat washes on this most textured paper since your pigment settles uniformly into the tiny valleys, but if you are using pen and ink with your watercolor washes, rough paper may catch your pen point and spatter ink where you don't want it. Experiment to find the paper that suits you best.

One of my favorite sketching papers is a small pad of watercolor paper in postcard form. These are of good quality, take paint or other sketching mediums nicely, and are small enough to be extremely lightweight. (These actually *are* postcards, by the way; you can make sketches of your travels, then turn them over, address them, and send them to a friend back home.) If the price for the commercial postcards seems steep, cut or tear watercolor paper to size (4 × 6 inches) and carry in a Zip-lock bag in your pack; 140-

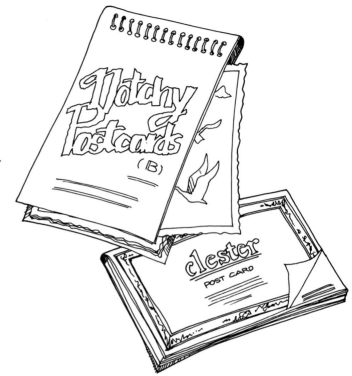

Bound postcards are wonderful for sketching. These have good-quality watercolor paper that takes pigment, pencil, pen, what have you. There are any number of brands on the market—these are but two.

pound paper this small won't buckle at all when wet. Working this size seems to keep me from overworking my sketches and trying to turn them into finished paintings.

You may like to work on toned or colored paper in the field, especially with colored pencils or pastels. The background tone becomes an integral part of your sketch, and can suggest the ambience or the predominant color of the scene. If you sketch the fire-colored rocks of Nevada's deserts, a reddish brown paper might be a good choice. If you're in a sunny mood, why not use a yellow background to capture just what you're feeling?

A toned paper can act as the middle values in your sketches, as well. Use a dark or black pen or pencil for shadow forms, accent light-struck areas with a white or pale colored pencil and your work is suddenly almost three-dimensional. It pops out of the flat surface of the paper as if it were alive.

I often cut a small stack of colored matboard scraps to tuck into my daypack; these give me a toned background, good drawing texture, plus enough support to work on. Give me a black fiber-tipped pen and a white, wax-and-pigment base colored pencil to produce three-dimensional effects, and I'm happy.

PAINTS

For centuries, watercolor has been used as a sketcher's medium, and with good reason. It's light and relatively portable, not messy, nonflammable, and versatile. No need to carry turps and linseed oil and rags, as you do with oil paints; brushes rinse clean on the spot. All you need is water, often found near where you are sketching—both for the actual painting and for cleanup afterward. And even if you must carry water with you, I'd still rather spill a little down my leg far from home than a splash of turpentine. But I'll admit, these are only peripheral reasons; I'm hooked on watercolor. For people similarly addicted to the joys of oil painting, those small inconveniences will be just that: small. It's all in what makes you comfortable, and what best expresses what you feel.

That said, I'll concentrate on watercolors; it's what I know best. Any good book on oils or acrylics should be able to suggest brands or colors.

Beyond the hard little pans of color we played with as kids is a wide range of watercolor possibilities. (But don't hesitate to buy a box of Prangs if you're just getting into sketching. They're dandy paints, just not as lightfast or intense—or subtle—as the more professional pigments.)

If you like what you see and the way these paints handle, you can buy semimoist pans of pigment in artist or professional grades. Actually, these are what you might think of as dry, very much like our first sets of watercolors. Moisten them with water to paint; the only difference between these and our childhood watercolors is that the artist-grade paints are of higher quality. Their colors are more pigment dense, and they're more likely to be lightfast. You can buy them in sets, with colors ready picked, or in individual pans to fill your metal paintbox. I buy them separately, because I have strong color preferences.

Be warned, though—these aren't Prang prices. A good metal box outfitted with professional-grade colors can set you back fifty dollars or more (*much* more), depending on the size of the box and which colors you choose.

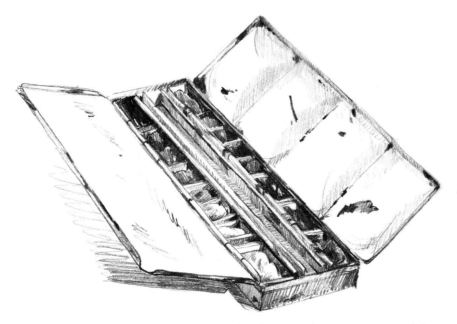

My old watercolor box has plenty of space for pigments plus two generous mixing areas; I could paint at least a half-sheet watercolor (15 × 22 inches) with this if need be. A good box will last for years; I've had this one for twenty.

Some especially rare pigments cost the sun—up to eight dollars for a single, small half-pan. More easily available pigments cost about four dollars for the same size of pan.

There are numerous brands of watercolors, both semimoist pans and tube paints. Winsor & Newton and Liquitex are among the best known, and are my personal favorites. I like the tube colors for versatility; I can use them immediately, straight from the tube for easy mixing with water, or let them dry for portability. Moisten with clear water, and they are as brilliant as ever. I often refill the half-pans in my metal paint box with these and allow them to dry (at least overnight) before taking them into the field, rather than buying half-pans already filled. It is less expensive and the colors are often more transparent in tube form. Re-wet with clear water a few minutes before you begin to paint, to avoid the necessity of scrubbing with your brush to loosen pigment.

A set of Oriental Sumi watercolors can be had for about sixteen dollars, but they are more opaque than traditional Western watercolors and handle somewhat differently; try them out.

Good-quality paints are worth the expense; they are pigment dense and go a very long way when mixed with water. If you are careful to pick light-fast hues, they are permanent. Even for sketching, I choose pigments that won't flake or fade with time. Check with your dealer for a chart on light-fastness before choosing a color.

If you like, use a limited palette; you can get by quite well with only a few colors. Choose one each of the primaries—red, yellow, and blue—and supplement with a few of the earth colors: burnt umber, burnt sienna, and raw sienna or yellow ochre. I usually use a warm and a cool of each primary: cadmium red (warm) and alizarin crimson (cool), ultramarine blue (warm), and Thalo blue (cool), and cadmium yellow medium—or new gamboge, a more transparent yellow—(warm), and cadmium yellow lemon (cool). With these I could mix all the greens, purples, and oranges I'd ever need to capture virtually any subject—add the earth colors (such as burnt and raw sienna, burnt umber) and I'm set.

Even simpler is the Velasquez palette: Indian red, light red, or burnt sienna stand in for red; subtle, smoky yellow ochre acts as yellow; black—believe it or not—represents blue. It sounds crazy, but try this simple, elegant color range at least once—black and yellow ochre really do mix to make an interesting olive green.

I do, in fact, supplement my usual palette at home with a couple of greens and a cadmium orange, but I could live without them—in the interest of saving money *or* weight in the backpack.

Opaque watercolors, or gouache, also come in tubes or pan sets. You might like to try these for sketching; they're very popular in England. As the name suggests, they are opaque; you can add as many small details as you like over your preliminary washes without worrying about retaining or regaining lights. Acrylics and oils also have this tempting advantage: acrylics can be used either in a thick impasto or as clear, transparent, watercolor-like washes.

INKS

Sketching with pen and liquid ink is a bit unhandy; it's too easy to overturn the ink in the field or to break that glass bottle as it rattles around in your pack. For that reason, when I *do* carry liquid ink, I wrap the bottle in plastic bubble packing and tuck it into a tightly sealed Zip-lock plastic bag to prevent disaster.

You can buy good-quality inks in many colors these days; I prefer a waterproof black India ink or a soft, brown sepia. I can add color later, if I wish.

For portability, try one of the Oriental ink sticks. As the name suggests, this is a dry stick-form ink that you mix with water. A small inkstone to grind it with doesn't weigh much, and you can make only the amount of ink you need on the spot. This ink is capable of a wide range of values, depending on how much water is mixed in. (So is India ink, for that matter— dilute it with water as you like.)

SHARPENERS

Unless you are working with a 0.7-mm mechanical pencil or a graphite block—or watercolors—you'll need a sharpener of some sort. One of the best is a simple pocket knife that will allow you literally to carve the kind of point you want: uniformly pointed, angled, notched, and so on. An X-acto

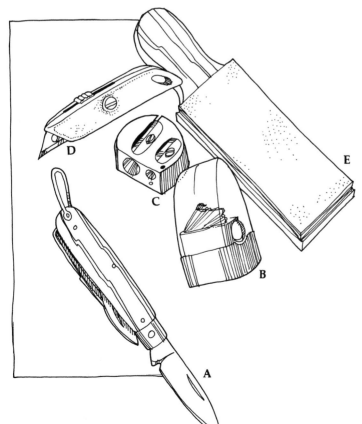

*A pocketknife (**A**) is really all you need to sharpen your pencils, but you may prefer a school-type (**B**), an imported technical pencil sharpener (**C**), or a tiny, retractable craft knife (**D**). A sandpaper block (**E**) can modify your point as desired.*

blade will also work, but be sure to get one with a cover; these blades are nonretractable and can be lethal. I have a small craft knife with a retractable, razor-sharp blade that hangs on my key chain; works great.

A wooden block with sandpaper works well to achieve a fine point or to sharpen some of the more exotic tools.

You may like an inexpensive school-type sharpener; these often have a hood to catch your shavings as well so you can carry *out* everything you carried *into* the field.

Whether you choose to sharpen with a knife or razor or a mechanical sharpener, you can run the lead over a piece of paper or fine sandpaper to make an angled tip. This will give you a fine point or a good, flat edge to work with for variety.

MISCELLANEOUS TOOLS

If you're working with watercolor and haven't bought a watercolor box to carry your paints and provide you with mixing areas, you'll need a palette. Choose a white plastic or porcelain one so you'll be able to judge accurately the strength and purity of your colors. (Having a white mixing surface lets you see with some accuracy what you'll get when you touch brush to white paper.)

At home or on serious painting expeditions, I use a large John Pike palette with deep, generous wells to keep colors separate and unsullied. This model has a large primary mixing area plus a lid that acts as additional mixing surface if I need it. A recent trip to the art supply store amazed me with the variety of styles and sizes of palettes; you can't go far wrong if you just remember to suit your *own* needs, buy a white background, and look for separate wells to keep your colors pure.

A supply of tissues or paper towels is handy for mopping up spills, lifting watercolor washes to lighten, texture, or otherwise alter them (and for catching sneezes).

A sponge can perform many of the same jobs. I buy mine in the hardware store; look for a natural sponge. You can even paint with a sponge for interesting texture effects, or wash off large areas of pigment with a sponge moistened with clear water. (An artificial sponge works as well to lift areas of color, and may be less expensive.)

Burnishing or scribing tools expand your capabilities.

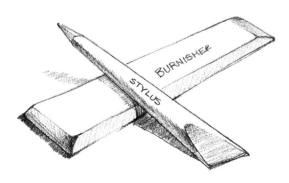

For special applications, you may want a burnishing tool or a scribing tool. With these you can regain the smoothness of paper that has become roughed up or scribe light lines to stand out against a darker ground (see Chapter 2).

Extremely miscellaneous are those tools that help us see. They open new worlds for exploration and inspiration, and although you may not have thought of them as artist's aids, they are. A telescope can bring a white dot on a distant mountain close enough to sketch the ridges on a bighorn sheep's horns. A microscope can introduce us to unseen beauty. Even a simple hand lens opens new horizons right under our noses.

Your miscellaneous tools list, in fact, may grow like a weed—as you work, you'll find things that seem suddenly indispensable; add them to your list. And don't hesitate to weed things *out* that you no longer use; a sketcher's kit is a living thing, always in a state of flux, changing as your needs do.

THE BACKPACKER'S ART—KEEP IT LIGHT

The "keep it light" rule applies to all of us who work in the field, not only to backpackers—we have a lot to learn from the dedicated packer's close attention to total weight. It's amazing how heavy your sketching supplies can get only a few hundred feet from the trailhead—or from your car!

My simplest sketching outfit consists of a small, hardbound book and my 0.7-mm mechanical pencil. That's all I really need, and it weighs only ounces. I can make color notes directly on my sketches to remind myself of what I saw, and add color later, at home. To work in color in the field, I add a few colored pencils.

If I plan to sketch in watercolor, it gets a bit more complicated—but not much. I carry a book of Notchy Postcards, a set of folding watercolor brushes, a graphite pencil for preliminary planning, or a Prismacolor colored pencil in warm, dark gray or sepia. For color, a wonderful set of traveling watercolors from Winsor & Newton works best for me in most cases; it's virtually indestructible in high-impact plastic. The tiny Cotman set has one tiny brush of its own, room for all the colors I need (twelve half-pans), three color-mixing areas, a small natural sponge, and its own water container and cup. At just around 5 ounces fully loaded with paint, water container filled, this is a backpacker's dream. It doesn't hold *much* water, but for small 4- × 6-inch sketches, it's at least sufficient. Since I'm not often in the desert and water is normally available, this is not a big drawback. There are several companies that make a similar product—shop around.

It seems everyone has jumped on the sketching bandwagon. There are any number of small traveling watercolor kits available, including a competitor for the Cotman set, complete with mixing wells and a water container. Cotman even makes its *own* competition in the form of a simpler and much less expensive small set of paints. The Russian Yarko set could be used out of doors, as could Pelikan's Transparent Watercolors. Both of these come in lightweight, unbreakable plastic cases, though Yarko's black container would make mixing a challenge. There are metal watercolor boxes that can be filled with cakes. These haven't changed in design in over 100 years. I still use mine.

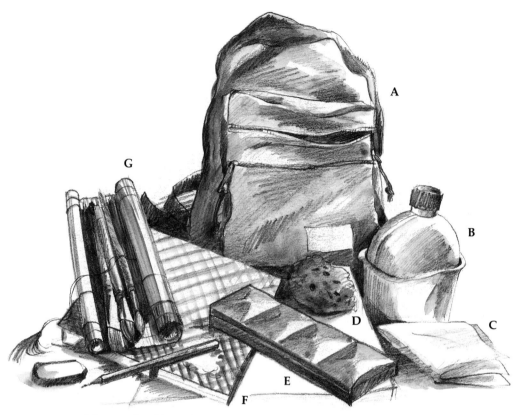

A longer sketching trip tempts me to take everything but the proverbial kitchen sink—including lunch. I use an old daypack as a traveling studio.

For a serious sketching trip when that's *all* I intend to do, I take the big guns. I have a daypack (**A**) especially outfitted for painting. It's at the ready by my front door so I have no excuses—I can't say I don't want to take the time to pack. The body of the pack is big enough to hold a metal paint box (**E**) *or* my big John Pike palette from my home studio, a 9- × 12-inch water-color block (**F**), an old army canteen with drinking cup (**B**) to hold paint water, a supply of tissues (**C**), a sponge (**D**), and my brushes. I use a bamboo placemat (**G**) to roll my brushes in to protect their hairs in transit; the open weave allows them to dry thoroughly after use. I may take as many as ten brushes in the daypack.

Two zippered compartments hold incidentals: small sketchbooks, pencils, sharpeners, erasers, and a sandwich and a piece of fruit or a candy bar, if I'm planning to spend the day. A thermos fits in the pack too, and in summer I take insect repellent and sunblock, neither of which I ever remember to use.

This outfit has gone cross-country on teaching workshops and traveled thousands of miles; it's gone with me as well to the park two blocks from my home. It seems to meet any need I've yet come up with—or it will do until I find that perfect tool.

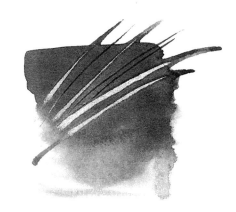

TWO

Getting Started

FINDING YOUR WAY around a sketchbook is largely a matter of learning
how to *see*—seeing what is there, seeing what you *want* to sketch,
seeing what makes a good subject, seeing how to get that down on paper—
seeing, in other words, like an artist. It gets easier with practice. Once you
have done that—and that's the fun part—the other techniques are gravy.
The process of sketching itself almost becomes second nature.

Of immediate importance—before theories, techniques, or tools—is
the art and nature of seeing, and your own response to what you see. There
is a lot going on out there; it's all exciting, but it *can't* all fit on a sketchbook
page. What should you choose to get down? That's the most personal decision you will make, whatever your primary purpose for being out there,
sketchbook in hand.

Unless you are sketching for a very particular reason—to draw all the
mushrooms that grow in late April, say—the first order of business is to let
yourself take the time to respond. There's no hurry—time spent in letting
the abundance of nature settle like flecks of gold in a miner's pan is never
wasted. Unless you are racing to catch the field marks of an unfamiliar bird
in flight, you can take your time, kick back, and let it soak in. What catches
your eye, begging to be explored? What asks a question or stirs a memory?
What strikes a chord?

FINDING WHAT YOU WANT TO SKETCH

It's often helpful to use a viewfinder to isolate your subject from the visual
confusion. A viewfinder gives me a movable "window on the world" and
helps to frame a possible composition. This needn't be anything complicated; take along an empty 35-mm slide mount and use it to sight through.

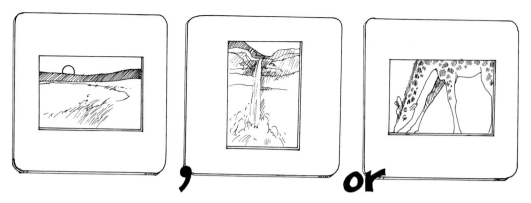

An empty slide mount or a homemade cardboard viewfinder will help you zero in on a subject and choose a format to best express that subject. Try it both ways—vertical and horizontal—to see what speaks to you.

Move it farther or closer to your eyes, or turn it sideways to help you to see the most pleasing aspect. Some subjects—the tall-grass prairie, a low, flat island, the broad meanders of a river—might work best horizontally, while the spectacular waterfalls of Yosemite or a magnificent sandhill crane beg to be sketched vertically. Don't overlook the more subtle handlings—an obvious vertical needn't be sketched that way if you want a fresh look at a familiar subject. That's where your slide mount comes in—see how that giraffe looks as an extreme horizontal, all legs and neck. It's a different look at the subject that helps to capture the unique *truth*.

If a slide mount seems too small, cut your own viewfinder from lightweight cardboard or heavy paper, any size you want. If you like, cut two holes (as shown), one for a "normal" rectangular opening (perhaps 3 × 4 inches) and another with more acute dimensions (2 × 4 inches) to frame an

You may prefer to cut two rectangles from your cardboard—one a "normal" shape and one more extreme, to increase your sensitivity to the possibilities before you.

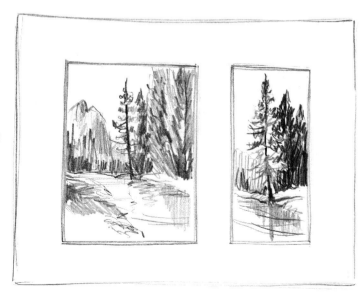

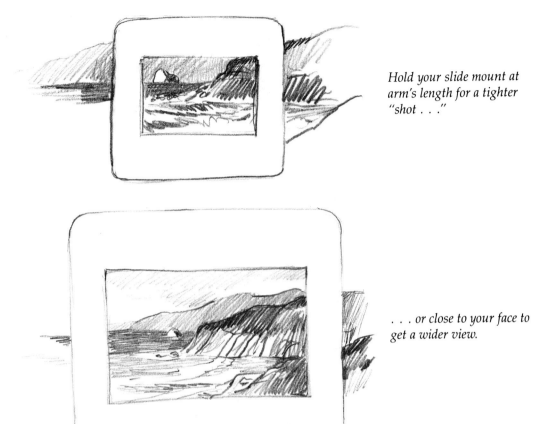

Hold your slide mount at arm's length for a tighter "shot . . ."

. . . or close to your face to get a wider view.

extreme vertical or horizontal (depending on how you hold it). There are even commercial versions of the viewfinder idea—check with your supplier.

Hold your cardboard "window" at arm's length for a tighter view, or bring it up close to your face for a "wide-angle shot" for the broadest possible range of choices.

My camera acts as a viewfinder, as well. As I aim it, I become more aware of pictorial possibilities. The rectangular format of a single-lens reflex camera allows me to look for a horizontal or a vertical picture possibility; it gives me practice in "seeing."

Another old artist's trick for isolating a composition is to frame it with your hands, a bit like an old Hollywood cinematographer (as shown), or make a box with your hands to work just like a viewfinder. Again, it's just a technique to help your brain translate what you see before you to the flat surface of your paper—and one advantage to the hands trick is that you can't forget and leave them at home.

Having a framing device helps our brains translate and isolate that confusing cornucopia of nature to something that will fit on a 5- × 7-inch sketchbook page—and even suggests ways to place it there.

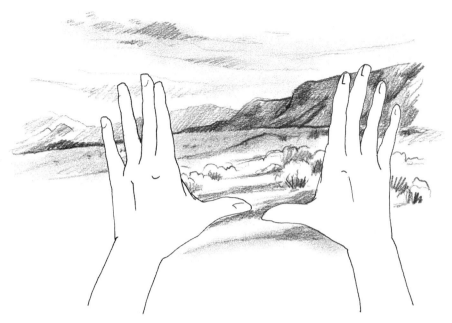

Your hands can help you "see" the vignette you want to sketch.

After a while, this framing trick may become so ingrained in your seeing that a physical object—your viewfinder—may no longer be necessary. You'll be able to imagine that frame around anything you see.

I often freehand a quick border on my sketchbook page to help me relate what I see through my viewfinder (even if I'm only using the mental one

An 0.5-mm fiber-tipped pen was used for this quick sketch of an immense root that reaches halfway across a ravine; the border helped me to correctly draw the angles.

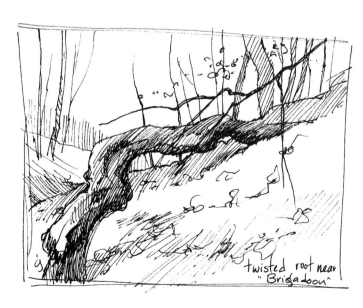

I've acquired through practice) to the edges of my paper. I can contain my sketch within this vertical or horizontal shape, and thus see more easily the relationships between what I see there and what I see before me. It's easier to correctly depict angles if I have the constant of the border to measure against.

SIMPLIFYING THE SCENE

Nature is full of details: the varied tapestry of leaves; a million pebbles, each with its individual shape and color; the lovely confusion of winter weeds. We take it all in with our eyes—or think we do—but there's no way to translate that to paper; no need to, either. In fact, the human eye sees much like a camera lens; what we focus on is sharp and clear. Other things tend to be hazy, out of focus—simplified. Artists simplify what they see, as well, distill it to its essence, translate it to form and volume and value.

Look for the major shapes to help you simplify your subject. Pretend you're doing a collage rather than a sketch, and outline the shapes you might tear from your imaginary paper. Notice their relationships to one another. Mentally overlap them to suggest distance, one thing closer to you in space than another. Or, if you like, *do* a cut or torn-paper collage of your subject to enlist your brain's capacity to see these shapes more clearly.

See how many details you can eliminate. It's that tangle of detail that often intimidates us when we begin to work. It's easy to become confused and produce something that looks more like camouflage fabric than a cohesive work of art—or even a readable sketch. See what you can do without while still expressing the basic truth of your subject—find the abstract *bones.* You can always flesh it out later with all the detail you could want, once you've established the gestalt.

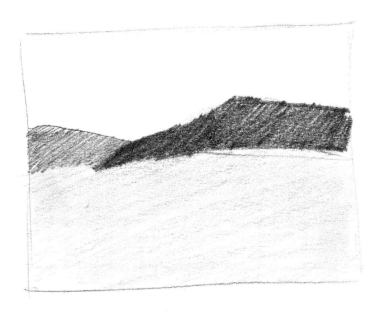

Simplify shapes and values by imagining your subject as a paper collage.

A MATTER OF VALUES

On a larger scale, the very patterns of light and dark can confuse the eye, especially if we try to get them all down on paper. There are so many gradations of value there, so many tones of gray. Color may confuse the issue, further—it's no wonder we sometimes have trouble accurately seeing what's before us.

Value patterns help our brain make the visual transition between the reality before us and the reality we've chosen to get down on paper. They are what gives form and volume to a simple line drawing—they "flesh out" this illusion we're creating.

Practice seeing—discerning—these values rather than details. From the lightest light—the white of your paper—to pure black, these values or shades of light and dark not only add the sense of depth and reality to our sketches, they also help us place things in relationship to other things. In landscape, light objects often recede (such as far, hazy hills) while things in the foreground appear sharp and dark. (Not always, of course; if your foreground is a sunlit hill of pale, dry grass and your background is a cloud-shaded conifer forest, your values are just reversed. The contrast helps suggest distance.)

But often it's hard to see how much gray there *is* in this brightly colored world. Unlike most of the other animals we share this earth with, we're not color-blind; we don't see only in black and white and the shades of gray in between.

To help you find these values, make a value chart or scale, with rectangles graded from light to dark. Use an HB or No. 2 pencil or watercolor washes with only black pigment. Punch a hole in each value area, as shown. You can hold this chart up next to the scene before you and look through the holes to find just where that bright yellow or rich green falls on the value scale. Match that shade when you draw, and your sketch will have the same sense of monochromatic reality as an Ansel Adams photo . . . well, maybe not. But it *will* have a sense of depth and light.

Carry a bit of tinted Plexiglas or cellophane to help you discern values. Look through this brightly colored stuff and some of the gradations of light and dark disappear—you see the major value patterns only. Dark or polarized glasses work almost as well, or just squint your eyes to simplify the shades of light and dark. This cuts out both detail and too wide a value range, and can be a very useful—and portable!—trick for the artist.

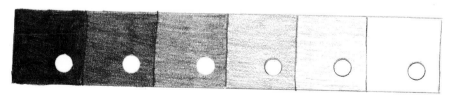

To help you see the values even in the brightly colored world out there, use a value scale. By looking through the small holes at your subject, you'll be able to correctly judge the value of your chosen subject.

This is an effective device even when sketching in color instead of black and white. We still use value in the shades (darks) or tints (lights) we choose, to give a sense of reality and depth. If we've learned to see value accurately, it's much easier to pick the right color to depict the subject or capture the mood we want to create. (An overall light or high-keyed sketch with only a few darks often suggests a sunny, lighthearted mood while the darker values are generally more somber.)

THE ANGLE OF REPOSE—PENCIL TRICK NO. 1

Sometimes it's difficult to see the long slant of that hill as it relates to the flat plane of your paper, or the angle between two limbs of a tree we've chosen to draw. The odd perspective of a long sand spit by the open ocean needs to be drawn correctly or our sketch threatens to pour all the water in the bay into our laps. We can *see* the line with our eyes, but getting it right on the paper eludes us.

It's easy, and the oldest trick in the book. Hold your pencil at arm's length, aligned with the angle of whatever it is you're drawing—line it up along the shoreline of that sand spit, say. Then lay the pencil *at that same angle* flat on your paper. That's where you draw your line. It's an old perspective aid that can be used in a hundred ways. Seeing that straight line (your pencil) out there in space, apparently on the same visual plane as what you're drawing, helps fix the line in your mind.

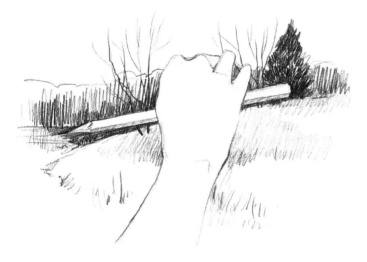

Use your pencil to find and transfer angles.

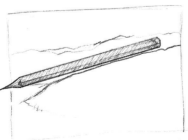

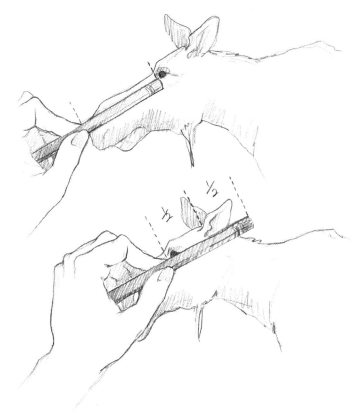

Use your pencil and your thumb to take a measurement. Move to the next area you want to measure, keeping your thumb in the same place on the pencil.

TAKING THE MEASURE—PENCIL TRICK NO. 2

Your pencil can act as visual aid and measuring device in another way, as well. At first glance, it's easy to overlook the spatial relationship between objects, or their relative size. The result can be a bear with eyes too close together or a moose with a nose entirely too long. To avoid these problems—and to help you see correctly—hold the pencil, again, at arm's length. Take one measure by holding the top of the pencil at one end of the area you need to measure and placing your thumb at the other end. Keep your thumb in place and move your pencil to the next area you want to compare. Notice the difference between these two measurements, and keep those relative differences when you translate moose to paper.

LINE IT UP—PENCIL TRICK NO. 3

This trick can help you find *alignments* you might overlook, as well. (Pencils are invaluable for a lot more than just drawing.) Hold your pencil vertical to what you want to draw; notice where other salient features fall (as shown) to see where to place them on your paper. This trick can help you see just where that wing covert comes in relationship to the nape of the neck, or where an animal's eye is in relationship to the edge of its nose.

Of course, all this squinting and posturing and pencil-at-arm's-length

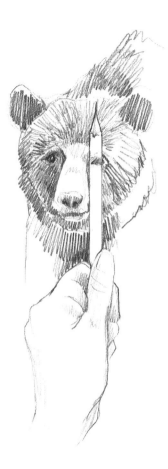

Use your pencil to find alignments—here, with the inside of the bear's eye and the outside of the muzzle. (If you are really this close to a bear, don't stop to sketch!)

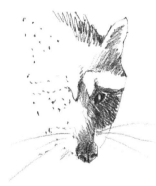

Make dots at important points to help you place your subject on the page—a dot is easy to cover or erase.

business is going to make you look a little strange to the general public. Grin sheepishly, say, "I'm an artist," and ignore the spectacle you're making. (Or draw where there's no one about, or develop a deeply contemplative attitude that can't be shaken by casual observers.) It's worth it if it helps you see better.

SOME HINTS ON WORKING PROCEDURES

If that blank paper still seems to bother you—we all have performance anxiety at times!—it helps to "image" your work onto your paper before you begin to draw. See your subject already down in black and white—or living color. Imagine that it's there on your paper, and then *trace over* that mental image. Getting your bearings by imaging is not only the province of artists, these days—Olympic athletes, rock climbers, dancers, fly fishermen, and others are finding that this *mental* practice helps improve physical performance.

Make phantom lines above your paper's surface to plan placement of major elements, or touch only the point of your pencil to the paper at important points to make your own dot-to-dot game to fill in once you've placed things to your satisfaction. And *think* of it as fun, by the way. It can

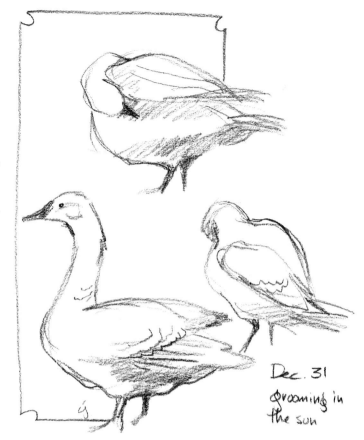

"Restate" lines along the way to find your subject on that white paper—it's there. Restatements aren't mistakes; they're a pilgrimage on the way to truth. (Berol Prismacolor pencil.)

be a game; Art—with a capital "A"—may be dead serious to some people, but sketching needn't carry such heavy baggage.

Making "shadow lines" or restating your subject works much the same way. These restatements are not mistakes; they're just a means of finding your way. Sketching is like a meandering walk; we discover our subject along the way. There's no need to nail it the first time—sometimes it's more fun to surprise ourselves. (Don't erase these restatements, by the way. They add a nice vibration, a sense that your sketch is a living, changing thing.)

HOLD IT!

How you hold your drawing tool affects your technique. Think about it; if you hold your pencil tightly near the point, as if you were going to write, you can use only the muscles in your fingers—or, at most, your hand. Loosening up, holding the pencil further up the shaft, or using the artist's grasp (shown) lets you use your wrist and forearm for a freer, looser effect.

Experiment with both of these to see which suits you—and your subject—best. A landscape might benefit from a looser hold on that pencil or pen, while a detail sketch of a weed or tree you find in that landscape might

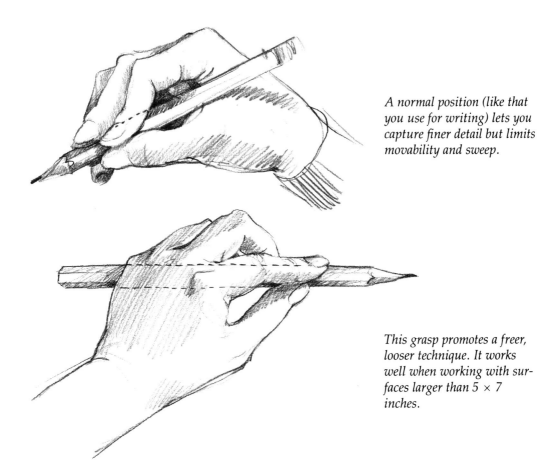

A normal position (like that you use for writing) lets you capture finer detail but limits movability and sweep.

This grasp promotes a freer, looser technique. It works well when working with surfaces larger than 5 × 7 inches.

need the increased control of a more familiar, tighter grip. Generally, you are capable of more graceful, sweeping marks if you loosen up a bit. This is especially important if you are working larger than, say, 9 × 12 inches. In a tiny sketchbook, there's hardly room for sweep. And I'll admit—I most often use a slightly modified writing grip; it's a holdover from being largely self-taught. The best rule here is—use whatever grasp is comfortable and *works* for you.

GET SHARP

How you sharpen your pencil, whether it's a No. 2 office pencil or a water-soluble colored pencil, makes a difference in the marks it can make. A modern pencil sharpener produces a cone-shaped lead with a good point for details or sharp linear effects. For broader effects, use the side of the lead or modify the tip by running it repeatedly over your paper or a piece of fine sandpaper.

Before mechanical sharpeners were available, pencil wielders used a knife or other blade to give their leads a point. And what a point! A knife-sharpened pencil has character. It will provide an extensive range of marks,

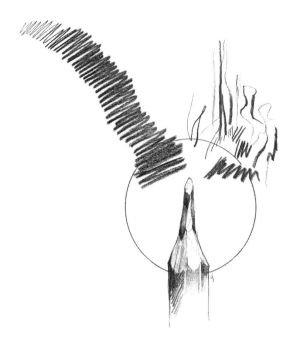

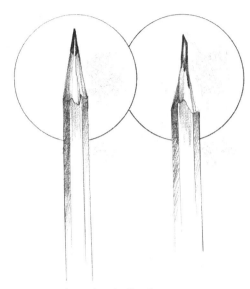

A knife-sharpened pencil can create a wide range of marks; hone the tip by running it over your paper or a sandpaper sharpening block.

A mechanically sharpened pencil, left, is convenient and has a sharp point, but the point quickly dulls. A knife-sharpened pencil, right, may have a stronger point; it's also capable of a wider range of marks.

depending on how you've chosen to sharpen it: a fine edge, a wider chisel, the long, flat side of the lead (shown). Often you can keep turning the pencil to maintain a fresh, sharp edge while keeping the chisel in fine order as well. Knife-sharpened leads are not likely to break or wear down as quickly as those sharpened mechanically.

To achieve this degree of versatility, I keep a tiny retractable craft knife among my sketching tools and wield it carefully, almost like sculpting. In the studio, a sandpaper block or sheet of scrap paper keeps an edge on my lead until it's worn nearly down to the wood; then I get out my craft knife and expose a new length of lead.

Look at my sample drawing, done with a knife-sharpened pencil; I used light, zigzag marks and rubbed them with my finger to make a soft, cloud effect. Then I put the chisel edge to work with repeated strokes to suggest the ranks of trees. The entire side of the lead made a smooth tone to suggest the dark hillside. Using the lead at an angle let me make open, scalloped strokes for the foliage on the light foreground trees, and the sharp tip of the lead made good bare limbs and twigs. (The light lines of the light-struck branches was another trick—I used a wooden burnishing tool to incise the paper, then rubbed my pencil over the tiny impressions; the graphite doesn't get down into the grooves. In the field, I've often used my fingernail to achieve the same effect, pushing hard into the paper's surface where my lights will be before I begin to draw.)

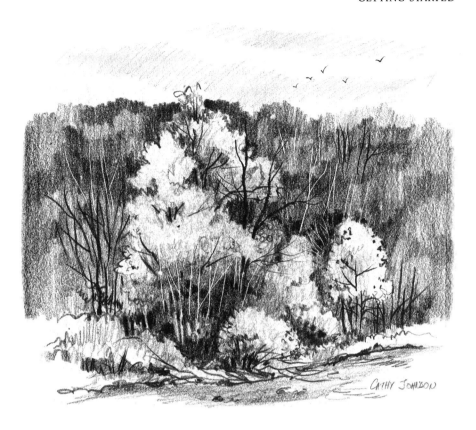

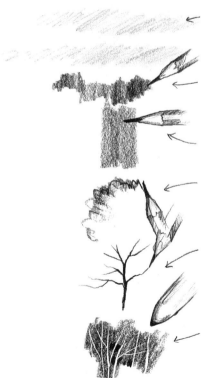

(a) Sky rendered lightly, smudged with finger for cloud effects.

(b) Use pencil on an angle with short repeated strokes (vary pressure).

(c) Use full length of lead on its side for smooth, quick, even coverage.

(d) Angle lead, and try zigzag or scalloped strokes for foliage.

(e) Use the tip of the lead, turned and twisted with varied pressure, for fine twigs and branches.

(f) Before *drawing, press light lines to the paper's surface with a burnishing tool, toothpick, or brush end— then work over the area with pencil.*

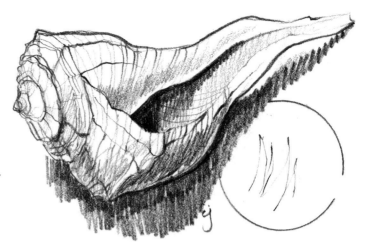

Linear effects. Follow the contour of your subject with your drawing tool to capture the sense of depth. (HB pencil.) Study early etchings to see how artists have used the direction of their lines to suggest form.

MAKING YOUR MARK

Use the direction of your strokes to suggest planes, the geometric forms of your subject. Angular rock forms or tree bark may be sketched in this way. Moving water can be captured with this trick as well—follow the direction of the flow with your strokes to imply dynamic movement. Follow the shape of your subject with your pencil lines to suggest roundness as well, as in my sketch of the seashell.

Use bold strokes for the foreground and a lighter pressure (or harder lead) for the background, or bolder strokes in the areas where you want to focus attention. One artist I know makes a darker mark at each turning of leaf or twig; another uses her boldest strokes to suggest those things closest to the viewer. Play with your sketching tools to find the effect you prefer.

This "play" is not confined to pencils, of course. You can use these same sketching techniques with fiber-tipped pens, art sticks, or vine charcoal; the same strokes apply to almost any sketching medium, even to watercolor if you are using a linear style.

And if this sounds like rather a lot of preparatory work—it is. No one expects to ride a bicycle the first time on, or play the piano after one lesson. You fell down the first time you tried to walk, didn't you? Like anything else worthwhile, sketching takes some practice, some preliminary research, some getting familiar with necessary tools. It shouldn't be daunting or discouraging.

The time you put in getting to know your tools in the preceding chapter will stand you in good stead here; you'll know which brush to grab to capture that rough, weedy patch beside the road, or what pen stroke to try to suggest a rugged rocky coastline. Remember that it *is* a kind of play; sketching should be fun. Relaxing, even.

Now you're ready to get out and get started. We'll explore some of the ways to enlist the brain's right side to translate these basics of seeing like an artist to the pages of your sketchbook.

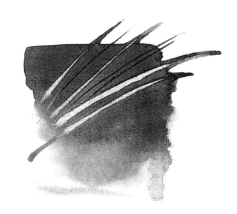

THREE

Putting the Basics to Work

ONCE YOU'VE STARTED down the road to seeing like an artist, sketching is pure pleasure. This is something we can do just for *fun*, just for ourselves, with no expectations at all; no one else may ever see your sketches, if you don't want them to.

Sketching can also be the most alive of all the visual arts; I'd often rather look at a fellow artist's sketchbook than at a painting he or she may have worked on for weeks. A sketch is vital, and catches some elusive, essential truth that's all too often buried under layers of paint and planning.

Knowing what each tool is capable of and what you need to do to make it live *up* to its capabilities is simply exploration and practice. Learning to see is a given. The basics of format, composition, and value are easy to use—with a bit of practice you can *break* the rules to give your work originality and power.

That's not to say your sketchbook isn't a good place to practice the more classical ins and outs of drawing. It is. I learn more about how to draw from simply picking up a pencil and sketching—seeing for myself what works and what doesn't—than from all the *reading* about art and techniques I may ever do. That's intellectual learning—essential, but not enough, not nearly. Sketching enlists hand and eye and brain, and puts them to a task together. It involves our whole selves.

Translating the technical into the sketcher's art is half the fun. By itself, a pencil can't capture the quizzical expression of a young raccoon. That takes the alchemy of human creativity that inhabits the right side of the brain.

Recent studies have taught us amazing things about the abilities of this brain hemisphere; everyone has creative aptitude, unless there has been

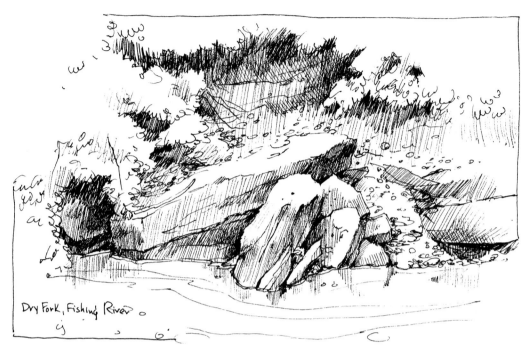

Dry Fork, Fishing River

An 0.5-mm fiber-tipped pen was used to render this sketch of rocks in the stream.

some massive trauma. It's simply a matter of unlocking that potential.

The right brain "sees" holistically—that is, whole systems at a glance. It grasps relationships between the parts, and how they fit together. It has a visual language all its own.

This side of the brain is intuitive. It *feels* its way. It is cognitive, nonlinear, and instinctive—even somewhat anarchistic. Rules don't apply; it has its own wisdom. We need to invoke it, invite it, enlist its aid—and then let it speak to us.

We can engage the more logical, linear left hemisphere to list possible solutions, suggest order to the steps along the way, and make final decisions *after* we've tapped into the right brain.

The left hemisphere is geared to the basic step-by-step of systems and techniques—even artistic ones. But without the right brain's input, the art produced might as well be computer generated. The right brain gives your work its power, its heart. (For an in-depth study of the right brain as it applies to artists, see Betty Edwards' watershed book, *Drawing on the Right Side of the Brain*, 1979, or her more recent *Drawing on the Artist Within*, 1987.)

We enter a different mode when drawing or painting—it's part of the creative function. You may have noticed that you don't feel the same—you don't feel "normal"—when you are creating. You've gotten on a different wavelength, somehow, hopped a creative freight. It may be meditative, contemplative; it may be a state of barely suppressed excitement, a kind of power, humming like Hoover Dam. Whatever *your* particular condition, it's hardly the everyday, nuts-and-bolts, get-the-job-done state.

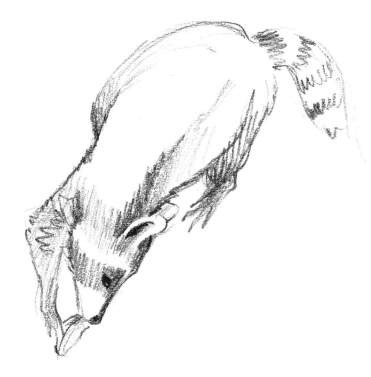

I kept this young raccoon for a day until it could be returned to the wild; it's sucking on an ice cube, the only way I could successfully get water inside its cage. (Berol Prismacolor pencil.)

I often find that when I'm teaching I have every intention of explaining exactly what I'm doing at each step—and why. Instead, my voice drifts off and stops, and I'm sunk knee-deep in the act of creating. When I come *back* it's as if from a long journey, and I have to think hard to remember what it was I wanted to say. I've been off in R-mode (as Edwards calls it), and the shift back to left-brain functioning—explaining, making verbal sense of the step-by-step process—isn't always smooth.

There are techniques for unlocking the right brain's capabilities, simple exercises to invite it out to play—or to advise. And there are "rules" to follow to help you suggest perspective, volume, and distance that have stood artists—and art *teachers*—in good stead for centuries. In this chapter, we'll explore some of these basics and, in the process, involve both hemispheres of the brain.

RIGHT-BRAIN EXERCISES

These right-brain exercises are good warm-ups for the most accomplished artist, but they'll also help the novice past that "I can't draw a straight line" stage. (Neither can I, and who cares? That's why someone invented rulers.)

At first, do the exercises in this order; later on, use only those that seem to work best for you. I seldom warm up by drawing my response now; I'm enough in touch with my own creativity that I can trust my feelings without seeing them in black and white.

I can't claim to have invented these exercises, or most of them, anyway;

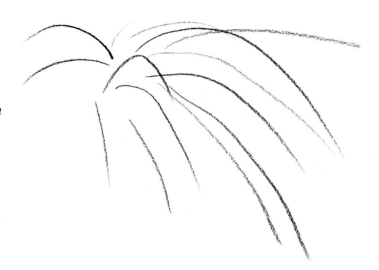

This is the feeling I got from a spray of water—kind of lighthearted and buoyant.

Betty Edwards, Clare Walker Leslie, Charles Reid, and others have suggested many of them before me. They *are* excellent practice, and they seem to provide a breakthrough experience for artists at any level of expertise.

—*Draw your response, not your subject.* This is great fun, and very freeing. Obviously, there's no right or wrong way to do this warmup exercise— no one but you knows how a subject will make you feel. This is the place to use symbols, if you like: long, undulating lines to depict peace, angular squiggles to express anxiety, cloudlike shapes, circles, dark scribbles, graceful sweeps—whatever feels right. You'll not only unlock the brain's creative right side—you're telling it you're ready to pay attention, after all—but you'll be warmed up and ready to draw further.

No response to the subject you've chosen, you say? You don't feel anything? No images suggest themselves? Then pick another subject. Why waste your time on something you don't care about?

—*Work fast.* Choose a subject—preferably one you can hold in your hand or sit close to—and do a three- to five-second "gesture sketch." Capture the overall movement, flow, shape, and direction of your subject. No need to worry about detail or getting everything right— and in fact, in this amount of time you can't worry about *anything*; there's hardly time to think. You can't expect to create a finished piece of art in three seconds, so you are able to break through your expectations of yourself and at the same time kill the curse of that blank white

I like these quick sketches—they're fresh and often amazingly accurate, in the sense that they capture essence. They have an easy grace. (They're also quite good practice for when you're drawing a moving subject. If the bird flies, you've still got something, and probably a pretty *good* something as your hand-eye coordination improves.)

—*Try a blind or pure contour drawing.* As the name suggests, in this exercise you look *only* at your subject—not at your paper at all. Pretend your

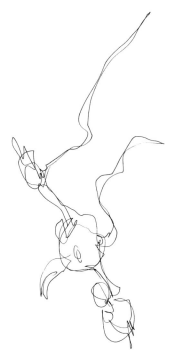

Root knot, gesture sketch

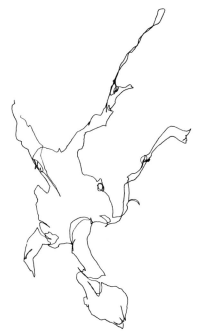

*Root knot, blind contour
drawing*

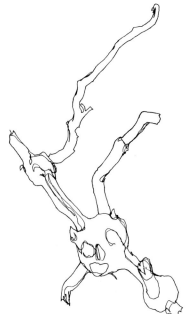

*Root knot, modified contour
drawing*

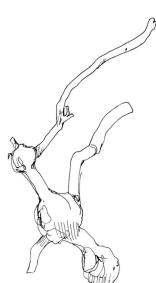

Root knot, memory drawing

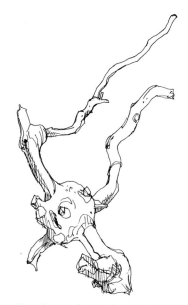

Root knot, direct observation

pencil point is actually crawling along the contours—the edges—of the object you've chosen to draw. Don't lift your point from the page; draw *into* the form if you want to trace the inner details, then return to the edge and continue drawing.

Take as long as you like with this exercise. Depending on the complexity of your subject, that could mean five minutes—or an hour. And again, you break down your expectations of yourself to produce a "good" drawing. How *could* you, without even looking at your paper? You may end up nowhere near where you began, or draw right over initial lines—and so what? (This exercise is good for overachievers like myself, especially those who also make their living from their art. I can't aim for perfection—and it's exhilarating!)

Beyond the inevitable inaccuracies, there *is* something wonderful about a blind contour drawing. It makes you look—and it lets you *see*. The finished sketch has a quirky freshness, an immediacy that captures the truth of your subject in a way no anxious, self-conscious drawing can.

—If you like, *do a modified contour drawing next*. Look down only when making a major change of direction to make sure details end up where they belong. Again, draw into your subject's form, and out into background areas without lifting your pencil from the paper; author-artist Charles Reid does wonderful paintings with this technique; his underdrawing shows through fresh watercolor washes.

Draw exactly what you see—never mind what logic tells you. You may *know* a twig is as long as the others on a branch, but if it comes toward you in space it will appear foreshortened. Your eyes see that, if your mind does not—trust your eyes and your drawing will look "real." This applies, of course, to an animal's foreleg lifted toward you as it begins to walk, a leaf that comes forward in the picture plane, a branch that's bent backward—anything that is three-dimensional and takes up a certain depth in space. Modified contour drawing—and faith in your own abilities—will help you capture that truth.

When you use this modified technique, you are still involved with something outside yourself, as you are with pure contour drawing, but you can be a bit more concerned with what's going down on paper. This can be an invaluable tool for creating an accurate and compelling image; if you've never drawn before, you'll be surprised at how right your drawing can be.

—*Do a memory drawing.* I especially like this exercise because it keeps my seeing ability in fighting trim. I pay attention. I'm there.

Look at your subject intently for three to five minutes—longer, if you like. Notice all the details. Let it soak in; imagine your subject imprinting itself on your brain cells. And at the same time, enlist the help of the left brain—ask yourself questions about your subject. If it's a leaf, for instance, what sort of edge does it have (toothed, lobed, smooth?), and are the veins opposite or alternate? What does it feel like—rough or hairy or smooth? Is it symmetrical or somewhat off center? Is it undamaged, or has it been chewed into a network of holes by hungry insects? How does this angle relate to that line? Just look— don't draw a thing, yet.

Don't be impatient with yourself. We're not used to focusing such concentrated attention—we do three things at once, normally. In a recent study on human concentration, subjects were asked to put up their hands as soon as their attention wavered. It took less than ten seconds, for most.

When you've looked all you can, turn your back on your subject or put it behind you. Draw everything you remember. Take all the time you like. When you're done, look again; your drawn image may be amazingly accurate—because you've allowed yourself to really *see* and to respond before drawing.

I use this exercise in my workshops to help my students tap the right brain *and* harness the left.

—*Do another sketch of the same subject, but this time from direct observation.* Use any combination of gesture, modified contour, and memory drawing that seems right; you will without thinking about it, actually. You're primed and ready, all warmed up.

FURTHER WORKOUTS

If you want to do more, try these exercises. The basics are sufficient for warming up, but artists often find they've fallen into *habits* of seeing—some good, some bad. We may have begun to draw all trees generically, for instance, or we've neglected the shapes around our subject—we need to broaden our focus. The bad habits need to be broken, or at least examined; even *good* habits need periodic review. These exercises help you do so.

—*Break away from symbols.* We're programmed in childhood to see an eye or a tree or a flower in symbolic terms—but we lose a lot by not upgrading our "program." To draw the fluid grace of a feline with two circles, two triangles, and a curved line for a tail—at any time past kindergarten—is to miss the point entirely.

If it helps you to overcome symbolic thinking—the kind that makes you see something other than what is before you, or at least makes you want to depict it in that way—and to see what you're really looking at, turn your subject upside down or look at it reversed in a mirror. Now draw that. It's just different enough to free us from that canoe-shaped eye or lollipop tree. (Contour drawing will also help to break free from the symbols we've been taught.)

There's nothing wrong with symbols used consciously, by the way. If you know what the object looks like and can draw it accurately, but just *want* to simplify it into symbolic form, you may be onto something very powerful.

—*Draw what isn't your subject.* That is, draw only the negative shapes *around* your subject, not the subject itself. Find the relationships

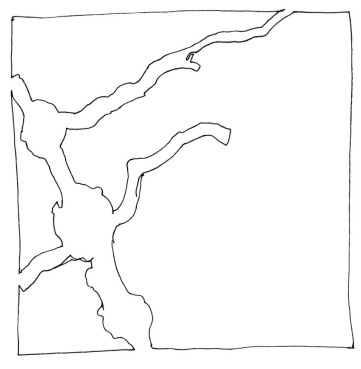

Root knot, negative shapes

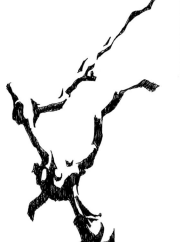

Root knot, chiaroscuro

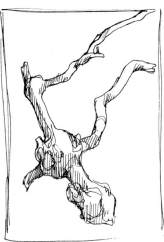

Root knot with border (helps to relate angles)

between shapes or areas; this exercise, too, helps break down those stereotypical images—my eye may *be* a canoe shape with a circle in it, looked at straight on, but the shape changes with the angle. By looking at the spaces around the shape, as Edwards suggests, you can accurately draw the eye (or anything else) while bypassing learned symbols.

An added bonus is that in looking at the negative shapes you can be sure to keep them varied and interesting. Rather than placing your subject stage front and equidistant from the edges of your picture plane, you can keep it slightly off balance. An asymmetrical placement is usually more pleasing to the eye and involves the *viewer's* right-brain functions as well.

—*Go one step further and use chiaroscuro*. Look for large lights and darks and draw *their* shapes; if the dark forms—and their relationships to the lights—are correct, your image will hang together and make sense.

Different from using the full range of values from white to black and all the shades of gray in between, here you simplify to the point of using *only* black and white. And since your paper is the white, all *you* need to do is look for the strong shadow shapes that define your subject. (Obviously, this one is easier to accomplish if what you are looking at is in full sun. An overcast day creates too many middle values and not enough contrast.)

—*Use a border*. An enclosure helps to find and relate the negative shapes and the angles formed by your subject. Measure against those straight edges (or even not-so-straight edges, as I freehand them in my sketchbook); if I can relate the angle of my subject to a constant horizontal or vertical line, I am much more able to discern that angle with accuracy.

—*See through your subject*. Pretend what you are looking at is transparent—visible, but transparent. Look for the continuation of lines and shapes behind other shapes. Draw these extensions with dotted lines or very pale ones. This approach not only helps you to see clearly—and logically, to the left brain's satisfaction—but also allows you to draw correctly. Say a bobcat is lying on its side with its legs folded over one another. By "seeing through" the upper leg, you can correctly place the lower one where it belongs.

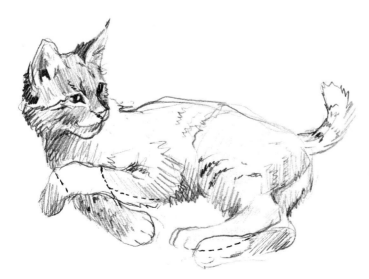

"See through" your subject to find the hidden logic. Here I've visualized what is going on behind the bobcat's upper foreleg, to make the lower one come out at the right place.

BASIC RULES AND THEORIES

Now that you've employed a number of *different* ways of seeing—some, perhaps, unfamiliar—your right brain should be fully engaged. It's a good time to try some of the more left-brain functions of organization and planning. These are the familiar "rules" of art, decked out in left-brain clothing. They're like a system of checks and balances, a way of using the combined artistic wisdom of the ages in your sketches. But as Bert Dodson, author of *Keys to Drawing* (North Light, 1985), says—"When rules conflict with seeing, forget them and draw what you see."

There are a thousand possibilities in nature, and compositions abound—some perfect just as they are, some not so perfect. Decisions as to what things to change and which ones to emphasize to make your sketch as effective as possible; decisions about values and how to use them to suggest form, distance, or mood; decisions about perspective, to suggest distance and relationship: that's where some of the *rules* of art can be a real help.

Remember, though, that rules were made to be broken, especially in the arena of creativity. They may better apply to the more formal act of painting, and can seem cumbersome if you are only sketching. They may get in the way. Listen to what you *want* to do; use the rules, if you like—and if they'll help. Ignore them, if they don't. You can always press them into service later, if you're translating a sketch to a more finished work.

COMPOSITION

You will already have made some decisions almost unconsciously. When you used your viewfinder (an ancient technique, by the way, that dates back to the early Renaissance—and beyond, for all I know), you chose an existing composition and a format to sketch it in. You may have been influenced by a number of things: what most pleased you in the scene; sketches and drawings you've seen and enjoyed; perhaps earlier teachings—you name it. And once you make the first tentative marks on your paper, you've already begun to plan a composition.

Use thumbnail sketches—tiny drawings no larger than 1 × 2 inches— to help you make some of these decisions. You won't have a lot of time tied up in these, obviously, so you'll feel more inclined to explore the possibilities. I can do one thumbnail sketch a minute—at least. It's fun, and instructive. Try out possible formats; modify your composition; use the values you see or change them to suit your mood.

Don't worry about detail in a thumbnail sketch; you're looking only at the major shapes here. It's a good way to discover those abstract "bones"— and it's another aid to simplification. And who can get too anxious about getting everything *right* when you can practically cover it with a postage stamp?

> —*One of the oldest rules of art is the Golden Mean*. It's a classical designation that puts the center of interest one-third of the way from the top and one-third from the side of your composition (as shown). It works

Horizon line too close
to center

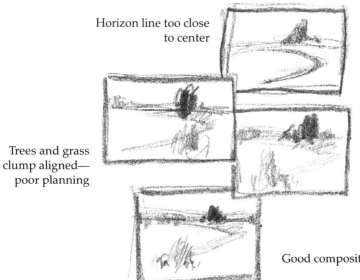

Trees and grass
clump aligned—
poor planning

Tree and grass clump
almost the same size
and shape—poor
planning

Good composition

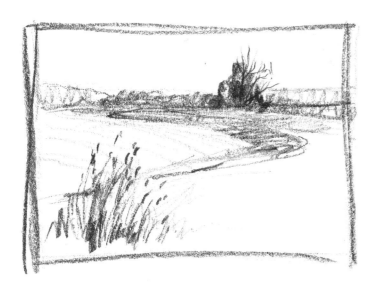

Uses not only a modified
S-curve, but a foreground
"arrow" as well

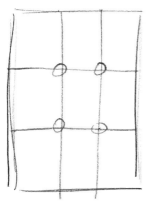

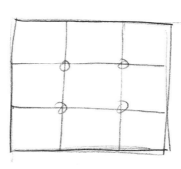

*The Golden Mean places the
focal point at one of these
intersections.*

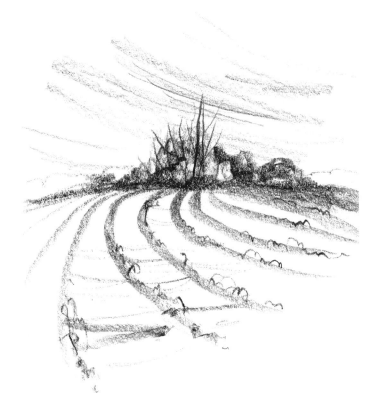

Focal point here is almost dead center, but softened by curving "invitational" lines in the foreground.

beautifully, whether you're using it with a wide-open landscape or a close-up of one of nature's details; it's a very pleasing proportion.

It *works*, and works well—but for sketching sometimes it's almost too perfect. Break that rule by just a bit, and you can create an interesting tension. There are times when I like to put my subject dead center when I am focused on it directly—especially for a botanical sketch—or far off to one side for a kind of lively "there it goes" feeling. This approach seems more suited to subjects that really *may* go; a bird or animal is always on the edge of flight. The more asymmetrical composition pleases me here.

—*Invite the eye into your composition*. There are a number of ways to do this, from employing a simple S-curve that leads into the picture plane to playing up—or inventing—a feature of landscape that will provide a "door." A road or trail can invite us in, or the curve of a river. A triangular "arrow" formed by a clump of grass or a group of rocks acts in the same way. A cloud shadow will also do. Used with subtlety, these ploys aren't obvious—just effective; such forms abound in nature. It's just a matter of seeing and emphasizing them.

Don't feel *bound* to include these shapes or S-lines. At times, when sketching the linear strata of a sandstone ledge, for instance, or low, flat undulations of the prairie, such a compositional "trick" would detract from the feeling I'm after. That linearness *is* the essence of the scene—another rule that can be broken, if you do it consciously.

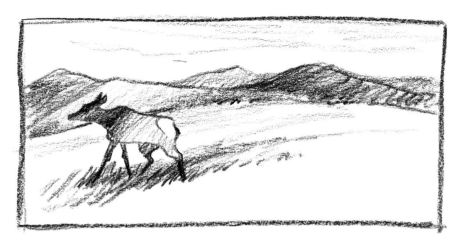

This sketch breaks a number of rules, but still expresses a lively truth *in the scene.*

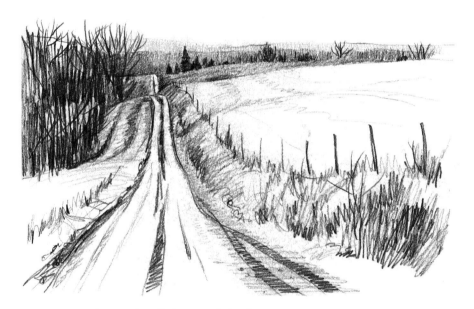

HB pencil used to render all three road sketches.

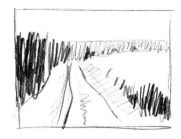
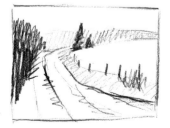

Unusual composition.

"Normal" composition;
"arrow" of the road points
the way into the picture.

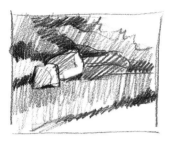

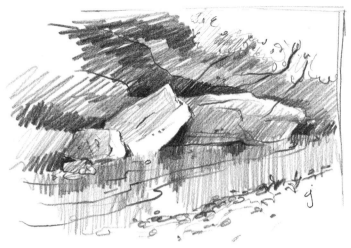

This sketch has three large rocks of varied size, shape, and value. Other shapes (shadows, lights, and darks) are kept varied, as well.

Mechanical pencil with HB lead was used on the final sketch.

—*Vary shapes, sizes, and numbers; try to avoid uniformity—it's boring.* Shapes should be somewhat different, even if you are sketching a line of ducklings. A large light shape should be balanced by a smaller dark one—or vice versa. Try to use an uneven number of things in your composition—three, or one, or seven, rather than two, say. (Again, use a bit of thought here, and if truth doesn't line up with the rule, go with truth. Canada geese mate for life, for instance, and if you draw three adults together the question naturally arises—which one lost its mate?)

In Oriental flower arranging, they follow the uneven number rule by designating one thing as heaven, one earth, and one man or mountain; works great for them, too.

—*Generally speaking, curved lines are more pleasing than straight ones—also, more common in nature.* Some tree trunks are straight, overall—but look closely to discern a narrowing near the top, a lean, a slight bending to the effects of prevailing wind over the years. Compositionally, these curves are more pleasing, as well—but do use straight lines where they apply (crystals, angular frost lines, sandstone layers, the horizon line on open sea). And be aware of the emotional impact you're creating, as well—straight lines can have a spiky nervousness that can be quite expressive.

USING A FOUR-VALUE SYSTEM

In the last chapter, I discussed learning to *see* the values in nature. Now we'll see how to simplify those values and to use them to suggest form, light and shadow, distance, and mood.

There are hundreds of subtle gradations of light and dark in nature; you'd make yourself crazy if you tried to reproduce them all in your sketchbook. Again, simplification is the key.

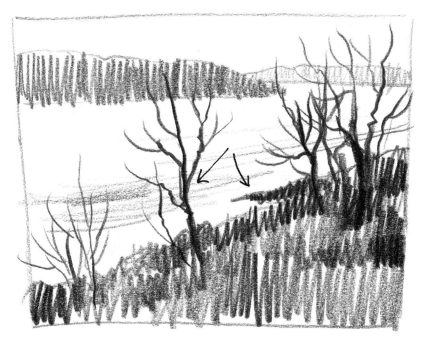

Using only four shades or values will let you render a believable sketch; here, you can "see" distance and detail, light and shadow, all within the confines of a single Prismacolor pencil—my usual warm, dark gray.

Try to limit your values to four: the white of your paper, your darkest dark (as close to black as the tool you've chosen will get—a fully saturated shade, at any rate), and two shades of gray in between.

Of course, there will be some variation in these halftones; unless you're cutting them from gray paper, your pencil lines or pen crosshatchings will naturally produce some variation. But in general, let these four stand in for everything you see.

They'll work quite well. Your eyes and brain will fill in the rest; that's one of the ways to involve the brain's right side.

The sky is usually the lightest thing in your sketch, unless you've included the sun—then *that* would have to be lightest. I use the white of my paper for the sky and for whatever the sunlight falls directly on—light-struck water, for instance. Then, I look for my next lightest area (distant hills, or a patch of pale winter weeds) and use a very pale gray. A good mid-tone gray may act for foreground objects—a tree, for example—or as middle shadow tones, and my black or darkest dark provides deep shadows and sharp details. Like a stage set, it's amazing how real this illusion can seem.

—*Use value to describe form.* Again, analyze where your lightest lights and darkest darks are, and try to catch their shapes and values accurately. Notice that *reflected* light sometimes bounces back up into shadow areas, lightening them, and that the darkest area may be just where an object turns from the light.

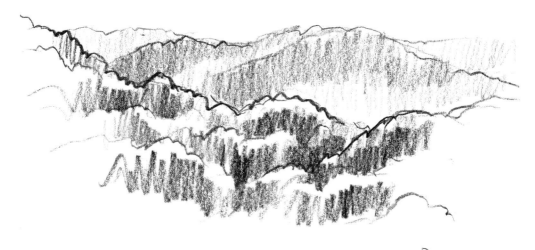

Ozark Mist

Values were used to suggest the receding planes of Missouri's Ozark hills. (Prismacolor sepia pencil.)

—*Use value to suggest distance.* Light areas seem to recede, and darker ones come forward. Often objects in the distance seem both lighter (and less detailed) than those that are close by. There is less contrast. It's a trick of atmosphere and light, of course—if we were on that far hill, we'd find it just as boldly colorful (and scrolled with details) as the one we're sitting on. But this particular trick of value can be used to give a sense of depth to our sketches, like that stage set analogy I suggested earlier.

Thunderstorm over Missouri hills. Overall mid-to-dark values give this little sketch a somewhat dramatic mood. (Prismacolor warm grey pencil with watercolor wash.)

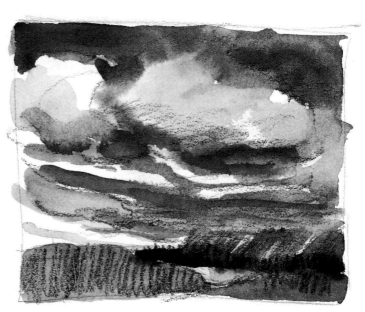

—*Use value to denote mood.* Lots of mid-tone grays and blacks make a moody, low-key sketch, indeed—reminiscent of a breaking storm or the coming of evening. A high-key sketch, with white paper and light tones, suggests a sunny day with the attendant lighthearted mood. Overall grays can be soothing or oppressive, depending on your subject matter. And a sketch with strong contrasts of light and dark may be dramatic, striking—even spectacular.

PERSPECTIVE

Even if you're drawing in the wide-open spaces without a building in sight, the reality of perspective remains unchanged. You won't see an obvious vanishing point, usually, as you might in a Manhattan street scene—but on the other hand, maybe you will. Perspective still applies. Things appear smaller the farther away they are—and again, lighter, and less detailed. *Aerial* perspective takes these things into account.

Natural features in the landscape follow the rules of perspective, in their own way, and can be used to define distance in your sketches. A road or game trail seems to narrow as it gets farther from the viewer. So does a river, though it might be just as broad a mile away as it is at your feet.

In an aerial perspective, shapes overlap—or seem to—also defining distance. Objects that are closest to us may seem lower, while things in the distance are apparently higher. Shadows are particularly graphic. Clouds obey these laws of aerial perspective, too, appearing to fold and overlap like origami—but unlike earthbound landscape elements, the closest *clouds* are high overhead, at the top of your page as you sketch them (unless, of course, you're above them in a jet).

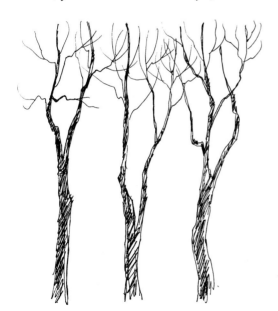

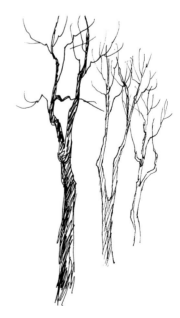

All the walnut trees in this group look close to us.

These three—same trees—recede into the background (lighter, smaller, simpler, higher).

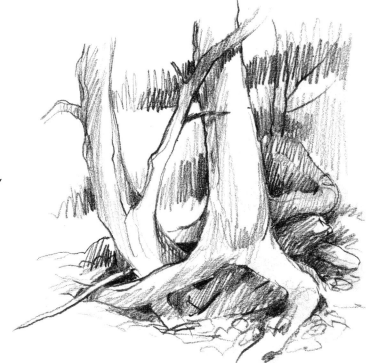

Overlapping shapes help to suggest perspective, even in close-up. (Mechanical pencil, HB lead.)

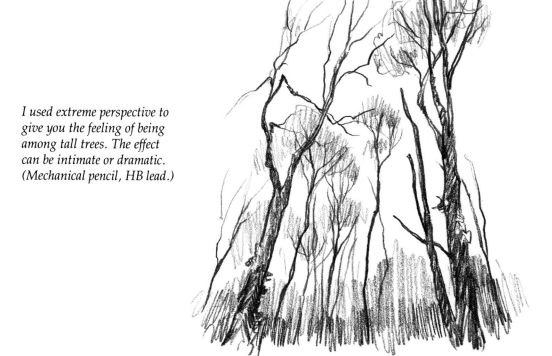

I used extreme perspective to give you the feeling of being among tall trees. The effect can be intimate or dramatic. (Mechanical pencil, HB lead.)

—*Use perspective to suggest distance.* Pick out a narrow trail or a creek, and try to sketch it to give a sense of space. Remember that things seem smaller or narrower, higher, and simpler as they go away from you.

Or do a cloud study, remembering that generally speaking (nature vigorously resists our generalities!) the largest clouds are closest to you and overhead. Smaller ones are farther away, near the horizon—unless there's a storm on the horizon and a cumulonimbus threatens.

—*Putting one thing apparently in front of another on your page helps to suggest a sense of aerial perspective.* Look for ways to overlap shapes, even at close range. The overlapping limbs of a tree give you a sense of intimate perspective just as clearly as do the layered shapes of Ozark hills.

—*Using an extreme perspective can give drama to your sketches.* A waterfall drawn from across the valley is lovely, sure—but one drawn from its base looking up at the precipice puts you *there*. A sketch from the same angle of a single tree gives it a sense of towering height. A look down a narrow canyon—sketched from a particularly good grip on the edge—makes you *feel* those passing ages that carved away the solid rock (or feel a good case of vertigo).

EXPRESSING LIFE WITH LINE

There's a kind of elegance to a beautifully done line drawing. Without benefit of value or local color, line steps out on its own, carrying the day. You will have seen what I mean in your contour drawings; even with restatements here and there, a line drawing seems exceptionally direct. There's a truth within those lines, pure and inviolable.

Lines can be as delicate as a spider's web or bold and black as steel cable; each has its special strength. (Remember, spider's silk is as strong as steel, ounce for ounce; stronger, in fact.)

Lines may be graceful, rhythmic, flowing; they may be nervous, spiky, or angular. They can be uniform or contain subtle variations of width or weight. They can even be scribbled or crosshatched to give the illusion of tone—all with a single tool.

—*Use line sparingly and capture only the details, not planes or values.* Try a seashell or a shelf fungus here—or the striations of a sandstone ledge, or a leaf with its fine network of ribs and veins.

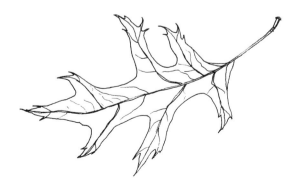

An 0.5-mm fiber-tipped pen worked well for an elegant linear effect.

—*Use varied lines.* Allow your line to darken at changes of direction or where you want emphasis—or just to give you a livelier, more interesting line.

—*Use darker or bolder lines to suggest areas closest to you*—the dark lines seem to pop out at you while the more delicate ones recede.

—*Use light or thin lines to suggest light-struck areas;* use darker, broader marks to depict shadows.

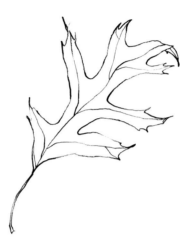

Varied lines add interest and suggest depth. (HB pencil.)

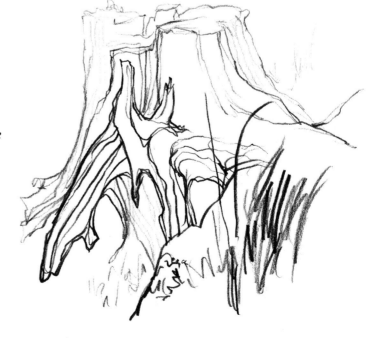

Bold lines come forward; pale ones recede. (2B pencil.)

—*Match your line to your subject—or to your mood.* A delicate wildflower could be sketched with a fine, uniform line while a gnarled tree might work best with a broad, varied line such as you might make with a calligraphy pen.

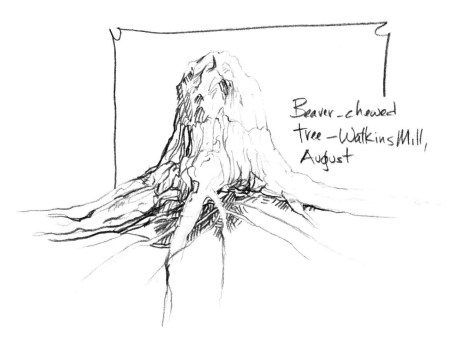

I used three different office-style pencils here to suggest the direction of light: a very hard No. 4 in the lightest areas, an F or firm in the middle tones, and a No. 2, or soft, in the shadowed areas.

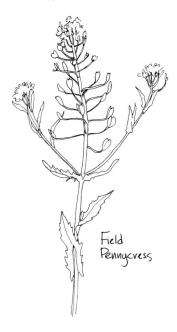

An 0.25 Rotring technical pen was used to sketch this field pennycress.

—*Finally, experiment with repeated lines.* These can provide a nice vibration; they can soften an area or contour; they can suggest tone, as well. Try out closely spaced zigzag lines or crosshatching to build darks.

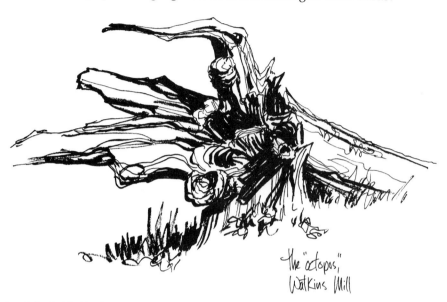

I tried a bold, black calligraphy pen on this sketch of a rugged tree stump and roots in raking sunlight.

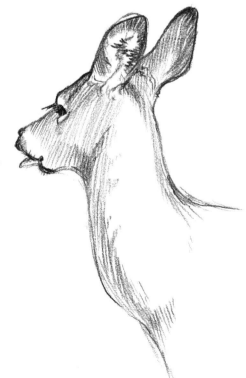

Repeated lines soften the contours of this young doe. (Prismacolor warm grey dark pencil.)

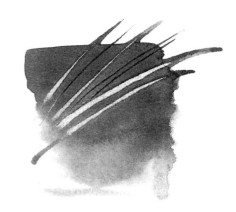

FOUR

Capturing the Illusion of Light

*L*IGHT DEFINES OUR WORLD, gives it visual form and substance. It's what keeps us going, day to day, sustains life on this planet. No wonder we're grateful for the sunrise.

For an artist, light is the most beautiful thing there is; it explains everything else. These nuanced patterns of light and shadow are an artist's best tools. We use them to make objects appear three-dimensional, to give solidity and form to what we draw.

Lights may be wonderfully vivid; luminous; dim and subtle; oblique; brilliant. They may bring tears to your eyes, and you won't know if it's the sun or the loveliness. Learning to use these nuances in a variety of conditions can impart a sense of reality and mood to our sketches.

Think of the quality of light for a moment: the blinding glitter of sunlight on water; the pervasive luminosity of sun burning off a morning fog. Think of mountain light, light above the clouds, English light, American light, summer light, winter light, the long fading of alpenglow. Think of light falling on the infinite variety of nature, itself changing every hour of the day—without it we might as well pack up our sketching kit and go home.

The dark side of all that light—shadow—helps us to describe form, volume, texture, surface, direction, and mood. Shadow patterns may be sprightly and expressive; they define the world like a dictionary—sans the Latin roots. Without these lovely, lively darks, everything would appear flat and one-dimensional in the glare. We wouldn't have a clue as to the true shape of, say, an apple—it might be flat as a sheet of paper, for all we could tell. We couldn't guess at the slope of a wooded hill without those cast shadows to etch their angular lines for us. We'd miss the richness of texture without shadows to highlight its endless variations.

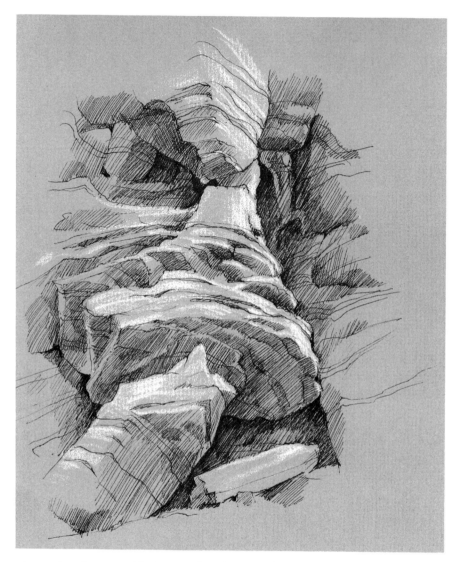

A gray-toned paper, a black razor-tipped pen, and a white Prismacolor pencil work together to define the sense of desert light.

We use the invaluable darks to help us capture the lights—like sweet and sour, high and low, male and female, we need both to fully express our world. Light, shadow, and line can give us all we require to make a paper image take on life. We conjure it up with a pencil.

USING LIGHT TO EXPRESS VOLUME

Without the effects of light, everything you sketched would be a line drawing—you could make no effort at shading at all. You wouldn't be able to discern the subtleties of the world around you; you couldn't draw what you couldn't see. *With* light, you can express all the varieties of form and volume you could hope for or suggest a thousand textures that add a tactile sense to your sketch. The practice in seeing and using values in the last chapters are your key, now, to a lively world of depth and volume and surface textures.

BODY SHADOWS AND CAST SHADOWS

Shadows—the patterns of light and dark—suggest volume in what would otherwise be a flat or linear drawing. Using them with panache gives life to your work.

Body shadows (the shadows on your subject itself) can be extremely eloquent, giving us a lot of information within a single area. They give roundness to a linear image; they suggest overall shape and define features within the outline. They can portray surface characteristics or textures.

Body shadows may have soft or hard edges. They may become quite light if they contain reflected lights; often they are darkest just where they turn away from the primary light source.

Cast shadows are usually darker in value than body shadows. They reveal the direction of the light, hinting at the time of day or season. Like body shadows, they tell us something about the shape of our subject, even passing along clues about the *back*, the parts we can't see.

These shadows help us describe the surface they fall on; we can tell if the ground is dead level or if it falls away from a tree, for instance, from the direction of the shadow—and also whether that ground is smooth or rugged. We can suggest bare or roughly weeded ground just by the kind of shadows we sketch in around the subject. We can tell if a mountain goat is standing on an incline or a flat area from the angle of the shadow—not so critical, perhaps, in person, when your eyes and brain make sense of the

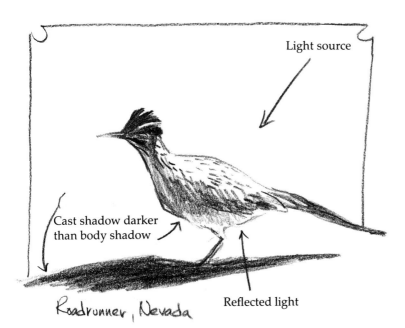

Light source

Cast shadow darker than body shadow

Roadrunner, Nevada

Reflected light

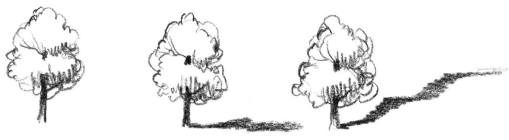

This tells us nothing about where the tree *is*.

This lets us know the tree grows from level ground.

This tells us the tree stands on the side of a gently rolling hill.

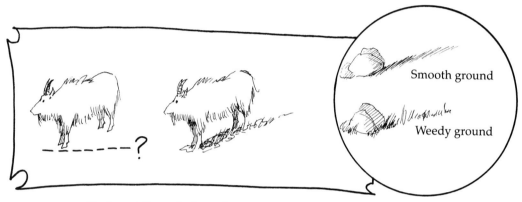

Shadows tell much about the surfaces they fall on: roughness, smoothness, angle, and so on.

scene, but in a sketch an unshadowed ground can make it look as if your mountain goat's backside is levitating. (And yes, a mountain goat is almost *always* on an incline.)

We can use shadows to invite the viewer into the picture plane. Shadows rushing toward us obey the rules of perspective; they point the way to the yellow brick road.

Don't overlook the *emotional* value of shadows. On an August day in Missouri, they're to die for; including a deep-shadowed area in a sunny sketch can be just that kind of welcome invitation. It gives the eye a place to rest. A dappled path can be inviting, as well, as cast shadows diminish into the background.

PRIMARY LIGHT SOURCES

Analyzing these light and dark shapes can be a challenge—but when you literally "see the light," your work seems to take on a life of its own. It almost pops off the page.

Knowing the direction the light comes from helps you to catch a sense of reality in your sketches and gives your work sparkle. When you sketch,

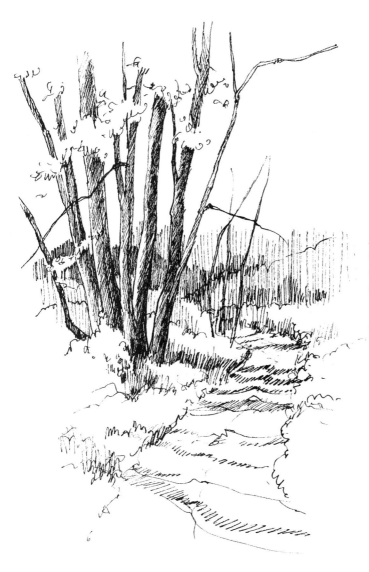

A dappled path tells something about time of day, contour, direction of light, and perspective; besides, it's inviting. (0.7-mm fiber-tipped pen.)

first ask yourself where your light source is. On a sunlit day in the desert, this source may be painfully obvious, but on an overcast day or when you sketch indoors it may be harder to pin down.

To help you see more clearly what light can do, bring a bit of nature indoors, where you can easily control the direction of illumination. Try a shelf fungus, a rock, an orange—anything small enough to put on a desk. Shine a strong light on it, and move the light around—overhead, to the side, low to your subject or behind it—and see what happens. Body shadows shift and change, along with what they tell you about your subject. Watch where the cast shadows fall, and how much information they give you, not only about the direction of the light but also about the shape and surface of your subject. Sketch these variations to become more familiar with the cause and effect of a single light source.

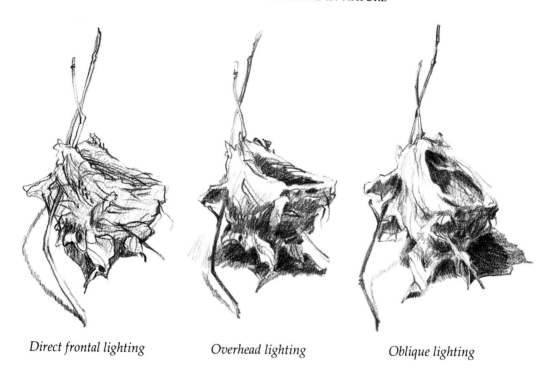

Direct frontal lighting   *Overhead lighting*   *Oblique lighting*

—*Direct light.* Shine your light directly on what you're sketching. Notice how many surface features seem to disappear; the light may expose a number of details, local color may be true, but often this direct light seems flat and uninteresting. You may see *linear* details but not the highs and lows that explain the *shape* of the surface. For instance, in strong, direct sunlight you can see where an animal's eye or nostrils are, but not the ridge over the eyes that casts a deep shadow, or the hollows in the cheeks. You might as well be doing a line drawing, for all the information your light source gives you about your subject's form.

—*Overhead light* is similar to direct lighting, but can be much more interesting. Think of the light of midday in July—tonal gradations are from the light-struck top to the shaded bottom. The shadows are rich and deep and thrown at an object's base. They are nearly the same size as the object itself—no long El Greco shadows as you find just before sunset, but a deep pool of darkness. One drawback of this light is that it seldom helps describe the volume or texture of the subject.

—*Oblique light* is the light we most often use to suggest volume in sketching. It is useful in describing both form and surface. Mountains sketched in oblique light have a sense of solidity; their textures are accentuated. Animals have roundness and life. The only drawback, in fact, with oblique light is that it *is* so familiar. It's almost the expected thing—and in scientific illustration it's the *required* thing, slightly above and from the left to throw the subject into slight relief and explain surface textures. Often it's more fun to play around with some of the other sources of illumination to capture a sense of drama or mystery.

—*Low side light*. You may have heard someone describe this as "raking" light. It makes for long shadows and a very evocative mood. Often in nature colors are intensified or tinted with gold or coral when these light conditions prevail. By all means, try sketching by morning and evening light. This light strongly accentuates planes and surface characteristics of your subject; it can be very dramatic.

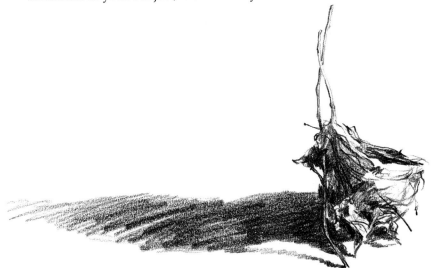

Low side lighting

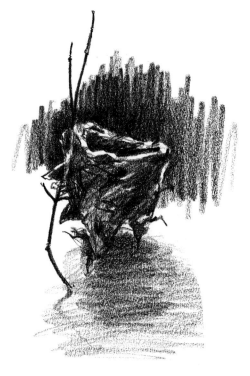

Rim or back lighting

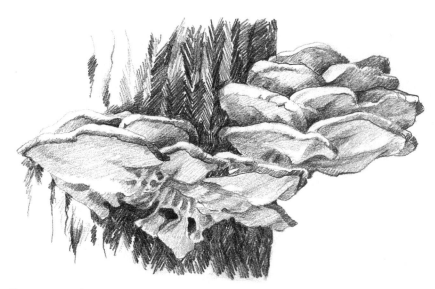

Overcast conditions suppress many sharp changes in value. (Mechanical pencil, HB lead.)

—*Backlight or rim lighting* occurs when the light is directly behind your subject, or almost so. What you are looking at may seem dark and nearly featureless, but the light catches fire at the very rim or accentuates the planes closest to the edge.

   You may see this lighting just at sunrise or sunset, or if your subject is silhouetted by the sun; it's a lovely light, very dramatic or very subtle. Place your desk lamp directly behind your subject to explore the ways rim lighting can be used to suggest mood or drama.

—*Overcast light.* On a cloudy or foggy day, the light may be diffused and even. Demarcation lines are smoothed; planes become more subtle and a bit harder to detect. But even under these conditions—difficult conditions, I'll grant, to duplicate with your desk lamp (try a translucent shade between the light source and your subject)—the principles of light and shadow still apply. Their values are just much closer together than they would be in strong oblique or even direct lighting.

Occasionally you may get confused when depicting the direction of your primary light source—more likely when working indoors, where there may be more than one kind of illumination, or when combining several sketches or photo resources in a single sketch, than when working outdoors on the spot. If one scene depicts morning and one afternoon, the conflict will show up in your work, giving you that uneasy something-is-wrong feeling. However, you can weld one to the other seamlessly if you alter the light source in one or the other of your resource sketches.

   Working from life, of course, makes it much easier to capture the light as you see it—except when it changes rapidly. That's why I often make a quick thumbnail sketch of value patterns to freeze-frame the lights and shadows before they travel.

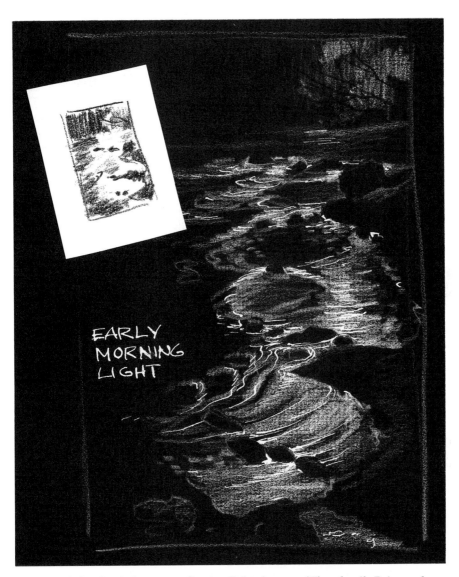

Thumbnail sketches help capture fleeting light changes. (Thumbnail, Prismacolor grey pencil; large sketch, white Prismacolor pencil and white ink on black paper.)

SECONDARY LIGHT SOURCES

There may be *more* than one light source, or you may find reflected lights in the shadows—don't count these out. Accurately seen and depicted in your sketch, they lend the undeniable ring of truth—but keep them secondary to your overall pattern of lights and darks. The strongest values will be in these primary patterns.

Indoors, lights may come from several directions at once. Sunlight streaming in the window may be your primary illumination, but reflected lights, lamps, or overhead fluorescents confuse the issue. It's not all bad.

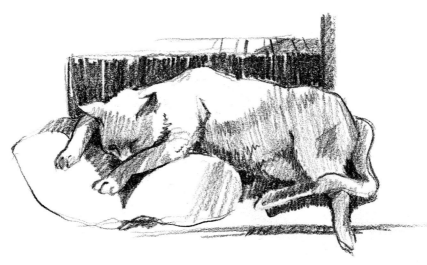

Indoors, you may get several light sources; here, light from the window provides strong backlight, while reflected light catches my cat's face and back foot. Soft indoor lighting keeps her fairly light in value even in shadow. (Grey Prismacolor from my field sketchbook.)

Such a "fill light" can give you lots of information about what is going on in shadow areas, and the varied light sources may lend richness and interest. (Fluorescents, by the way, offer a particularly flat, even illumination, not the best for sketching.)

Outdoors, reflected lights may form a light flare. Strong sunlight on water shines almost as brightly as the sun itself, and seems to pulse upward. Sunlight striking a very pale object may create a glow of secondary illumination. Fire lightens on its own, adding its secondary lightness to the sun's—so do foxfire and lightning bugs.

Very strong outdoor light seems to provide its own candlepower when it strikes a light object. This mushroom was in deep forest; a beam of strong summer sunlight broke through and created a flare. (Prismacolor pencil.)

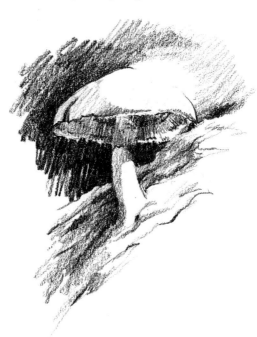

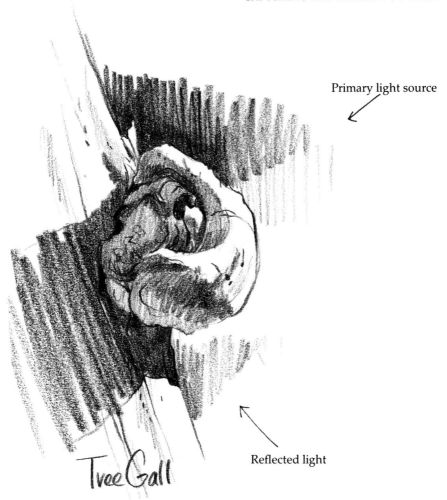

Primary light source

Reflected light

Tree Gall

Indoors or out, a reflected light bouncing back into a shadow area gives a special luminosity to what you see, and keeps your shadows from being dead flat. When working in color, I like to flood these areas with a bit of local color from the nearby objects to capture the liveliness of reflected light. In black and white, a simple lightening of shadows captures the effect.

Once you've located your *primary* light source, these lesser lights really shine.

HARD AND SOFT EDGES

If it helps you to "see the light"—and the dark—try the chiaroscuro exercise in the last chapter. Train yourself to find the dark shapes; for practice, draw a visual map of these areas, then fill them in with darks (shown). Simplify form and value until you've got it down.

But shadows are seldom so simple as our map suggests—not so black and white (sorry, pun intended). Reflected lights change the intensity of darks, as we've seen; so do fill lights or secondary light sources. Shadow edges may be hard as a chiaroscuro drawing—they may not. The surface characteristics of your subject affect the quality of shadows.

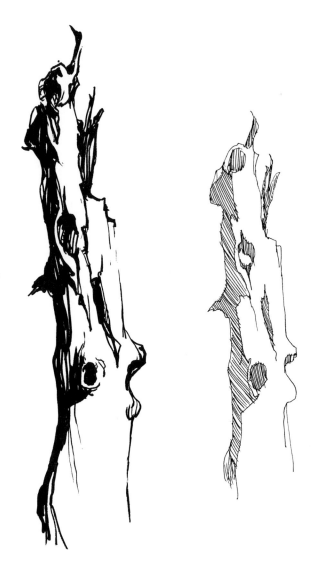

Map your darks, as at right, if it helps you to better find their shapes. (Map, razor-point pen; sketch, black fiber-tipped brush pen.)

The body shadows on a smooth, rounded object will have softly graded leading edges, while a rough or angular surface may produce hard-edged shadows.

—Sketch something rounded and relatively smooth—a walnut husk, an egg, a puffball mushroom—and try to capture the smooth gradations of light and dark, the soft edges of the shadows. Watch for reflected lights as well, to help describe roundness, and notice that often the darkest area within the shadow shape is near the leading edge of that shadow as it turns away from the light.

—Now sketch a more rugged subject—a *hulled* walnut, a rock, a chunk of tree bark—and play up the hard-edged shadows. Keep it simple, like your visual map, or look for reflected or fill light to help you make sense of areas obscured by shadow.

Direction of light

Soft-edged shadow

Darker

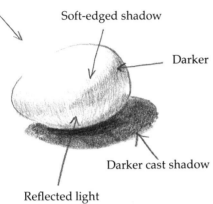

Darker cast shadow

Reflected light

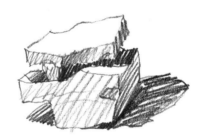

Direction of light

Hard-edged shadows

Darker
cast shadow

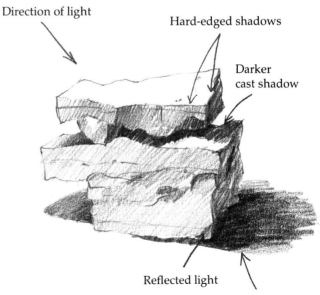

Reflected light

Darker cast shadow

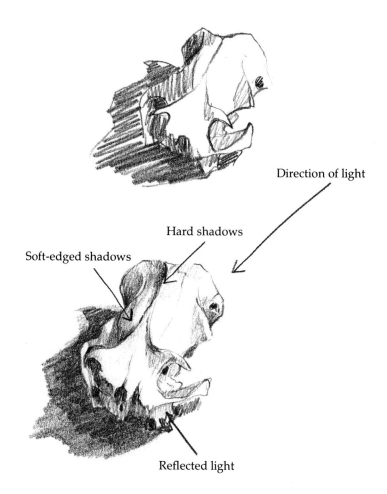

Direction of light

Hard shadows

Soft-edged shadows

Reflected light

—In nature, things are seldom one thing or the other, but a combination. The same rock may have rounded areas and jagged ones; a bird's head may have a smoothly rounded crown, with soft, graded shadows, but an angular beak that makes for hard-edged darks. Combine these hard and soft edges to graphically suggest the shapes and shadows you see.

"LOST AND FOUND"

Look for "lost and found" edges—areas where the lights touch and seem to blend, or where cast shadows and body shadows are lost in one another and boundaries begin to blur. Lost and found edges involve the viewer's imagination; they're an open invitation to complete the picture—the brain's right side is called into play.

Open up your light edges here and there to suggest a light-struck surface; let your darks share a common value. This simple trick is deceptively powerful; it lends a bit of mystery, and almost everyone loves a mystery.

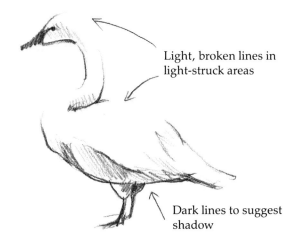

Light, broken lines in
light-struck areas

Dark lines to suggest
shadow

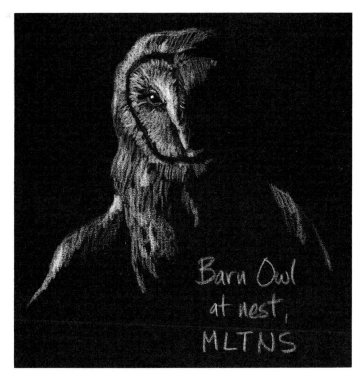

Lost and found edges involve the viewer and contribute to a sense of mystery. (White Prismacolor pencil on black paper.)

HIGH KEY AND LOW KEY

As we discovered in the last chapter, values can be used to express mood; values are the artist's way of capturing the varieties of light and dark.

A high-key sketch uses light values to capture the sense of illumination; this might be effective when sketching a day at the beach or the deep snows of Wyoming's Jackson Hole. You almost have to squint your eyes against the glare. (If you're working in full sun, you *will*—all that white paper needs to be shaded by your body or a broad-brimmed hat.)

On the other hand, a low-key sketch is dark and foreboding or full of a kind of brooding drama. The light is dimming, almost gone. You may even sketch at night; I have. What is night, after all, but Earth's own shadow? At night the illumination is from the moon—a secondary light source that reflects the sun's glow—or nearly nonexistent. But even here the sky is lighter behind the trees. If you need proof, go out for a midnight walk but leave your flashlight at home—let your eyes' rods and cones adjust. A low-key sketch with only a few lights would capture this sense of night.

Your practice in using values will help you to depict these conditions with accuracy—and besides, it's fun to sketch at night. Eccentric, maybe, but fun.

—As an exercise, choose a very high-key subject and see how to create the impression of strong sunlight. Let the white of your paper shine through, and use only a few well-placed darks.

—Try a toned paper to capture a low-key mood, or create your own low tone with charcoal or a soft pencil. Coax your lights up out of this tone by using white—or a kneaded eraser, if you are working with pencil or charcoal. Experiment with creating an aura of mystery.

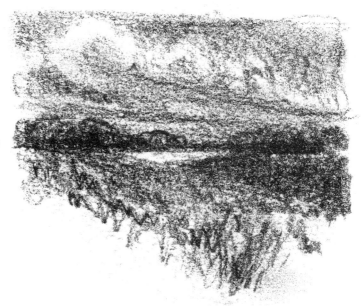

A moodier sketch results when you use predominantly dark values; this low-key sketch was done on the inside cover of my sketchbook with a 2B graphite stick.

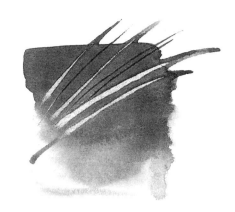

FIVE

Field Sketching

FIELD SKETCHING is more than simply planning for a future work or keeping your drawing hand in practice. It's more, even, than learning to see. It is learning, period. About the world and our sometimes precarious place in it. About the creatures, large and small, that share this island Earth with us. About life in general—and in delightful, intimate particular. It's a search for answers—to questions both as vast as infinity and as microscopic as the hidden workings of DNA.

The small mysteries, especially, are fascinating to naturalists; we tend to maintain a childlike interest in the world as long as we live. We *expect* the infinite to be somewhat inaccessible; but the questions of bird song and animal sight and the doings of insects we find compelling by their very intimacy. They're on a scale we can comprehend.

Field sketching is a necessity for anyone wanting to learn from what he or she is drawing. Not only artist-naturalists, but also botanists, biologists, zoologists, archaeologists, geologists, astronomers—all benefit from the discipline of recording our own "visual aids."

John Muir, founder of the Sierra Club and one of our most respected naturalists, used his sketches as tools of discovery. As he camped in the High Sierra, he not only recorded the magnificent landscape but tracked the slow passage of glaciers, inch by inch, to find how much and how fast they moved. He chronicled the path of a grasshopper—"a singing, dancing grasshopper over North Dome" in his field journal, a line itself dancing and annotated with the phonetic sound of the insect.

Louis Agassiz Fuertes discovered his world through field sketches and translated them into wonderful paintings that teach us all. John James Audubon did the same, as did Thomas Bewick, whom Audubon admired

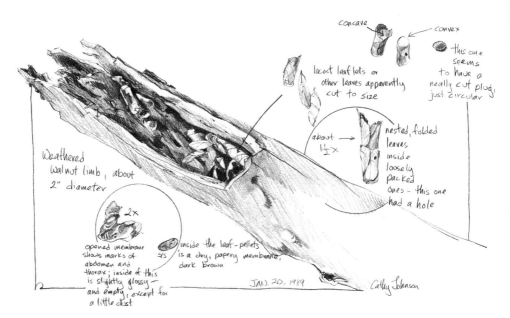

Insect eggs in branch. (0.5-mm mechanical pencil, HB lead on plate surface paper.)

enough to visit in England. Alexander Wilson sketched many of the findings of Lewis and Clark as they made their way up the Missouri River, adding their names to the annals of taxonomy. Abbot Thayer used his field sketches to explore the mysteries of the protective coloring of animals as he worked.

The tradition continues into the twentieth century with the field sketches of Olaus Murie, Ernest Thompson Seton, Charles Tunnicliffe, Winifrid Austen, Francis Lee Jaques, Eric Ennion, Roger Tory Peterson, Ann Zwinger, Clare Walker Leslie, and others—all maintaining that sense of wonder we felt as children, and that keen questioning.

Recently, I broke apart a piece of punky, rotten wood as I looked for kindling. Inside the hollowed branch, to my surprise, were tucked hundreds of small leaflets from a black locust tree. As I sketched, my curiosity was piqued and kindling was forgotten. I felt like a kid with a map to buried treasure. How had the leaflets gotten there? What creature had cached them, and to what end? Ants, spiders, flying insects? With my pencil point, I explored a long, tubular cavity stuffed with leaflets and discovered, even deeper inside, a stack of tiny pelletlike objects fashioned from the leaves, each as perfectly formed as a prescription pill.

Each pellet was no more than one centimeter long, slightly rounded on one end, slightly concave on the other so that each protectively cupped the next. The concave end was sealed with a perfectly cut circle made from leaves, like the rest of the tiny time capsule, and fastened in place with something crumbly, like an earth and saliva mixture. Inside was hidden a tough, brown membrane that must have been meant for protection. It worked. I could barely cut through it with my X-acto knife.

I knew these must be egg capsules or chrysalises of some kind, but what?

Detailed sketches allowed me, after a year of off-and-on search, to come a bit closer to the answer: it may be that wasps parasitized the eggs of a locust-wood borer, taking over the territory and providing a meal for their *own* progeny.

By keeping a field journal—a permanent place to record these specialized and purposeful sketches—we are able to ask and answer these questions, either for ourselves or with the help of field guides, textbooks, or experts.

A hardbound book seems to work best, and withstands the rigors of field work, although anything handy can be used; you can always transfer your sketch later. Look for a book with neutral-pH, acid-free paper from your art supplier, to ensure that your field notes will last. The pages of such a hardbound book stay in place, encouraging you to keep chronological records of your rambles. Date each page, and add the time of day. Include any weather notes you please—temperature, precipitation, etc.

Carry a 6-inch ruler with you, and measure the details you draw; note if you are working life-size or otherwise. This information may help you later with identification. If you have forgotten a ruler, make comparisons with the joints of your own fingers, a hand span, or the length of a stride and make more accurate measurements later. Even apparent measurements can be helpful; see how big the setting sun or a full moon look in comparison to a dime held at arm's length, for instance.

Occasionally, I tuck a small plant or leaf or feather I've found between the pages for reference. All this information—the date in particular—can be quite helpful.

As I write this, on January 19, I've just discovered the pale, tender shoots of crocuses in my garden. These normally key to the lengthening days as well as to changes in weather, but this year's long drought has continued through the winter months and the earth is as bare as July. They've become confused by mixed signals.

It's a good news, bad news kind of thing; the welcome crocus shoots, tiny, brave as ever, set against the oddity of this odd season—what could it

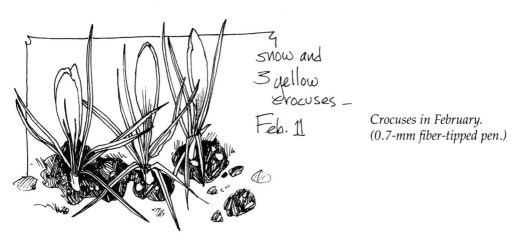

snow and
3 yellow
crocuses —
Feb. 11

Crocuses in February.
(0.7-mm fiber-tipped pen.)

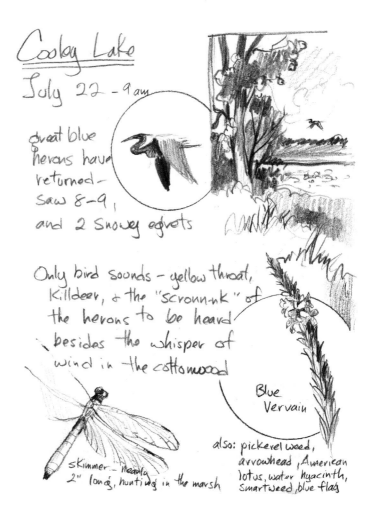

Cooley Lake. (No. 2 pencil.)

mean? Will the drought continue, bringing hardship and starvation? Will the orchards bloom in March, only to be nipped in the bud (literally) by the inevitable return of cold?

But perhaps not. I find my journal from two years past; the crocuses *bloomed*, not simply emerged, on February 11, only a few weeks away, and life was normal that year—or as normal as life gets in the Midwest's changeable weather.

The "rules" of art are less important in field sketching; composition and perspective and value still apply, but only tangentially. The details—plus good observation coupled with intelligent questions—are important here. Don't worry unduly about your drawing skill; use a gesture sketch to begin with, or a modified contour drawing to get down what you see. No matter how rough, these field sketches will help you identify what you've seen—and to see it with new eyes. Written notes will supplement your quick sketches, keeping observations fresh in your mind.

How you design your page depends less on the particulars of good art than of good *use*. Leave yourself plenty of room for those written notes, and allow space for detail drawings. Later, if you like, you can add borders or enclosures to clarify or separate things and to add a sense of design; I often do.

Normally, in my field journal pages, I include my subject, detail sketches, or close-ups if I can get them (a bison or a bobcat generally won't hold still for this one!), written notes as suggested, plus a small, rough habitat sketch that reminds me where I am (or rather, where I've found my subject): deep forest, open prairie, desert, or shore. If my *theme* is landscape, of course, the whole sketch is a habitat sketch and my details are peripheral, but it's best to subordinate one to the other: tiny landscape with large details or large landscape with smaller details, depending on what interests you most.

LEARNING TO OBSERVE

With a field journal, you can sharpen your powers of observation, focus your mind like sunlight falling through a magnifying glass. When I *stop* and take the time to sketch—whether the field marks of an unfamiliar bird in

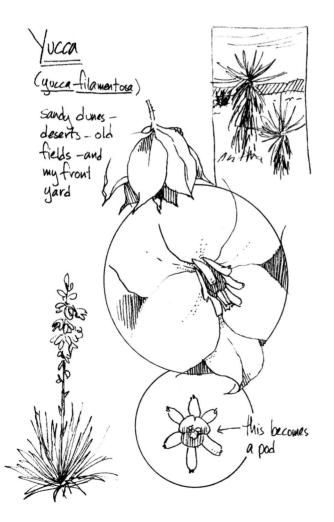

Yucca.
(0.5-mm fiber-tipped pen.)

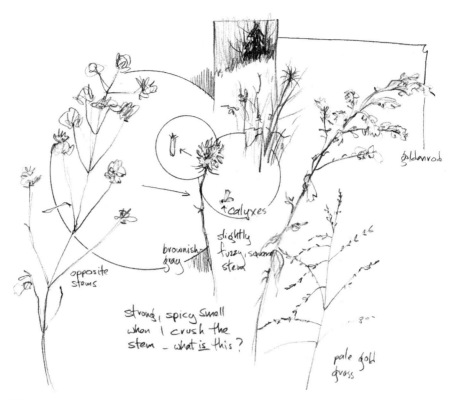

The scent of this late November weed was familiar, but I couldn't place it. Knowing from the square stem that it was a mint family member helped me to find it in my field guide when I returned home—it was bergamot.

flight or the spring-loaded details of a jewelweed's seed capsule—I see beyond the surface.

I notice things I would never see as I walk by in a hurry to get from here to there. Not even with my camera can I capture the wheels within wheels as I can when I stop and begin a careful field sketch. If a flower catches my eye, I can get it down on paper—and its leaves, and their shape and surface characteristics. I can notice what is *eating* those leaves, and if it has left its eggs in a honeycomb pattern on the back or sewn them into a silken comforter in an origami fold. I can sketch pistils and stamens and what creatures may visit for the nectar, carrying the bright pollen as gift. I can look for unopened buds and wilted flowers, and the forming of seed cases—and I can look inside to the seeds, and wonder how they are dispersed—by air, by birds or animals, or by jet propulsion, like that jewelweed. I could pass an afternoon—or a week—with a single flower. It could become a lifetime's study.

Choose a subject that interests you, even if only peripherally. Use your field journal to explore it microscopically, and you will find your interest deepening as your observations become ever more involved. Include a habitat drawing, not much larger than a thumbnail sketch—say 1 × 3 inches. Explore the details, first sketching them, then getting inside each one, either literally, as you can with a seed pod, or figuratively, armed with a few good questions. Note those questions on your sketch as they occur to you. Try to find the answer for yourself through empirical evidence. Trust your eyes and mind, but don't be afraid to dig in and do some research when you return home. Search your field guides; look in the encyclopedia. If you've made good notes along with your sketches—including, as usual, the date and perhaps time of day if it seems to make a difference (as it sometimes does in the flowering of a plant or the activity of a nocturnal or crepuscular animal)—you'll be able to get help from an expert in the field. Your local university or college is a good place to start—it's amazing, to me, how generous with their time these busy professors can be. I'd be lost without the people at the University of Missouri at Kansas City and at William Jewell College in Liberty, Missouri.

KEEPING TRACK OF CHANGE

We can record change as spring becomes summer and fall, as a seed sprouts and flowers and seeds again. We direct our own field of study with these sketches; we draw our own visual aids as we go along, making tangible what was only conjecture or book knowledge before.

In your field journal, you can track the path of drought or monsoon, note growth patterns, watch the autumn begin the long slide into winter, all with the point of your pencil. A lifetime could not be better spent than in learning more about this complex world of ours. Your drawings become learning tools, as surely as any electron microscope.

Choose a simple thing to sketch, something to which you can make a minor commitment: the sprouting and leafing of a single seed, the slow building of a paper wasp's nest, the hatching of a backyard bird's eggs. (Tracking the life of a tree can be deeply satisfying, but will take considerably longer than most of us are able to invest.) Make a sketch in one corner of your page and date it. Note any interesting details, either as a sketch or with words—does only one wasp work on the nest or are there several? How often does she make her rounds? Where does she get the wood cellulose to mix with her saliva to form these hexagonal chambers (the answer, here, is my back fence).

Come back the next day—or in two days, or a week—and make another sketch on the same page, noting changes. Track the progress, returning time after time until your page is filled and your curiosity satisfied—you may need to devote another page or two. (My intentions were foiled this summer when the entire wasp's nest inexplicably disappeared, with only the tiny goblet stem and its attaching rosette left on my porch ceiling to mark where it had been. I never did find what had happened, leaving my sketch unfinished.)

These sketches are not only fascinating in their own right, but can also be important records of change. You may note the first turning toward the greenhouse effect in your area; you may be instrumental in proving that the warming is only cyclical after all. You may track the acidification of a body of water and the effect it has on the life there. You may record the evidence,

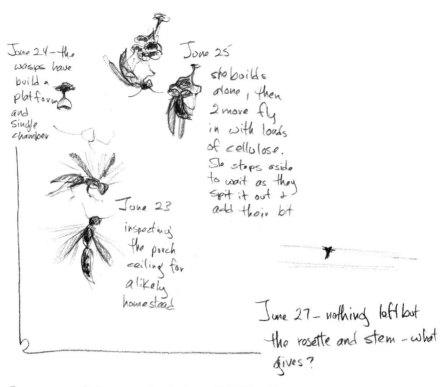

June 24—the wasps have build a platform and single chamber

June 25 she builds alone, then 2 move fly in with loads of cellulose. She steps aside to wait as they spit it out & add their bit

June 23 inspecting the porch ceiling for a likely homestead

June 27—nothing left but the rosette and stem—what gives?

Paper wasps. (0.5-mm mechanical pencil; HB lead.)

over the years, that scientists need for verifying their theories or confirming their own findings; they can't be everywhere at once, and your input may become vital, if your records are well kept and documented. Don't be afraid to "waste" your time on this work; your amateur observations could be crucial, if you've been a faithful and careful witness.

COMPARING NOTES

Comparing the results of your own findings—what you've seen with your own eyes—with the published facts can result in quantum leaps in your degree of understanding. At the *least*, it is fascinating. Your field sketches will give you the ammunition you need to be your own best teacher or to enlist the help of experts. If you've seen a bird—or a mammal, or a spider—you don't recognize, your sketch making note of field marks will allow you to clear up the mystery when you return home to your bookshelves.

Your notes—taken in your particular part of the country—can be checked with records in other areas to tell much about migration patterns or changes in global weather.

You can compare notes with a friend, as well; two minds working together more than double the combined information—it's chemistry. Brainstorming enhanced with field sketches can be most productive.

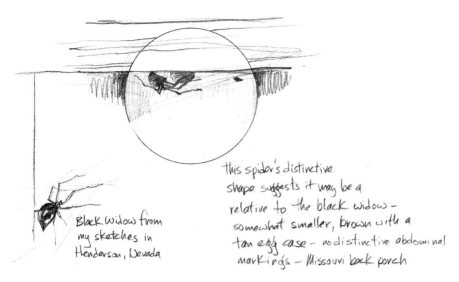

This spider's distinctive shape suggests it may be a relative to the black widow – somewhat smaller, brown with a tan egg case – no distinctive abdominal markings – Missouri back porch

Black widow from my sketches in Henderson, Nevada

Spider comparisons. (0.5-mm mechanical pencil; HB lead.)

BEYOND LEARNING

Beyond a simple learning of the facts is another dimension entirely, a dimension of experience and response. When I do a field sketch, I see with my mind as well as with my eyes. I take time for wonder *and* for logic. I notice; I appreciate; I learn; I respond. I've deepened my experience. You'll be amazed, as well, with the interest that you've generated within yourself.

Your field notes needn't be only factual, though a listing of, say, the other wildflowers you've seen this day as you sketched your chosen subject tells you much about seasons and cycles. Write your observations, but write your feelings as well. If the singing of insects on languid summer air makes you feel at peace, say so. If you are tense just before a lightning storm, write it down. If you are awed by the sight of Yosemite's deep valleys and stony towers, who could blame you for taking note of such a feeling? Later, these written notes may serve as memory jogs as well.

Written conjecture about your subject will help you remember the things you've noted, the questions raised in your exploratory sketches. Expound your own theories; make a guess. Later, find out if you were right; it's a humbling experience when you're not, a gratifying one when you are. (Once, I was quite eloquent in the margins of a sketch of a small, dying cedar tree; I was sure acid rain had affected its life cycle here in the open winter woods. I called a forester for confirmation—and he reminded me, gently, that in summer these tiny sprouts probably don't get enough sun in the deep woods where I drew them. The huge cedars nearby got that way when the rest of the second-growth forest was too small to shade them. Oh.)

As artists, we may wish to make color notes, or written notes as to mood, especially if the tools we've brought are of the most basic. If I have a full contingent of watercolors, I can capture mood; if I'm confined to a single

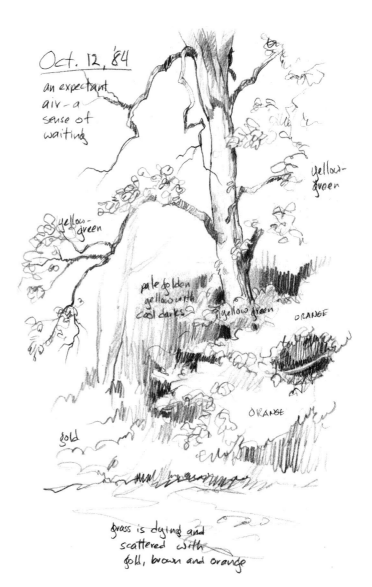

October 12, tree study with color notes. (HB pencil.)

black pen, I may have a bit more trouble with visuals. Then my written notes become invaluable.

As an exercise, make a field sketch of anything you choose; make the normal notes of date and time and weather, and the questions you may have raised about your subject as you drew its details. Now, stop and listen to what else is going on. What birds sing? What insects hum in the grass? Do you hear a rustling in the woods, or a coyote's wail? Do unraveling skeins of geese trail across the sky, recalling an unnameable longing for no reason you can logically explain? Is there a scent of rain on the air, or the sharp brimstone of lightning? Write it down. Read it back to yourself later to see if you haven't noticed far more than you normally do—about your subject, about what is going on around you, about your own response.

GETTING CLOSE ENOUGH TO SKETCH

If you are drawing a rock, a tree or a flower—or a habitat sketch—getting close is normally no problem. An animal, on the other hand, presents a challenge. Unless you've caught a turtle basking in the sun—or incapacitated by the cold—most animals are gun-shy. I applaud their caution—especially in hunting season—but I'm frustrated in my efforts to sketch more than a quick scribble. I can't tell if a bird is bright as a parrot in the deep summer shade, or simply another little gray bird.

You can sketch at the zoo, of course, and it's great fun as well as great practice. But you won't learn much about an animal's normal behavior there. Often the animals are listless, or agitated by overattention. They respond to their captive condition and to us—though often with boredom rather than their normal feral caution.

Many city zoos share another serious shortcoming for naturalists, at least those interested in their own areas: the animals in the zoo are mostly exotics. That's fine if you want to sketch a rhino or ring-tailed lemur, but I'm quite fond of our indigenous animals. I want to draw a mountain goat—on

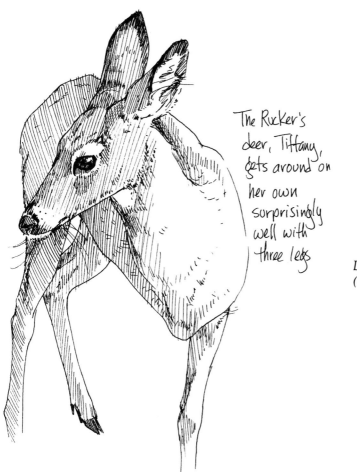

The Rucker's deer, Tiffany, gets around on her own surprisingly well with three legs

Deer Study.
(0.5-mm fiber-tipped pen.)

the spot. I want to sketch a white-tailed deer, or a raccoon, or a prehistoric opossum. I want my drawing of an American bison to be unhindered by bars.

I'm privileged to have a good relationship with my veterinarians, Ed Piepergerdes and Pete and Vinse Rucker. When they get a wild animal in after an unfortunate run-in with a human or car, they often give me a call. I've drawn a great blue heron at arm's-length range; I've sketched a red-tailed hawk and a kestrel. I've drawn Tiffany, the Ruckers' three-legged white-tailed doe, brought in after a mowing machine killed her sibling, and a young male fawn still drinking from the bottle after being separated from his mother. I've gotten to watch a young screech owl released back into the wild.

Wendy McDougal, a young friend who works with another nearby vet, also volunteers at a nature sanctuary. People often bring animals there that they had thought to hand raise, or creatures that have been injured. When Wendy has a wild charge to release, often she comes to my acreage. Thanks to her interest, I've sketched raccoons and owlets and a baby bobcat some-one guiltily delivered to the Lakeside Nature Center in Kansas City's Swope Park. (It is rightly illegal to have these wild creatures in private hands.)

The information officer at my local police department knows of my work with wildlife; when peregrine falcons took up a winter roost on a downtown

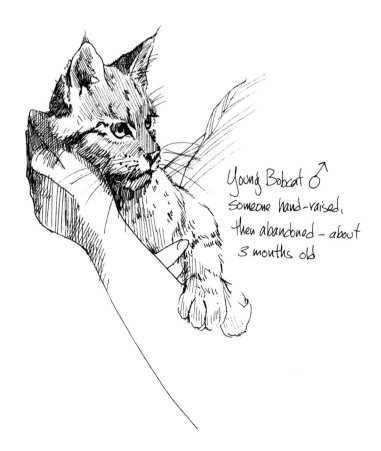

Young male bobcat.
(0.5-mm fiber-tipped pen.)

Young Bobcat ♂
Someone hand-raised,
then abandoned — about
3 months old

building, he called to let me know about it. A tiny shrew was caught in a window across the street; my neighbor called me in to draw it. People call me to report the incursion of a snowy owl here in northern Missouri, far from its normal range; they let me know when eagles are spotted nearby, or when the snow geese have arrived at Squaw Creek National Wildlife Refuge. They tell me where hawks are raising their young.

Let your friends and neighbors *know* you'd like to be contacted when they see a wild animal. Tell them why, and follow through if at all possible; it's gratifying to most people to be instrumental in your work. If you don't show up, next time they don't bother.

For a naturalist, these contacts are invaluable—not to mention one of the most pleasurable parts of my profession.

Under these circumstances, make notes as you normally do; there may be differences in behavior or stance, which need to be noted for accuracy's sake, between a bird in the wild and one in a cage. My great blue heron drawings are invaluable to me, but they don't reflect its normal behavior. The 52-inch bird stalked restlessly in its confinement and stabbed at the tiny fish provided it as if angry. In the wild, a great blue moves like a glacier, slowly and deliberately—until it strikes, a lightning attack too quick to track.

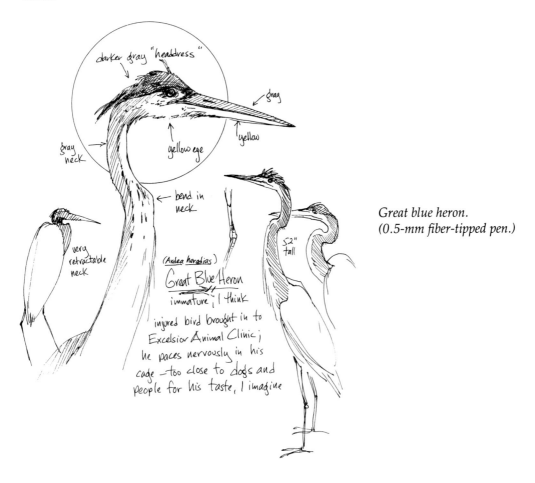

Great blue heron.
(0.5-mm fiber-tipped pen.)

These sketching opportunities, gratifying as they are, are still not *wild*. For true field sketches, that's where you need to be—in the field. And getting close enough to sketch is still a problem.

Study up on stalking techniques. Read Tom Brown's book, *The Tracker* (1984), among others. Study the ways of our Native American predecessors, who moved like smoke through the woods, or the colonial hunters who followed them. Don't wear perfume or aftershave lotion; our own scent is threatening enough. Mask it by burying your clothes in leaves for a few hours, or sitting next to a campfire until your clothing—and your person—is redolent of smoke and not humanity. Don't eat or smoke tobacco in the field.

Walk as silently as possible; watch where you step to avoid the brittle twig or dry leaves that may give you away. Best of all, find a comfortable place and *sit*. As long as you can—until nature forgets you're there and gets back to business. I've gotten to sketch a woods wren and a common yellowthroat—not to mention the inquisitive chickadees and titmice that inhabit our woods—by simply sitting quietly until they lost interest in me, realized I was no threat or forgot I was there.

Deer hunters sometimes use a tree perch to sit above the line of sight of the big mammals; there are chairlike shelves that put you high enough to be out of the line of sight. Simpler is to find a comfortable and sturdy limb to sit on. If you don't suffer fear of heights, you may be in fine shape. The deer walk right by, allowing you plenty of time to sketch.

Plan a spot ahead of time; look for animal trails in the area—footprints and droppings are your best indication of a well-used trail. Then put out a salt block to attract wildlife near your chosen place. It may work; it may not. The deer on my place have decided they prefer the other side of the creek for their passage—my salt block hasn't been touched in weeks. I've seen them only from a distance.

If you are walking rather than sitting, try moving when the animals do, stopping when they stop. With their black and white vision, they may mistake you for a tree, if you are downwind. Look away when an animal looks toward you, or shade your eyes—our bold looking is very unsettling. A wide-brimmed hat or sunglasses may help. Crouch or sit to disguise your two-leggedness; instinct tells them that upright beasts are dangerous, and instinct is correct. If it isn't a hunting human, it may be a grizzly; either way, animals don't like it, and how are they to know we're only sketching?

A small sketchbook works best to capture animals in the wild, by the way; those large white sheets of paper flapping in the wind are like a warning signal. The animals bolt.

At times only a blind (or a *hide*, as they call it in Britain) will do. Fashion one from brush and leaves, or use camouflage cloth or even a small tent; animals may come quite close. Edwin Way Teale built a permanent brush pile, hollow in the middle, from which he could closely observe wildlife. In a marsh, borrow a waterfowler's trick and hide behind marsh grass or cattails. Cut some and lash them to saplings for a portable blind. Often a canoe works well; even uncamouflaged, the odd shape allows us to get close enough to draw—the shape and that wonderfully silent moving.

Improvise an extremely portable blind that you wear. A camouflage-

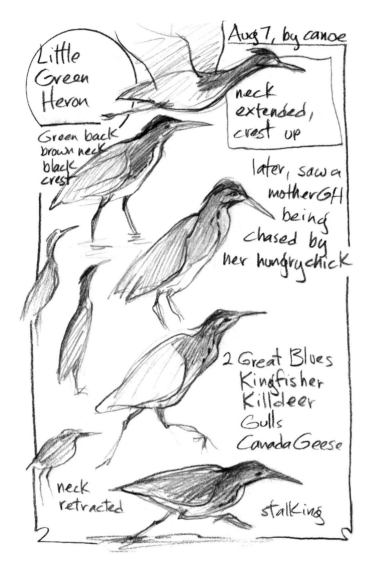

Little green heron.
(0.5-mm mechanical pencil
with HB lead.)

cloth poncho can be spread out around you as you sit against a tree; a wide-brimmed hat sits like a big mushroom on a rock—and that's just what you'll look like. Keep your sketchbook hidden under your poncho, and do a blind drawing, or lift it only enough to see what you're doing without scaring your subject away.

FIELD SKETCHING IN FAMILIAR SETTINGS

You needn't go far from home to find subjects for your field sketches; you needn't leave home at all. Our backyards teem with life, both plant and animal. There are even things to sketch and study indoors, if you look. Houseplants make good subjects, as do their pests and parasites. Sketch that spider or waterbug. This oddly mild winter, we've been invaded by box elder

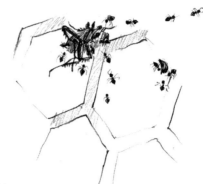

Waterbug and ants.
(0.5-mm mechanical pencil.)

Dec. 28

One of the kittens
killed a waterbug
in the bathroom
this morning, early
Already the tiny
lithe acrobatic
ants have found it
and are efficiently
dismantling it
before my eyes.
They are so strong—
they can maneuver
this behemoth like
the Lilliputians did
Gulliver!

bugs, normally killed off by frigid weather—they've found every tiny crack and used it as an entryway. Why *not* sketch them? I'm outnumbered, by far, and they're fascinating little creatures.

Keep your bird feeders full—all year, if you want to attract subjects. Use a variety of feeds, from black sunflower and niger seeds to cracked corn. Put out apples and suet; make a squirrel feeder at some distance from your bird feeders, and keep water out through the winter. At night, a flying squirrel may be tempted by your offerings. In the summer months, add a hummingbird feeder, and keep the syrup in it fresh to ensure lots of action. (Do take it down in the early fall; hummingbirds have been known to linger too long in the temperate zones by an accessible and famliar feeder. They can't survive the rigors of winter.)

If you want to attract butterflies to your yard, plant blooming shrubs and flowers with plenty of nectar.

Although most people don't care for foraging mammals on their deck at night, I like to leave out food for the raccoons and opossums. I can sketch them, too, if they become accustomed to a low light. Make your backyard an attractive place to wildlife, and you'll have all the subjects you'll need for field sketches. If an occasional Romeo tomcat also sings a duet with his lady there, who cares?

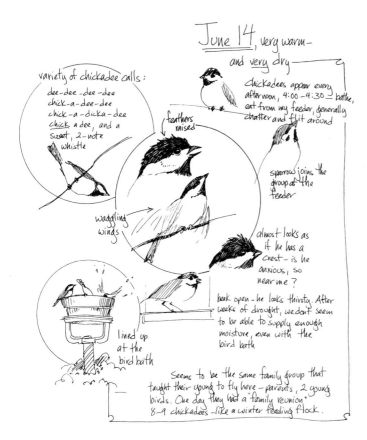

June 14, chickadees.
(Pilot razor-tipped pen.)

SPECIAL EQUIPMENT

You may find you need your own faculties boosted from time to time. Mountain goats are, after all, notoriously shy of people no matter what our intentions; they won't let you near them. You may admire the patchwork of colors as lichen encrusts an ancient granite rock, but that's all—you can't see the wonderful variety of form. Near and far, we need help!

An inexpensive hand lens will aid your eyes' ability to see close up; mine, from Bausch and Lomb, is capable of magnification from 5× to 12×. A field microscope reveals even more; Radio Shack carries one little larger than a pocket flashlight that magnifies up to 30×, with built-in illumination. At home, a hobbyist's microscope lets you into the secrets you've only guessed at.

Binoculars are indispensable in the field for sketching birds and wild-life—if you've been unable to get closer than thirty feet, you'll need your vision enhanced to be able to sketch those details. I like a very lightweight pair for convenience when sketching. For serious wildlife drawing, you'll need a telescope, usually a refractor-style spotting scope. Used with a tri-pod, a telescope lets you draw comfortably for hours without disturbing the animals you see.

USING A CAMERA TO SUPPLEMENT YOUR SKETCHES

There are times when you want more information about the scene than you are able to sketch on the spot; perhaps you don't have time to record all the details, or you only want to do one habitat sketch of the area on this particular page, but there are so many other possibilities to record. You may be with people who aren't interested in waiting around while you sketch. (A bad situation, to be avoided—if possible—at all costs!) You may be traveling in a hurry, and *you* don't have the time to stop at each place to record the landscape and its features in depth. An animal may stand still for only seconds before it bolts—time for a quick photo, too late for a sketch, unless you've developed your visual memory to a high degree. A camera is your best friend in these circumstances.

I use a 35-mm, single-lens reflex camera to gather information. This allows me to see what I'm aiming at, and to get a reasonable likeness. I'm not really a professional photographer, though I've done all the photography for my own books—that's under controlled studio conditions, and has nothing whatever to do with waiting on a rocky ridge for a coyote to pass at dawn. I don't expect my shots to end up on the Sierra Club's wilderness calendar; they're for my information only.

A good zoom and/or close-up lens will let you get close to your subject—one way or another. I have a zoom-macro lens that is convenient in the field—no need to tote a camera bag and five lenses for my purposes, and certainly no need for the extra weight in addition to sketching supplies. I can't get quite as close as I might like for detail studies of flowers or fossils, or take a photo from quite so far as if I had a powerful zoom, but the convenience is an acceptable tradeoff.

The practice gained in looking through a viewfinder will be invaluable in helping you to plan a composition—but don't be trapped into copying from photos, your own or anyone else's. They simply don't give you enough information. A fast shutter speed may have frozen an animal in an awkward position. The details may be distorted by angle or closeness.

Color film tells you something about what you see, but unfortunately— especially for amateur photographers—often the color isn't true. Color print film is less true than slide film. Try to remember what you saw; trust your notes. Train yourself not to depend on the developer's art for information about coloring, either in a landscape or in an animal's pelt.

Use your photos as resources, tools; pretend you are there, and use them as you do any other bits of information. Change, delete, mix and match, enhance, zero in on details. A photo is not a field sketch, no matter how wonderfully composed or beautifully colored.

But sometimes I *do* stick a photo in place in my field journal; it simply adds to the information I already have on my subject and increases my understanding—and my pleasure.

As you might have guessed, this subject is close to my heart. I'd rather be field sketching, enjoying the *being* there, learning as I draw, than painting the best watercolor I've ever done back in the studio. I prefer the immediacy, the challenge, the experience—both mental and physical.

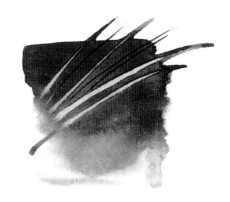

SIX

Sketching in Color

COLOR IS MAGIC; we knew that as children, discovering the world with new eyes. We know it now, each time we see an indigo bunting flash like blue flame across the sky, or a late winter sunset paint the snow with peach and gold. We itch to record those ephemeral, affective hues.

There are as many *reasons* to color sketching as there are artists to do it—and as many methods. Perhaps you love color, feel comfortable with it, and jump right in; you may be an instinctive colorist. Or maybe you prefer to explore in color, finding your way like an orienteer, choosing your way with no safely marked trail to guide you. If color makes you a bit nervous (there's such a lot of choice, after all), try a limited palette with only three to six hues—or plan your drawing first in black and white. I often translate in this way, doing my quick sketches with a warm dark gray, then taking off from there in color, either directly over the monochromatic underdrawing or as a separate piece.

You may want to plan the color scheme of a future painting or drawing; you may want, instead, just to capture the lovely color you see—if you don't get it down right *now*, you'll never remember it later. You may need to record a wildflower's color as it occurs in a varied environment; color often differs in shade or full sun. Color may define a bird's field marks; it's the color pattern more than anything else that lets us distinguish an indigo bunting from a lazuli one—or a flicker from a red-bellied woodpecker. Color sketching can meet all these demands and more.

Sketching in color can be as liberating as finding yourself suddenly unaffected by Earth's gravity. I feel like a kite, a hot air balloon. Freed from the constraints of black and white and carefully written color notes—the need to translate what we see through a monochromatic mental screen—I tend to go a bit giddy.

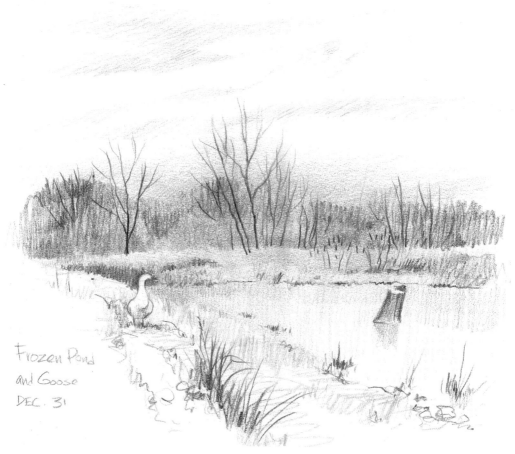

Frozen Pond
and Goose
DEC. 31

Pond sketch, Niji colored pencil set.

To counter my own tendency toward craziness, I carry only a few colors to the field. A limited palette often has more emotional impact—more piz-zazz—than an attempt to faithfully depict each hue and gradation. Oddly, it seems to capture more of the truth than a sketch in which you've used every color in your crayon box. There is, after all, no way to sketch *all* the hues in a winter sunset or wildflower-studded meadow, not without getting garish—and working very large indeed. Even a rainbow needs to be han-dled with subtlety.

An additional advantage to using a limited palette is that having only a few colors lets you work with more speed. The very nature of sketching out-doors often demands quick work—much of nature is in motion, and often I am, too.

Keep it simple, for the sake of weight as well as speed. Carry a few care-fully selected colored pencils; let the season or time of day be your guide, or the animals or birds you expect to see. Pick the colors you'll be most likely to need before leaving home. If you prefer, choose a single color that best expresses your subject; a tawny cougar could be done quite well with an ochre or sienna pencil. Add one color for shadows, another for eyes, and you have a sketch that seems to be in full color—but isn't.

You might want to include one of each of the primaries for good measure. You may *expect* only an overcast summer day with lots of subtle greens and blues, but you may be surprised by a brilliant scarlet tanager.

Rather than the sixty-four-color box, take along a small set of crayons, pencils, or colored felt-tips. In a traveling watercolor box, selection is automatically limited by space, but even so, simplify colors for best effect.

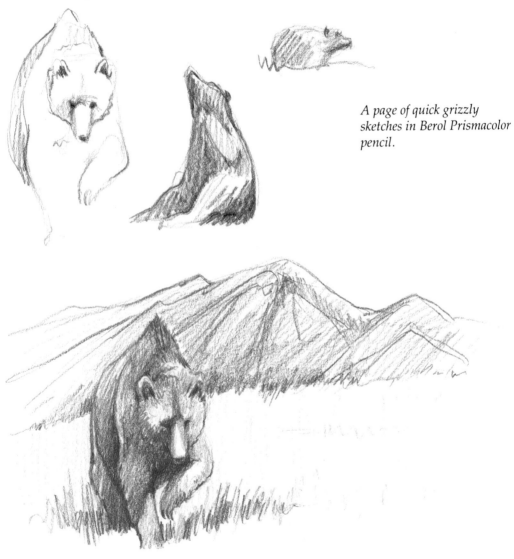

A page of quick grizzly sketches in Berol Prismacolor pencil.

I used Berol's yellow ochre, violet, and terra cotta to complete this drawing, adding elements from several grizzly sources as well as my live grizzly sketches. I used warm tones to suggest the light-struck areas, and deep violet to suggest shadow. I used that same violet pencil to capture distant mountains.

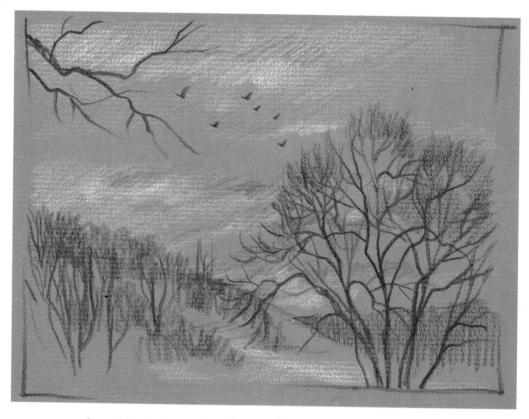

I carried only six pencils with me to depict this late winter sunset; the color of the paper itself, a grayish blue, stands in for others and gives unity to my drawing. (White, sand, rose pink, true blue, ultramarine, and indigo Prismacolors.)

Only three pencils were used for this lioness: Prismacolor warm grey dark, sienna brown, and deep yellow in the eyes. The sand-colored paper added the final value. (Notice the loose strokes; my first attempt was far too tight to make a good sketch. The strength of this feline seemed to call for sure handling.)

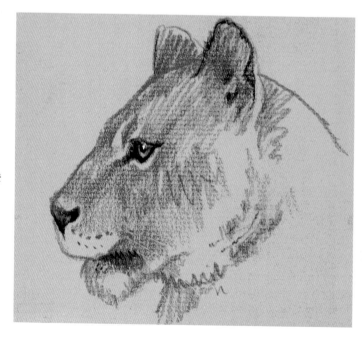

A BRIEF REVIEW OF COLOR THEORY

What you see doesn't absolutely have to be what you get. You can move color around, emphasize one over another, suggest a mood or time of day— it's your choice. (A detailed handling of color theory is beyond the scope of this book; this section is only intended as a review. If you would like further information, any number of texts have handled the subject in depth. Check the bibliography for a few of my favorites.)

A color wheel is often used to explain color theory; see my rough demonstration in the color section of this book. Red, yellow, and blue are called the *primary colors*, as you'll probably remember from elementary school— this simply means that they can't be made up from other colors. They just are.

The *secondary colors* are mixed from these primaries: equal amounts of red and yellow make true orange, and greater amounts of either will tilt the balance of power, producing what are called the *tertiary colors*. Mixed in various formulas, these two produce a variety of oranges, yellow-oranges, and red-oranges. Blue and yellow make the greens, and blue and red will yield all the purples you'll ever need, in theory if not in practice. (I usually take along a few greens, oranges, and purples for speed, especially when using colored pencils.)

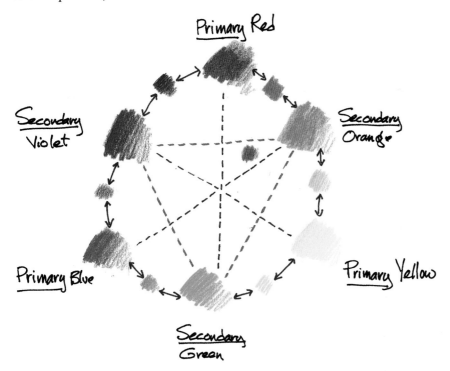

A simple color wheel shows opposites—the complementary colors. A triangle of lines link the secondary hues, mixed from the primaries, and between them lie the tertiary hues. In fact, there can be as many variations as you wish between each of these colors, depending on the strength of each color in the mixture. A small spot of reddish brown shows the position of less intense versions on the color wheel.

Lighter forms of these colors are called *tints* (pink is a tint of red, for instance). Darker incarnations are the shades, and duller mixtures produce colors of lower *chroma*—they're less intense than pure colors. For example, orange is quite intense, but its lower-chroma version, brown, is correspondingly less so—and occurs much more frequently in nature. The pure colors are delightfully rare—maybe that's what makes them precious.

Vary color value, using lighter and darker versions of the same hues. Use the somewhat lower-chroma hues for larger, more dominant areas and save the bright colors for accents, in most cases—unless you're doing a close-up study of a poppy. Then go for it.

—A *monochromatic* color scheme is made up of the tints and shades of a single hue—nice for depicting the coming of evening or a snowy arctic scene.

—*Analogous* colors are closely related and automatically work well together; these colors lie next to one another on the color wheel. The warm colors—reds, oranges, and yellows—suggest one mood or nuance, cool colors—the blues and greens—another.

—*Complementary* colors appear opposite each other on the color wheel and can create a strong impact. They vibrate nicely when used next to

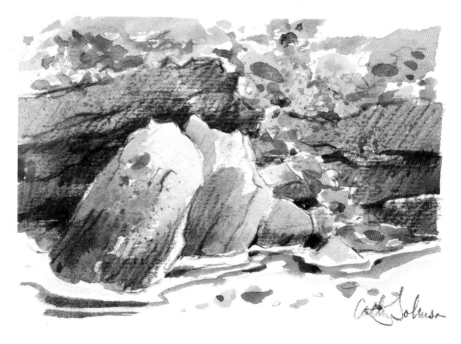

Autumn produces complementary color schemes in this sketch, with all the rich warm oranges contrasted with cool bluish shadows. Look for these complements, or opposites on the color wheel, at any season—a red flower against green foliage, for example.

each other, but you'll usually want to vary size or intensity. Tone one or the other down a bit to keep your sketches from appearing garish, or use a large area of one color balanced by a small splash of another. Examples—other than the familiar Christmas combination of red and green—are blues contrasted with a warm orange or orange-brown, or cool violet shadows within a yellow form.

—A *triad* scheme simply uses any three colors equidistant on the color wheel. The primary colors are triadic hues, as are the secondaries. You may have a bit of difficulty imagining a scene in which you'd *want* to use orange, purple, and green together, but with nature's own good taste in placement and balance, they often occur.

Repeat colors for unity in a picture or sketch, if only once or twice. Keep the two areas of color different sizes, or they will compete with one another and you won't know *where* to look.

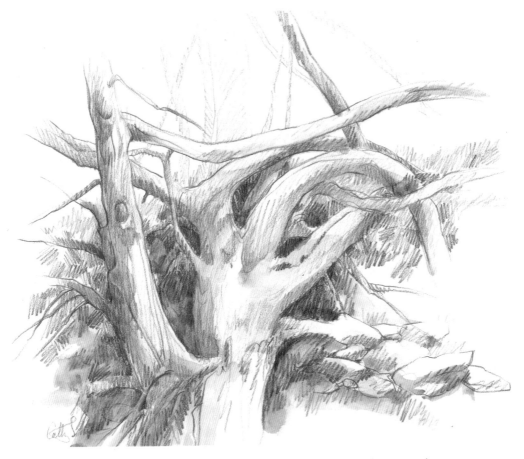

Water-soluble colored pencils were applied dry, then moistened with clear water in selected areas—those that I wanted softened or blended. Later, when everything was dry, I added sharp accents, again with dry pencils.

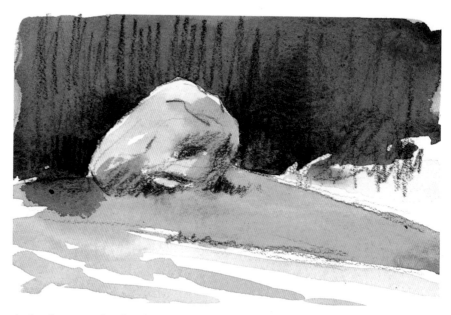

A simple watercolor sketch—see the larger version of this in Chapter 4, "Capturing the Illusion of Light." This was done on a Clester Postcard, and colors were encouraged to blend where they touched other wet pigments. The rock itself was laid in first and allowed to dry thoroughly so that I could maintain a sharp, light-struck edge against the dark foliage.

MEDIUM RARE—OR FAMILIAR

The "best" medium for color work is a strictly personal decision. If you've tried out some of those suggested in Chapter 1, you'll have a good idea of what will work best for you. I often use colored pencils, either the wax-based Prismacolors or the tiny, mechanical-pencil-style Niji set—they're lightweight, clean, and versatile. Used directly or layered to create new colors, these tools have great versatility. Art sticks or crayons work as well.

Water-soluble colored pencils are a hybrid between watercolor and colored pencils; they're great fun to experiment with. Draw first with the dry pencil—complete your whole drawing, if you like—then add clear water with a brush to blend selected areas. That's usually more satisfactory than prewetting the paper or wetting the whole drawing once it's finished—I lose too much detail that way. If you *do* find that everything has become a bit hazy and indistinct, let your sketch dry thoroughly, then go back in with sharp pencil details.

As noted elsewhere, the intensity of these pencils often changes dramatically when wet; a color chart, as suggested in Chapter 1, will be a great help in letting you know what to expect. As time goes by, you'll develop personal favorites that will be like old friends—you'll know what to expect of them, and a chart won't be necessary.

Watercolor is extremely versatile but somewhat more complicated than most sketching mediums. It requires a bit of explanation; it is handled in a separate chapter.

USING A TONED GROUND FOR COLOR WORK

A colored or toned ground (paper or board) will let you further simplify supplies; the paper stands in for one of your colors for an overall hue to enhance mood or presence. Here I've used a warm-toned paper with wax-based colored pencils to suggest the red rocks of Nevada. Opaque pencils were used with a heavy pressure in the sky area to completely cover the toned paper. (See color section, as well.) Or, if you prefer, work into a medium-toned paper with a dark pencil or pen and add light color accents—your work will take on new life and a visual "third dimension."

The color you choose for your background can suggest season—a light yellow-green for spring, perhaps, or a rich gold for autumn. A medium blue could suggest twilight, and a sunny yellow might be midday at Colorado's sand dunes. Colored pencils or opaque watercolors work well on this toned ground, but transparent watercolors may be too sheer for best effect.

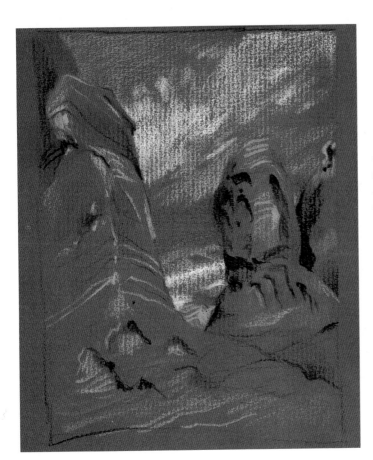

Choose your background to complement or enhance season, subject, or mood. Here, a rich terra-cotta paper expresses the overall Nevada desert color scheme. Opaque colored pencils cover the medium-toned paper to pick out the lights and suggest the sky; dark accents were added in the shadows.

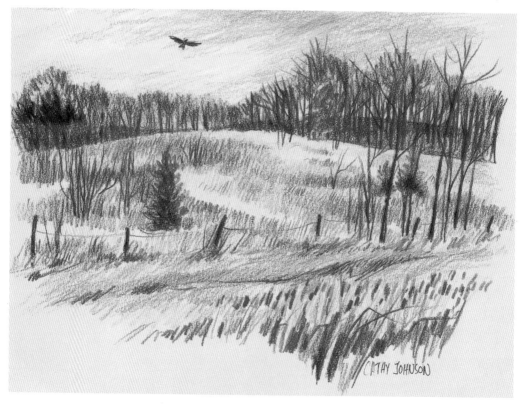

A light sand-colored background let me lay in the colors of an early winter day in opaque pencil.

LEARNING TO SEE AND RECORD COLOR

It may sound easy to see color, but in fact it takes a bit of doing, even if you are *not* colorblind. Too often, we react to what we see through the smoke-screen of what we've learned in some dusty classroom. We use symbolic colors, or what "should" be.

In fact, the only argument I have with color theory is that it's just that. Theory. Learned. Cerebral. Sometimes the magic is in what is actually there before us, that wonderful, impossible color, that subtle hue, not in what we've been *taught* is there. Or have been told will "work."

How many times have you seen tree trunks painted a warm, cozy brown? Not many of them actually *are*; they're a range of soft grays, instead.

Grass doesn't have to be a flat grass-green. It may blush with ruddy lights if the seed heads are ripe, or turn to gold in autumn. It may look almost blue in shadow—or in Kentucky bluegrass country. Against a low sun, each blade is a bright yellow-green, lit from behind like stained glass.

And in nature, water is blue only if it reflects a sunny sky or washes crystal clear over white sands. Even then it's really a hundred shades of blue—the deep blue of the North Atlantic is a very different color from the pale aquamarine of the Caribbean. In flood, water is every shade from café au lait to brick, depending on the type of soil it erodes; in winter, a creek looks black against the whiteness of the snow, like an etching. In hot summer sun, water can be white—at least if you want it that way, to convey the feeling that all color has been burned away. *You* are the artist.

The nuances of color and the values contained there take a bit of practice to see accurately, as well. You may want to make a color chart using each of your chosen mediums, from the most saturated hue to the lightest tint of each color, to help you recognize what you're seeing. Note the color name, or set yourself up a system of numbers or letters for each color to identify them later.

Use the *value* chart from Chapter 2 to help you see what degree of lightness or darkness is present in the colors you see. Which pencil should you choose for that stand of cedars or icy snowdrift? Shadows are darkest near the object that casts them; as they fall away, their value lightens. Seeing just takes a bit of practice—and once you see what *is*, you're in a better position to take off from that point with your own interpretation and to choose the color you need.

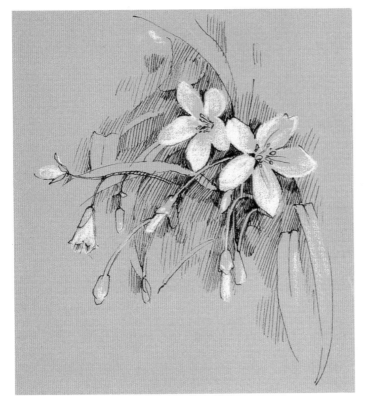

A colored ground with only one light and one dark drawing tool lets you introduce color, mood, or temperature as well as the feeling of dimension. Here, a grayed-blue paper was used with a razor-tipped pen and white Prismacolor colored pencil; the flowers seem to stick out from the surface of the paper.

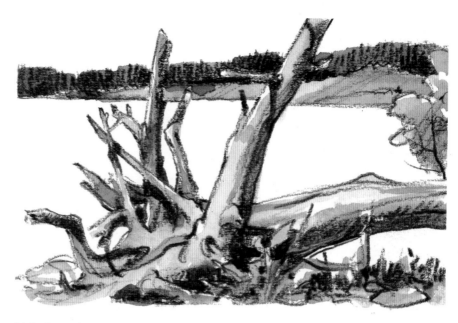

I left sky and water white to suggest the relentless August sun. Don't feel you have to cover every centimeter of your paper; leaving white gives sparkle, suggests emotion or mood, and can be a powerful compositional device: it directs the eye. (Prismacolor grey pencil and watercolor wash.)

TAKING COLOR NOTES

Obviously, taking these notes is almost instantaneous when sketching in color, but remember that the simplified or limited colors you've taken along can stand in for a much wider range. You can still note in the margins that a color appears grayer, bluer, more subtle, brighter—what have you. Use your color chart to supplement your notes; once you're thoroughly familiar with your own system, you can substitute a letter or number for a longer written note, and you'll know exactly what you meant. With time, you won't need this shorthand at all.

ENHANCING WHAT YOU SEE

Enhancing what you see is not so much a matter of changing what is before you but of really seeing what is there—becoming sensitized to color. An overcast day doesn't have to appear on paper as a monochrome handling of shades of gray; there's a lot of color in those tones. Shadows are not monochromatic, either; they pick up color and intensity from what is nearby. Reflected color in shadows is one of the artist's best tools. Use it well, and your work springs to life. Look at the shadows beneath this nuthatch's belly as it stands next to the apple; the warm, rosy light reflects upward to modify that single-color tone. The same thing applies to color bounced up into the shady understory or the pale hues of a flower reflecting back into the cast shadows on a white house.

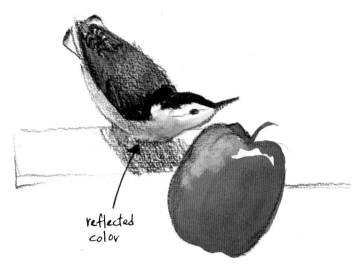

reflected
color

Local color in shadow areas can be affected by the direction of light and what is nearest your subject. Here, the warm glow of the red apple is reflected back into the shadow on the nuthatch's breast. (Prismacolor grey pencil and watercolor wash.)

EXPLORING WITH COLOR

Colors are magic. They move and vibrate and seem to shift position in the picture plane. They have temperature that can be used to express what you see—or what you *want* to see. Cool colors recede—the blues and greens and chilly lavenders. Think of the blue haze on distant hills or the cooler tones of tree trunks deep in the forest. Warm colors (reds, yellows, oranges, warm browns), on the other hand, seem to come forward.

I use this trick to give my work a sense of aerial perspective, even when dealing with relatively short distances. Warm colors used in foreground areas help them "feel" close, while cooler colors keep the background where it belongs.

Use quick color sketches to explore what is and what is not. Now you may be seeing your subject on a gray day, but that's no reason why you can't think back to the day you caught it bathed in buttery sunlight or at blue twilight. Change the mood or time of day in an instant with quick color sketches, then choose the one you like to develop further. Sketch the forms you see, but use the colors that have emotional content for you.

Or say you are sketching in autumn but would like to simplify the scene to a winter one. Color sketching lets you do just that, and easily. My colored pencil sketches didn't take long, but let me discover which had the most impact. I much prefer the subtle colors of the winter sketch, and if I paint this subject, it will be from the second sketch.

You can layer colors to get new effects, whether working in colored pencil, crayon, or watercolor. This not only saves carrying additional colors to the field but also lets you find subtle new effects not possible with someone else's formulated mixtures. Crosshatch your pencil or crayon strokes in different directions or apply smoothly, one over another, until you get the effect you're after. If you're using watercolor, be sure to let your first washes dry thoroughly, or they'll lift and muddy subsequent ones. Lay a cool color over a warm one, or a less intense color over a bright one for new effects.

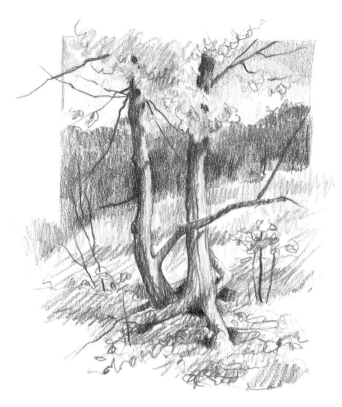

This colored pencil sketch is pretty much as I saw things, still leafed but turning ruddy in the fall.

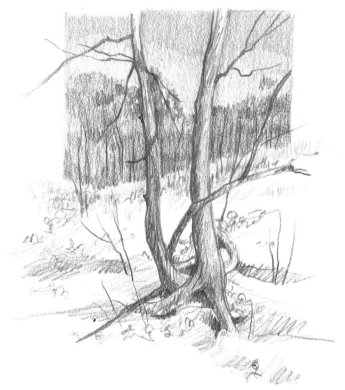

In minutes, I changed the scene to winter by switching color schemes and deleting details.

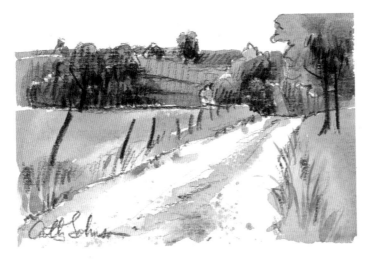

I made a Berol Prismacolor underdrawing, using only the bare minimum of detail. Later, back at camp, I added washes of the colors I remembered, pushing them somewhat for atmosphere. The white of the paper stands in for the pale graveled road and the bleached summer sky.

TRAINING YOUR COLOR MEMORY

Here's a trick I use to sharpen my powers of observation. I carry only my sketchbook and a single pencil—it's lightweight and allows room for spontaneity. This works especially well for field work, where I usually prefer the simplest of sketching supplies. I work in black and white, often with a wax-based colored pencil that won't be affected by subsequent watercolor washes. Generally, it's a pretty linear handling, with not too much attention given to value patterns; that can be included with the value of the colors I choose. I try to absorb the overall color sense as I draw—the mood, the feeling, almost, of what I see. I take no written color notes, although I may mentally tick off what I see—a certain warm glow in a reflected light, a rich green line of trees—to reinforce it in memory. Then, later, at home or when I've reached a convenient place to get out more complicated supplies, I lay in my colors.

This encourages closer on-the-spot observation while freeing me from an overanxious copying of the colors I see—matching the exact hue is not so important as value, composition, and form. I may intensify the colors in my sketch, pushing them a bit for dramatic effect. Sometimes I tone them down for a smoky subtlety. I may limit colors to two or three, and let white paper stand in for large areas; it's not necessary to cover every inch with color. I use this technique more often, now, than written notes or even sketching directly in color and seem more able to absorb what I'm seeing. I pay attention; I'm there.

BUILDING ON A MONOCHROME BASE

You may want to do your sketch using a single hue—say a dark gray or blue—then build up layers of sheer color over that. Laying in the preliminary sketch in a dark neutral will let you find the "bones" of your sketch, plan the composition, achieve a good balance of lights and darks—here, I *do* include the value pattern—before beginning the sometimes confusing work of adding color. The sketch could stand on its own, as is.

I often use colored pencils in this manner, but again, watercolor washes over a pencil drawing will work quite well. You can use this technique in the field or as a memory aid similar to that mentioned earlier; I've done both.

The best thing about sketching in color is perhaps the thing we all know from the time we're handed our first box of crayons as children. This isn't work—this stuff is *fun*.

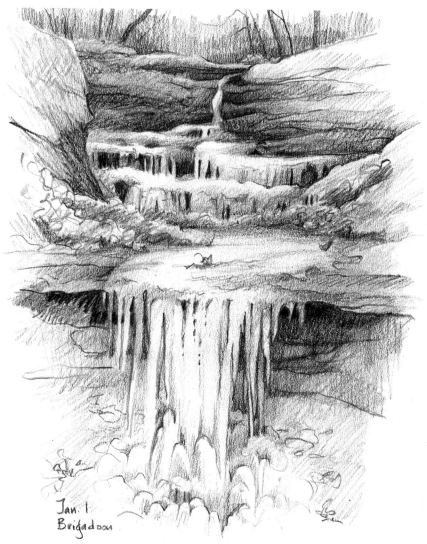

This sketch of a frozen waterfall was begun with a black, wax-based mechanical pencil and could have stood on its own as a monochromatic drawing before other colors were laid over it. The Niji colored pencil set with a variety of leads made this sketch easy to accomplish in the field, but this technique can work well when you only want to carry a single drawing tool—or when you are unsure about jumping right in with color. It gives you a chance to capture value patterns and details, then finish at leisure.

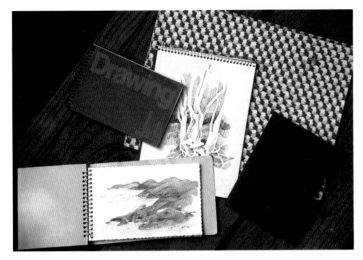

Try out a variety of sketching surfaces; the smaller sizes are most portable—and less obtrusive. Clockwise from left, surrounding the central 8 × 10-inch spiral-bound pad: a 5 × 7-inch drawing pad, a 9 × 12-inch watercolor block (which fits a daypack nicely), a 5 × 7-inch sketchbook (hardbound for durability), and a book of Notchy Postcards.

Keep watercolor boxes for field work light, sturdy, and relatively simple; it's not necessary to take along supplies you'd need for a full-sheet painting. My favorite is at lower left, a lightweight, high-impact plastic box that carries its own water supply, mixing areas, and a small brush.

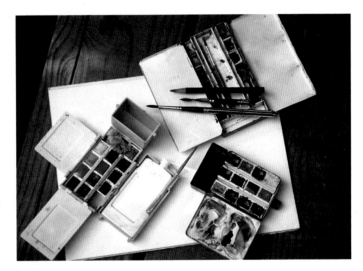

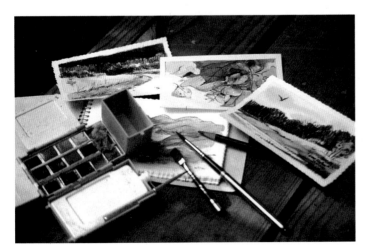

All you need for watercolor sketching: a field box, small-sized paper (in this case a book of Notchy Postcards), and a few brushes. I include a colored pencil for line work.

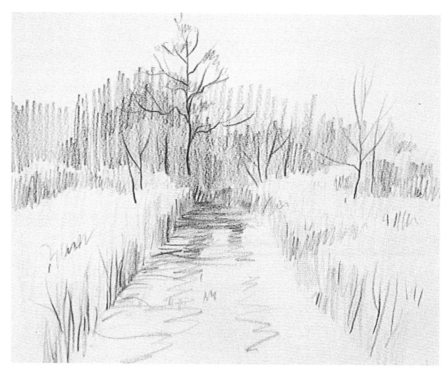

Colored pencils are handy for quick sketches as well as more complete works.
A limited palette with only a few colors makes for a lightweight pack.

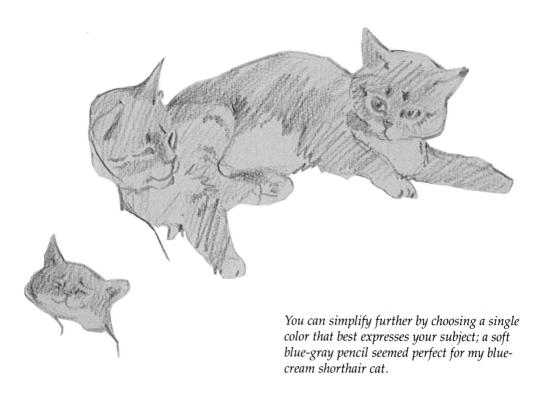

You can simplify further by choosing a single color that best expresses your subject; a soft blue-gray pencil seemed perfect for my blue-cream shorthair cat.

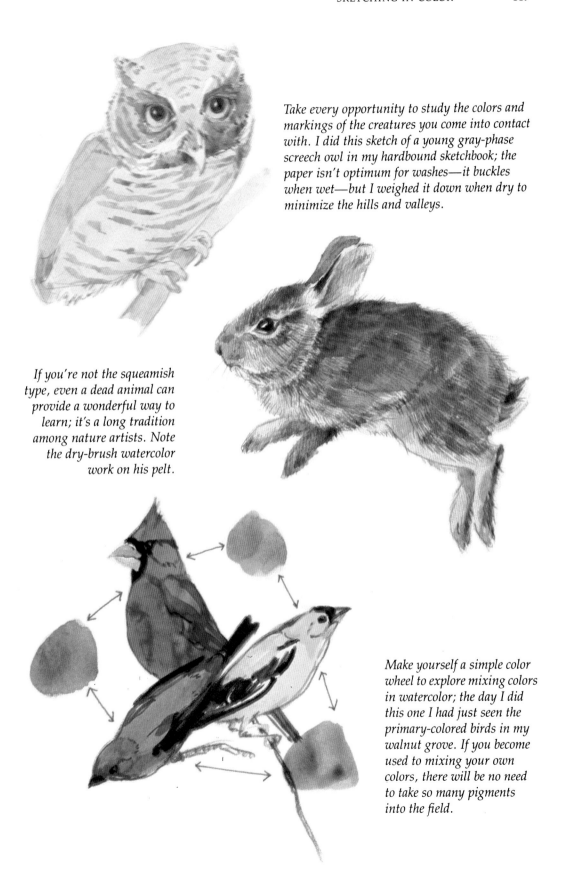

Take every opportunity to study the colors and markings of the creatures you come into contact with. I did this sketch of a young gray-phase screech owl in my hardbound sketchbook; the paper isn't optimum for washes—it buckles when wet—but I weighed it down when dry to minimize the hills and valleys.

If you're not the squeamish type, even a dead animal can provide a wonderful way to learn; it's a long tradition among nature artists. Note the dry-brush watercolor work on his pelt.

Make yourself a simple color wheel to explore mixing colors in watercolor; the day I did this one I had just seen the primary-colored birds in my walnut grove. If you become used to mixing your own colors, there will be no need to take so many pigments into the field.

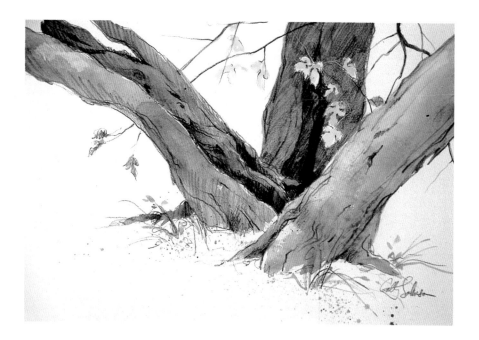

Mixed-media works just as well for a painting as for a sketch. Here, I used my favorite warm dark grey Prismacolor pencil to lay in the mulberry tree with a suggestion of values on a half-sheet of watercolor paper—on the spot. Later, in the studio, I added watercolor washes. For a more traditional approach, I repeated the same subject using pure washes on hot-pressed (smooth) paper.

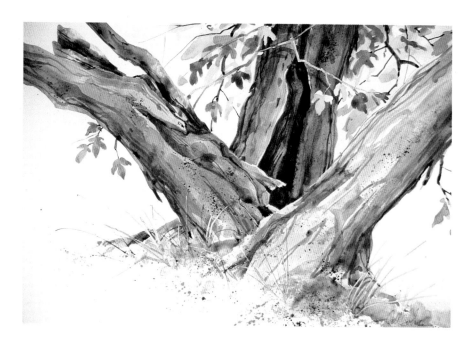

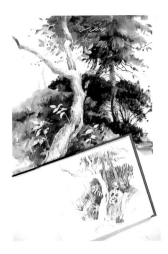

A simple value sketch may be all you need to plan a finished painting. Here, you can see both sketch and painting. I use only four or five values when sketching, including the white of my paper; more than that breeds confusion.

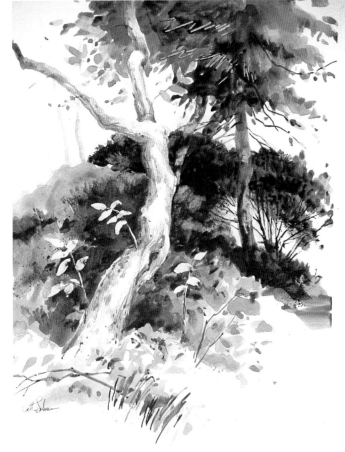

The finished painting follows the value sketch fairly closely, with some allowances for spontaneity. This was one on hot-press illustration board, a very slick surface that allowed puddles of paint to create textures complementing those I had planned.

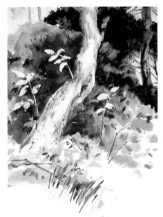

I used the end of my brush to scrape light lines through damp pigment, a fan brush in lower left to suggest rough foliage, and a small brush or palette knife for linear effects in twigs and small branches.

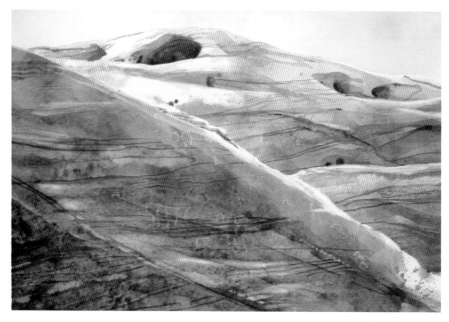

Don't feel that you must reproduce a scene exactly; it may fall flat. Here, I was too close to the colors and values of the scene—and too far from my feelings *about it.*

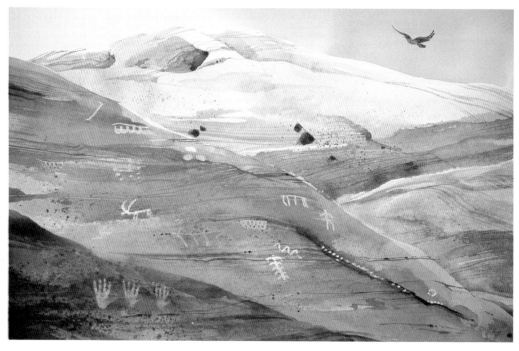

I tried again, this time using the bright, clear colors of the Southwest desert. The dark desert varnish reflected the cool blue of the sky, and the sun-struck rocks were hot—and they look it.

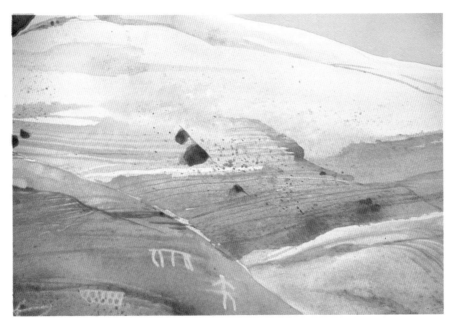

Separating, sedimenting colors like ultramarine blue and burnt sienna helped to express the feel of sandstone rocks. To keep the petroglyphs light against the dark wash, I used a wax candle and liquid maskoid over the first layer of color, then added my secondary washes.

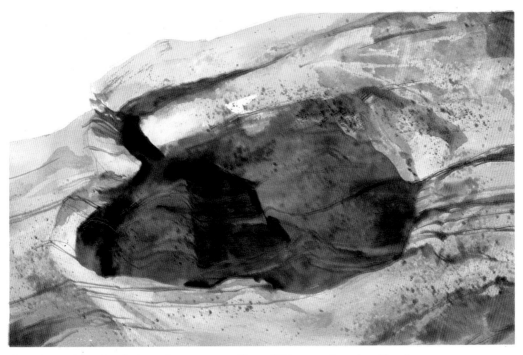

I used a variety of techniques here: among others, lifting a wet wash with a damp paper towel, scraping through a damp wash, pressing plastic wrap into the wash, then removing it. Simple texturing tricks work as well in the field as in the studio.

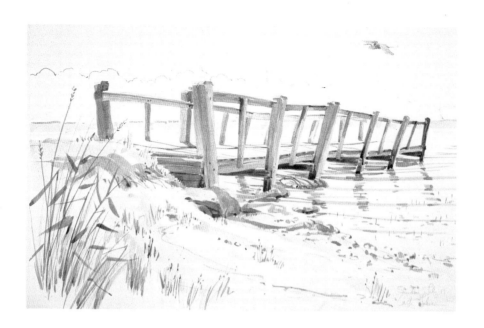

Above. Don't be afraid to alter color to fit mood or other circumstances. Here, I painted on the spot on a scorching summer day; cool greens didn't seem to work, but an extremely limited palette did. This painting was done with only two brushes, a half-inch flat and a No. 6 round; note the calligraphic, linear brushwork that captures all the necessary detail.

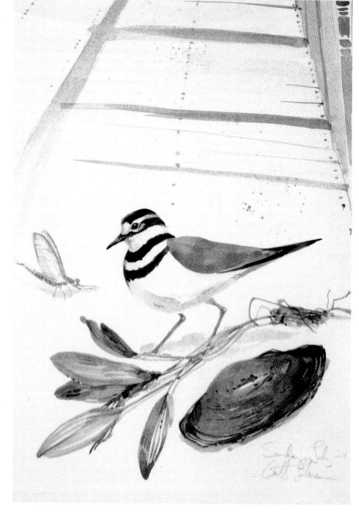

Right. As a naturalist, I'm very interested in the details of habitat. Here, I painted the old dock, then added the things I had found nearby— a killdeer, a mussel, a golden mayfly and water weeds—to make one of my favorite paintings.

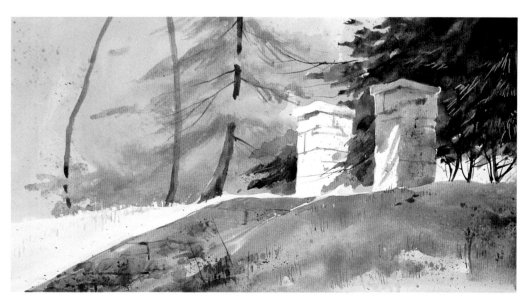

A wet-in-wet handling let me blend areas of color freely; this was a very quick watercolor. The contrast between the manmade stonework and the natural forms of the trees caught my eye.

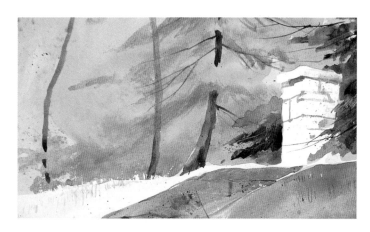

Here, you can see the effects of spatter into a wet wash (background trees) and light-struck grasses scraped into the wash when dry.

Only a bit of detail was used to suggest the stonework. Note the use of a scraping tool to suggest foliage in a damp wash at right.

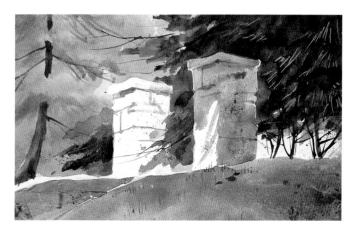

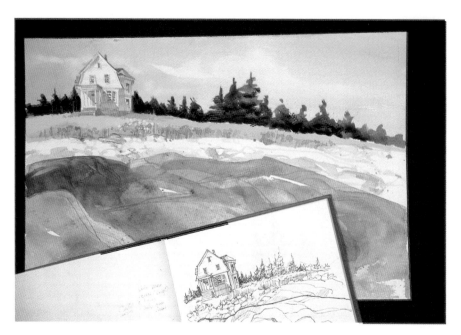

Annotated pen sketches provide plenty of information for a finished painting; notice the remarks in the margin.

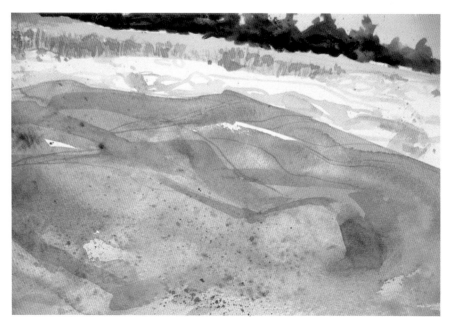

Loose washes, scraping and a bit of spatter suggest the texture of the granite rocks.

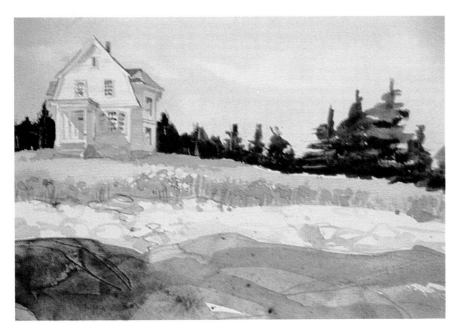

I used a fan brush and some scraping to depict the grasses of the lighthouse-keeper's home.

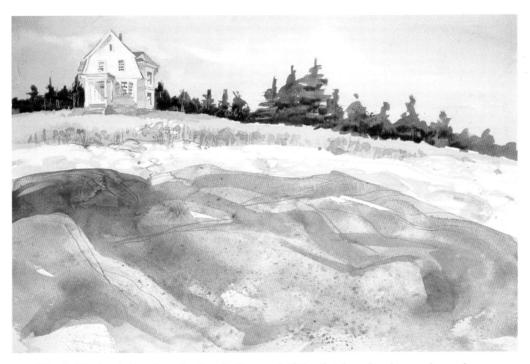

The finished painting is quite close to the mood of the sketch and makes good use of the information there, both in the sketch itself and in the marginal notes. I was interested in the play of color and distance and the rough granite rocks of the headland.

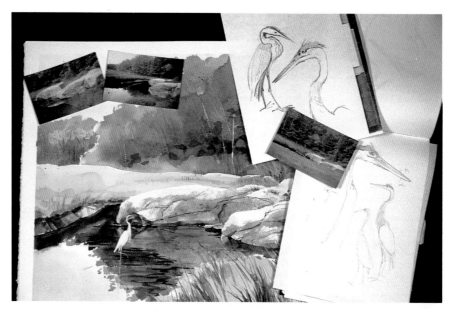

If there's no time for prolonged sketching (the black flies and mosquitoes were murderous near this salt marsh), you may have to make do with photos and sketches from other sources. These resources were used just as if I were sketching on the spot, combining freely to capture the effect I was after.

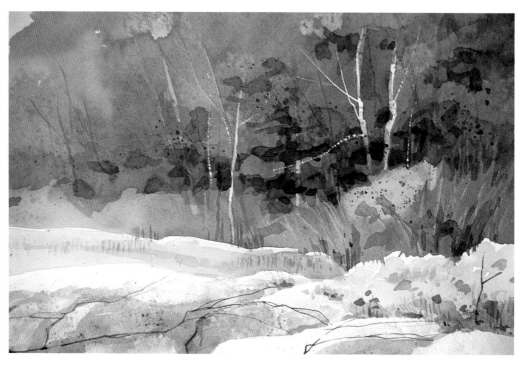

I used maskoid applied with a palette knife to preserve the light trunks of the birches, and rapidly added washes, glazes, and textures.

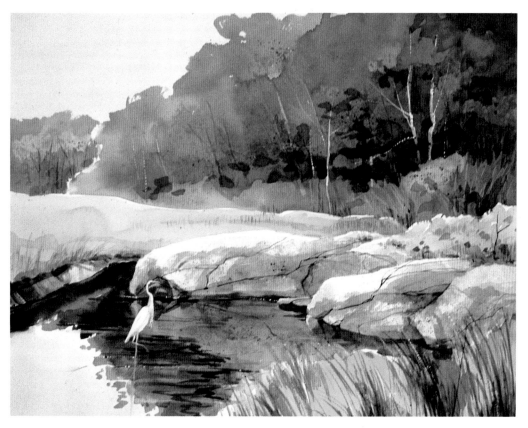

The finished painting combines three of my photo resources plus a heron-turned-egret from last year's sketchbook. I had sketches of a great blue heron, but when it came time to add pigment, I hated to lose the contrast—I decided to keep the bird pale to allow it to show to the best advantage. I paid special attention to the negative shapes in the distant foliage to suggest the complexity of tree forms.

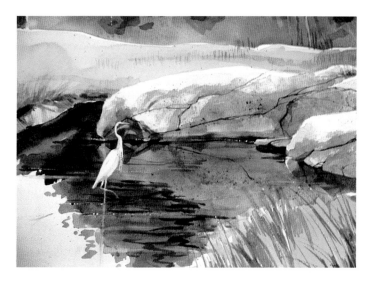

There were no egrets about when I took my photos, but I knew they might be seen at another time; I added this one in contrast to the tannin-stained water of the marsh. Successive glazes, drybrush and fine details gave substance to the granite rocks.

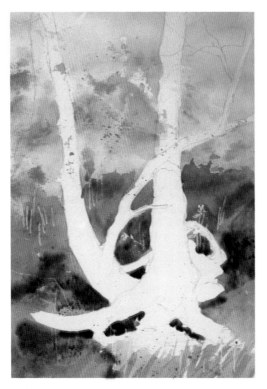

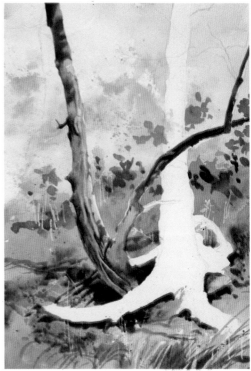

Above. Working on the spot requires flexibility. Here, I've simply painted around my tree forms and laid in rough preliminary washes in the negative shapes.

Above right. I've added the first washes on my trees, paying attention to shadows and form.

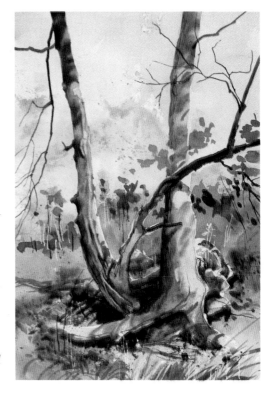

Right. Detail is added with a smaller brush and with a palette knife.

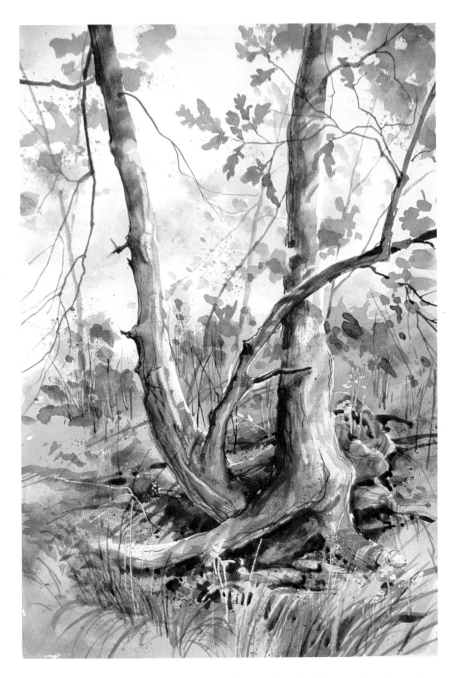

The finished painting was shot back in the studio with different film; hence the color difference. It is still almost a sketch, rough and free to capture the rugged Missouri woods.

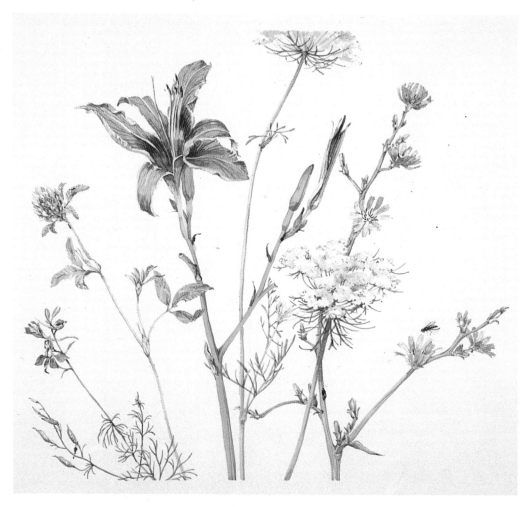

An on-the-spot painting can be much more tightly rendered than the previous land-scape; here, I painted from wildflowers picked along the roadside. Such a painting can become a contemplative exercise—a nice change from sketchier works.

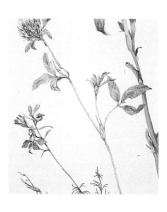

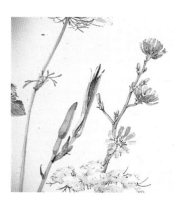

Left. The largest brush was a No. 6 red sable folding travel brush; it worked well to lay in the larger washes as well as to paint small details.

Right. Look for subtle color changes (as in the spent day-lily bud) and for ways to sim-plify without losing the sense of your subject.

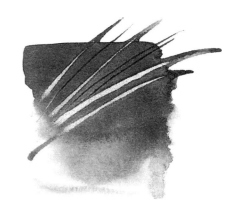

SEVEN

Watercolor as a Sketching Medium— and Beyond

WATERCOLOR IS WONDERFULLY versatile for field work, capable of everything from the roughest of sketches to complete—and intricate—paintings. Depending on the supplies you choose, you can do virtually everything in the field that you could in your home studio.

Generally, though, the pleasure of watercolor for field work comes from its simplicity and spontaneity. With a minimum of supplies, you can suggest a sweeping landscape, create a contemplative wildflower study, or capture a bird's field marks and subtle coloration for later identification.

As noted in Chapter 1, you can get by with a tiny field kit of colors, a few small brushes, a miniature watercolor block, and a container for water—in most cases you won't even need to carry the water itself. Unless you are painting in a desert or where all the water is ice, you can use what is at hand. Purists will tell you it's best to paint with distilled water to avoid pollutants and town-water additives that might affect pigment handling or longevity of your work, but it isn't necessary. I have dipped water from a creek, a lake, and an ocean and painted on the spot. Salt water isn't optimum, it's true—it reacts oddly with pigments—but the others work fine. If there's a bit of texture in the water, it will just give interest to your washes.

WATERCOLOR BASICS

For those of you familiar with watercolor, this is indeed basic stuff; bear with me. I encourage anyone who *isn't* an old hand to try the medium out, for the reasons stated earlier. It may be a bit more complicated than picking up a colored pencil, but don't let that deter you. The variety of washes, textures, and other techniques possible with this medium make it well worth the time spent getting to know your way around a watercolor palette.

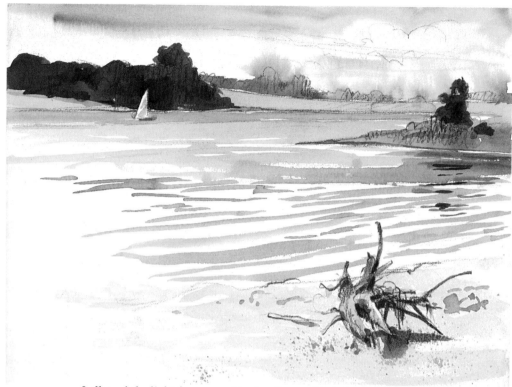

I allowed the light foreground to dry thoroughly before adding the old driftwood stump and its shadow for optimum control with no blending or running. In the background, however, I let the trees blend with the sky for a feeling of softness and distance. (Prismacolor grey sketch with watercolor.)

You may find it easier to control watercolor if you start light and work to successively darker washes, ending with small, dark accents. If you lay down darkest areas first, they may lift and muddy subsequent washes. For *most* control, allow these first washes to dry thoroughly before adding new color. But don't be afraid to add one color to another while washes are still quite wet, if you prefer. You can get exciting results that way.

Use the biggest brush you can for as *long* as you can; tiny brushes seem to encourage tightness. You can always go to the smaller brushes for details after you've laid in the preliminary washes.

And speaking of washes, that's where the difference lies when using watercolor as opposed to the linear effects of pencil, felt-tips, or pens. Large or small, areas of pigment mixed with water are called *washes*; learning how much water to use in relation to the amount of pigment requires practice. Finding out how the various brushes behave and how to apply the washes to achieve the results you're after may *sound* difficult, but it's really not. You fell off your bike the first time or two, didn't you? It's the same with anything worth doing; just takes a determination to *do* it and a willingness to keep trying.

MIXING PAINTS

I use tube colors, but not usually fresh from the tube. I let them dry on my palette or in my watercolor kit to a consistency much like that of a kid's set of paints—that way they don't run in my pack. To restore brushability, I wet each mound of color with clear water before I begin, either with my brush or with a sprayer. I'm ready to mix in minutes.

Pigment choices are up to you. I like a warm and a cool of each primary and a good assortment of browns for mixing neutrals (try any of the blues mixed with browns for lovely, atmospheric grays). Then I add a few other colors for good measure, depending on mood or subject. Again, as mentioned in the previous chapter, I prefer a rather limited palette for any one painting, using about five to seven colors as a general rule.

Even a white palette, which I recommend, is not an entirely accurate gauge of color; a wash on the palette usually looks a little darker than it will on your paper. To get around this inaccuracy, some artists use a scrap of the same paper they're working on to make test strokes.

The hardest thing a newcomer to watercolor has to learn is how *much* water to mix in with your pigment—especially if that newcomer is proficient with oils, acrylics, or other opaque mediums. It's partly a matter of personal technique and taste, partly a matter of how large you are working, but generally speaking you need to mix in *plenty* of the wet stuff. There's nothing more frustrating than reaching the middle of a perfectly tinted sky wash and running out of color. You can't match it exactly, and by the time

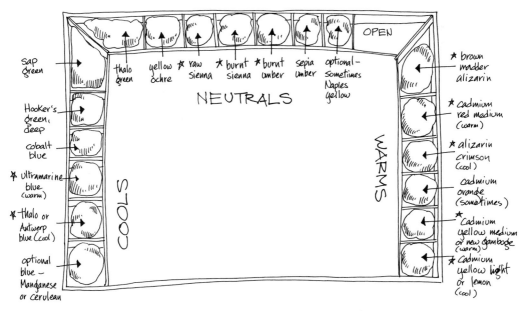

This is my personal palette—by no means **right**, *just mine. Starred pigments are those I must have, though in fact I use reds very little. I keep a few spaces open or optional to allow for spontaneity.*

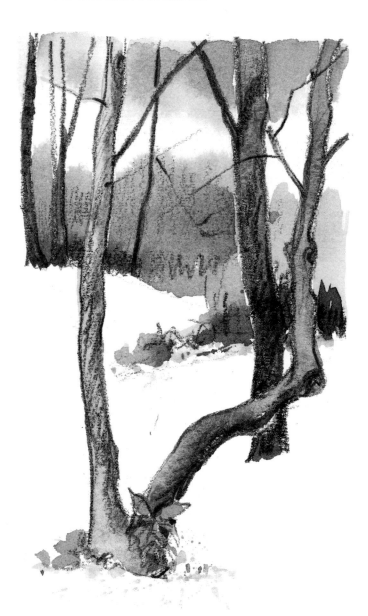

The background was painted wet-in-wet to suggest a diffuse focus and lend a sense of distance. (Prismacolor grey with watercolor.)

you've tried, the first wash is too dry to add color—it would just make hard edges. This is usually not such a problem when doing small sketches, but if you're planning to work outdoors on a full or half-sheet watercolor, you may need to bring along cups or other containers to mix large washes in.

Mix washes completely on your palette when you want smooth, homogenous effects, flat colors, and the like; do part of the mixing on your paper for livelier, more varied effects. One artist I know deliberately drops bits of almost pure pigment into his washes for exciting "jewels" of color. Try this with the triad of purple, orange, and green; mixed on the palette, these colors produce a neutral tint, rather gray-brown. Mixed more casually on your paper, however, the same colors retain some of their individual characteristics. It's all in the effect you're after at the time. I generally like a *combination* of the two techniques.

Timing is very important in watercolor—and that's something you learn with practice, like riding that bike. When aiming for smooth transitions of color, act fast while the wash is still quite wet and your paper appears shiny; when you prefer a visible line to form between color areas as one pushes against another, you need to wait a bit longer, until the shine has become more of a glow. If you want a hard edge, a little more time must pass (your paper will still feel damp but will have lost its shine). And if you want no blending whatsoever, but a glazed effect (see below), you need to wait until the first wash is completely dry. Sometimes all this time juggling makes me feel like a character in an H. G. Wells story—and sometimes I wish I could turn *back* the clock—but it's worth it. Usually I can pull it off. Usually, but not always.

And don't panic. Sometimes things happen that look *awful* at the time—because they're not what you wanted to happen. Wait a bit; you may have what watercolorists call a "happy accident," the perfect effect in a given area with no real work on your part at all, as in my sketch of Watkins Mill Lake. I put two areas of color next to one another, expecting them to blend. Something about the timing or the makeup of the pigments themselves caused the lighter color to push the darker one up, forming an interesting edge that looks for all the world like the zones of vegetation at water's edge; I was delighted. When this happens, sit back and take the credit; you deserve it. There are plenty of times when the accidents aren't so happy.

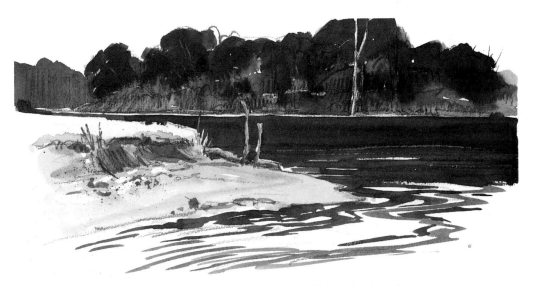

Notice the line of bushes on the far shore. Dropping wet, light color into the drying darker hue gave me an interesting edge that suggests foliage. Calligraphic brush strokes with a ½-inch flat brush suggest the action of waves. (Prismacolor sepia pencil with watercolor.)

APPLYING PAINT TO PAPER

Flat washes are pretty much what they sound like—an area of color laid on as smoothly as possible. In sketching, they're seldom needed—and in working from nature, I can't think of many places where they are useful, either. Even a blue sky has some variation in tone or a cloud or two scudding across it. Still, it's like learning to play the scales—good to know and good practice. *Small* flat washes of a single brush stroke or two are considerably more versatile.

Mix a sufficient puddle of pigment and thoroughly charge your brush—either a round or a flat brush as you prefer. Slightly tilt your paper and make a line of color. You'll notice that a "bead" of wet color—like a continuous drop—forms at the lower edge. Refill your brush and make another line of color just below the first, picking up this wet bead with the tip of your brush. Continue on down the page for as large an area as you wish. You can pick up the bead with a tissue after the final stroke. (A small wash of a single brush stroke or two doesn't require a tilted paper surface; strokes will blend together as is.)

A variation of this technique is to first wet your page with clear water, then lay in your color; often you can get a smoother wash this way.

A *graded wash* fades from dark to light or vice versa. It is made much like the flat wash, but instead of recharging your brush with color from your puddle of paint, you add clear water until your wash is as pale as you wish. You can work the other way, of course, from clear water to more and more pigment, but it's much easier to do this way. Gravity is a great helper; turn your paper upside down if you want the gradient to go from light to dark in a specific area.

A graded wash—two, in this case, with the first allowed to dry completely before glazing (overpainting) with the second. Greater and greater amounts of clear water are added to the pigment to let the color trail off smoothly.

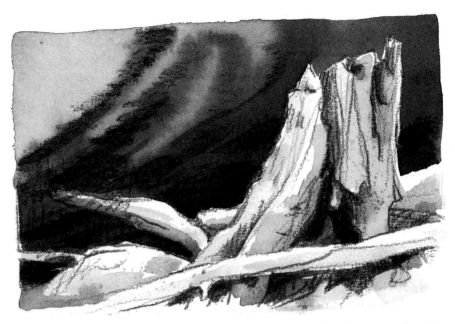

I laid in the dark lines of the waves while my wash was still quite wet, and used warm and cool colors to suggest a bit of distance. (Prismacolor pencil with watercolor.)

You may want to do a graded wash of one color in one direction, allow it to dry, and come back from the other direction with a graded wash of another color. Or add progressively greater amounts of a second color instead of clear water for a lovely color transition.

Again, you may get smoother results if you first wet the paper with clear water.

Unlike a flat wash, a graded wash can be useful in any number of situations—to paint the fading colors of sunset, to suggest roundness on a tree trunk, to show the shadowed area of a softly rounded hill or the tonal variations in a still mountain lake.

You may have heard of painting *wet-in-wet*; this simply means one color is added to another while the first is quite wet. You can get soft, hazy effects this way, gradual color transitions—lovely for suggesting trees in a distant forest, cloud shadows in landscape, and so forth. But it is quite tricky. Timing is everything. Do it when the first application of paint is too wet, and it's impossible to control; do it after the preliminary wash has lost its shine, and you'll get hard edges as one degree of wetness meets another. This technique takes a little practice; you may want to reserve it for smaller areas rather than doing an entire wet-in-wet painting. I often do a wet-in-wet underwash, then lay other, more controlled washes over it when it's thoroughly dry for sharp details. It's easiest to control on the generally smaller-sized sketches than on a full-sized painting.

A *varied* wash, as mentioned before, is simply one in which you mix all or part of your colors on the paper instead of on the palette, or drop in bits of contrasting, more intense, or even thicker color (using the pigment fairly thick will make it stay put rather than run or blend excessively). This is the one I tend to use most often. Very similar to painting with the previous technique, it's very spontaneous, and can be modified instantly—as long as your wash is still fairly wet.

When you *glaze* with watercolor, you lay one area of color over another. In this transparent medium, the first wash shows through and affects the second; you can get endlessly subtle effects this way. Let each layer dry completely before adding the next to avoid lifting or muddying, and you'll find this may be the most controllable of all watercolor techniques—or at least second only to true dry-brush. You can get nearly any effect this way but a soft, graded one—and even that you may pull off if you soften one edge of the wash with clear water and a partly wrung-out brush.

Try a *dry-brush* technique for areas of broken color. This works well to suggest rough ground, weedy patches, distant foliage, old weathered wood, sunlight on water—you name it. If you're using a classical dry-brush technique, saturate your brush with color, then squeeze most of the moisture from the brush with a tissue before touching it to paper. Apply as many layers as you like to achieve the texture you're after.

A somewhat less classical dry-brush approach has more to do with

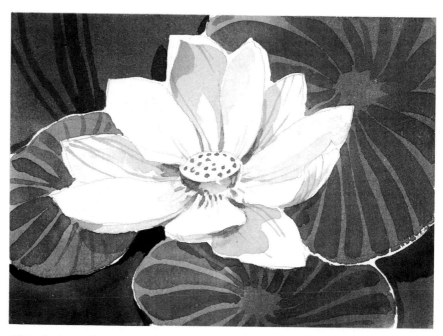

This glazing technique is rather traditional. I allowed each wash to dry before adding the next, with virtually no blending. You have the most control with this technique but the effects can be somewhat flat and decorative. I used complementary color to act as shadows in the water lily. This is often more satisfactory and fresher than simply using a darker or less intense value.

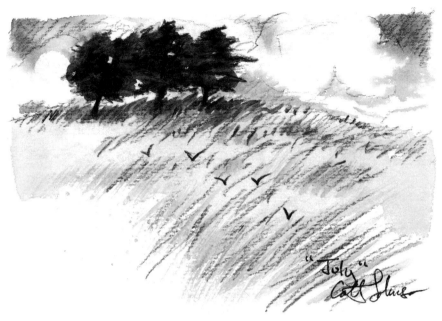

A brush well loaded with pigment and only a little water gave me a nice dry-brush effect for the grasses in the foreground. The repeated strokes seem to stand in quite well for blowing grass forms. Suit your technique to the subject for best results with watercolor, if you are going for a realistic effect.

brush handling than with the amount of pigment in that brush. Try it out: hold a charged brush vertically and pigment is forced down into the tiny hollows of your paper's surface, making a flat wash. The same brush charged with the same amount of pigment but held close to the paper— almost parallel, in fact—will make a broken wash. This is most useful when sketching—quicker and more spontaneous than the traditional dry-brush technique, which seems to cry out for egg tempera and Andy Wyeth. You can suggest that rough cedar bark or a bison's woolly pelt with only a few quick strokes.

For muted effects, you can dry-brush first, then glaze over that once it's thoroughly dry. Some of the color will pick up—not all—and edges will soften somewhat.

SPECIAL EFFECTS—BEYOND WASHES

Because watercolor is a transparent medium, generally speaking you can't paint light over dark as you can with oils or acrylics. You have to *plan* to save those light areas. You need to paint around whites to preserve them, or use one of the masking techniques such as masking tape, liquid maskoid, or rubber cement; then you can paint freely without worrying about the some-times tedious necessity of preserving small white bits of paper. Once your wash is dry, remove the mask and there's a clean white, ready to be touched with color or left as is.

You can *lift* a wet or damp wash for soft color gradations as well, although you'll seldom get pure white paper as you can with a mask. If you use a dry tissue to lift with, you often get harder edges; a dampened and wrung-out tissue or paper towel will result in a softer-edged lift.

It's possible to lift small areas with a brush. Wet it first with clear water, then squeeze it almost dry on a tissue or paper towel. This is called a "thirsty" brush, and when you touch it to a wet wash, you'll see why. The pigment is sucked up into the brush almost by capillary action, leaving a small area of lighter value. This same thirsty brush can be used to soften an edge, if you touch it while the wash is still shiny.

It's even possible to lift a wash that's completely dry, but with somewhat different results. Depending on the lifting technique you use and the paper surface you're painting on (hot press, cold press, or rough), the effects can vary widely. It's possible to lift an area almost back to white paper by going over it with a sponge dampened with clear water, although harder-surfaced papers like Arches will take this kind of abuse more gracefully than the tender English papers; they tear. Blot immediately to remove loosened pigment.

You can erase to lift as well; use a gentle white vinyl eraser if you want to paint back over the area, an ink eraser if you simply want to regain a white.

Some artists get good results by *sanding* dry washes to lift; use a light touch and fine sandpaper. It may be possible to go back in with a bit of color

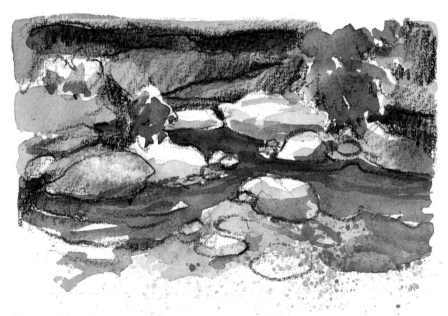

The grayish rock on the left had become too dark; I sanded it with a fine-grit sandpaper to regain a bit of lighter value. Sanding before painting bruises the paper fibers, making them more receptive to paint—the area would have gone on darker than my pigment mix would indicate.

over this roughened area, but the paper may be somewhat more absorbent; your wash will look darker than you expected. This technique works best if you use a fairly sturdy paper like Arches or Strathmore's Crescent; my favorite Fabriano is a bit too delicate.

I often lift pigment from my damp wash by scraping it with a fingernail, brush, or an old credit card. The operative word here is damp; if the wash is still shiny wet, the opposite effect will occur. Your scraped area will be darker since the paper surface will bruise, making it absorb more pigment. Wait to scrape until the paper is just beginning to lose the shine and you'll have a lighter area as you squeeze pigment from your paper or push it out of the way. This technique will not return your paper to pure white, but will provide a lighter value of the color you scrape into, as in the distant water in my Florida sketch.

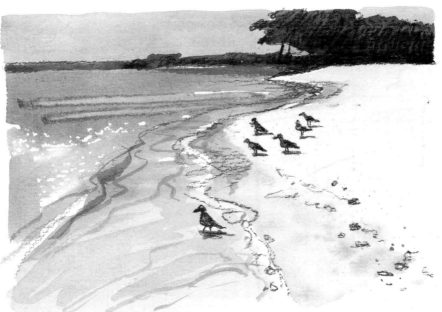

Aquarelle brushes are equipped with a diagonal end for scraping and manipulating paint—I didn't have one with me, so I used a plastic spoon found nearby to lift lights from the water as my wet wash lost its shine. A fingernail would have worked as well. (Prismacolor warm grey dark pencil with watercolor.)

Use this to suggest rough weeds, cracks, or planes on a rock face, distant tree trunks, weathered wood, lights on fur or hair—it's quick and effective.

Wait until the wash is *too* dry, and this particular scraping technique will have no effect at all. But all isn't lost if you still want a light line. Use an X-acto knife or the tip of your pocketknife to scratch through the wash to pure white paper. It works for light-struck grasses or twigs, the sparkle of light on water, foam in a waterfall, highlights in an animal's eyes, and many other applications.

BRAVURA BRUSHWORK

Brushwork becomes especially important when sketching. How you handle your brush can mean the difference between capturing the scene and missing it entirely. I like a somewhat calligraphic approach when painting outdoors; I let my brush follow the lines of my subject, suggesting it in as few strokes as possible. Single brush strokes stand in for the movement of water—waves in a lake or the falling cascades of a waterfall (see some of the demonstrations in this chapter). Bare twigs are suggested with the dancing tip of a round watercolor brush. Quick upward strokes can capture a weedy field; you may like the fan brush here—lots of grasslike lines from a single stroke. I often try to paint a flower using single strokes for each leaf or petal; there's something of Oriental simplicity in this approach that seems fitting both to the medium of watercolor and the action of sketching.

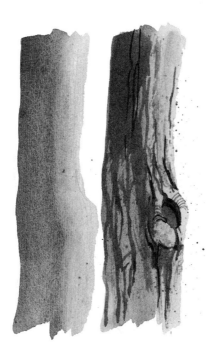
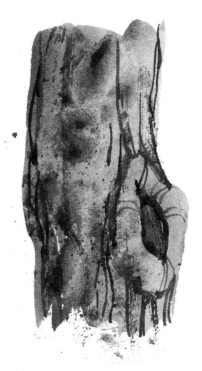

A graded wash was allowed to dry completely (left) before various texturing techniques were added. Detail work with a small brush and with drybrush and spatter helped suggest bark (right).

More direct texturing was used on this tree trunk. While the graded wash was still quite wet, I pressed a crumpled bit of plastic wrap into the surface on the upper trunk, then touched the lower area with the side of my hand before it dried. Spatter into a wet wash added to the texture. I finished with normal techniques of detail and drybrushing.

SUGGESTING TEXTURE WITH WATERCOLOR

Often, suggesting texture is simply a matter of applying successive washes as each one dries. The texture of tree bark, for instance, can be rendered by laying in a graded underwash for form and color, suggesting roundness and shadow areas. When that wash is dry, a little dry-brush work and some attention to detail to paint the characteristic bark pattern is probably all you need; in a sketch, usually not even that much, unless you're doing a close-up of a very specific tree. This same logical series of steps can suggest rocky escarpments, fur, feathers, or distant, lacy foliage; just takes a bit of patience and good observation of what you see.

Perhaps more fun—and a more spontaneous technique—is to texture the washes themselves as you lay them in. While an area of color is still somewhat wet, you can touch it with your hand, blot it with wadded tissue or a sponge, and spatter it with fine droplets of pigment or clear water from your stencil brush or toothbrush. Lay crumpled plastic wrap in a wet wash and let it dry in place, or move it after only a few minutes for softer effects. When field sketching, I generally use what's closest at hand—just that, the side of my own hand, for texturing a wash. Try it—there's something of the freedom of childhood's finger painting in this technique. (For more information on special effects, see my *Watercolor Tricks and Techniques* from North Light Books, 1988.)

The sketching technique mentioned in the last chapter for training color memory works well here, as well. Texture is mostly suggested with the underdrawing of wax-based colored pencil and just a bit of spatter once the sketch is dry, here done on toned paper. Again, it's fast, fresh, and effective.

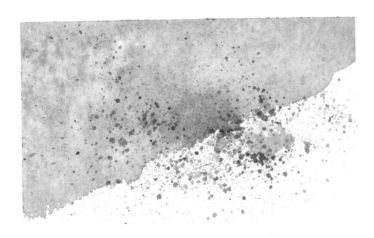

Pigment spattered into a wet or dry wash suggests texture. I used a small stencil brush for most control; an old toothbrush works well, too.

OPAQUE WATERCOLORS

Unlike transparent watercolor, opaque colors or gouache can be used in any order you like—dark to light, light to dark, back and forth, and then some. It's much like painting with acrylics; funny their use hasn't caught on in this country as it has in Europe.

But it hasn't. Americans are in love with fresh, transparent watercolor, and I am, too. I've used gouache in the studio and for commercial work, but seldom for field sketching.

I wouldn't presume to tell you *never* to use body color (opaque pigments) as many watercolorists do. To me, the point is to do the job. Make art. Get the image down. If you can do that better and easier with opaque paint, go to it.

At times it makes more sense for me to lay in a spot of opaque white to suggest the light in an animal's eye—or a lot of spots of falling snow, for that matter—than to try to preserve the white paper or scratch the lights out later. Retouch white (a commercial artist's tool found in art supply stores) applied with a spattering technique makes great snow, and for the highlight in an eye or on a moist nose, it's much easier to control and place correctly than a scrape through to white paper. Natural history and botanical illustrators use retouch white often and well.

Opaque color works great when I'm working on toned paper. Often, I'll do most of the sketch with transparent color, then lift light-struck areas with a little opaque white added to one of my transparent colors to lighten it only slightly.

FROM SKETCH TO FINISHED PAINTING

Usually, my field sketches are an end in themselves. They're enough; they don't need to go any further. I like what they have to teach me; I absorb much more deeply when I've taken time to get out my watercolors and really observe. I enjoy looking at them in much the same way you might look through photos from a favorite trip.

But sometimes sketches are meant to travel a bit farther down the road. They're studies for future paintings. I can use several of these small sketches to put together as a montage, or pick up bits and pieces to give a sense of veracity to a painting, especially an intimate landscape or a botanical work where I've zeroed in on the small details.

We all work differently, and at different times for different purposes. Usually, when I'm actually *painting* in the field as opposed to sketching, I work with only the roughest of references—a black and white thumbnail sketch no larger than 2 × 3 inches. I prefer to work this way when I'm doing more than a sketch outdoors. Too often when I work from my color sketches, I'll fall in love with their freshness and color and the wonderful things that it's easy to pull off when working small and almost impossible to duplicate on a larger scale. I attempt to do exactly the *same* thing—only bigger. I'm always disappointed.

See the color section for examples of painting progressions from color sketches back in the studio and on-the-spot works photographed more casually and without benefit of tripods, tungsten film, and studio lighting.

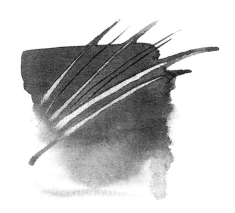

EIGHT

The Landscape

*L*ANDSCAPE HAS POWER. It touches us in ways we find difficult to explain, and on a level far below the conscious. We're taken captive. You know that feeling—that catch in the breath when you turn a corner on a mountain trail and the earth falls away, or when you see the ocean for the first time. There's a visceral response.

The vastness of landscape can't be confined to paper or canvas; we can only just begin to suggest the scope. Its multiplicity staggers the mind. There's no way to include all the details; such a drawing would be hopelessly complicated, a lifetime in the making.

But there's something magnetic in that power, something that draws us in and makes us try to express that response on paper. We want to make it ours in some indefinable way; instead, the magnetic field reverses and we are owned by our own attempt. What I have drawn has a claim on my imagination that never fades. Something of me belongs permanently in that most particular place.

We approach the task symbolically, as artists, not camera lenses; there's no other way than to *suggest* the complexity, hint at the vastness. We use tricks. We try calligraphy to define forms. We simplify elements in order to call up something of what we see, as if we could do magic—and so we do. We call the image up out of blank paper like shamans. Like homeopathic doctors, we use bits and pieces to affect the whole.

With time and practice, you will develop your own style, your own visual shorthand. Certain marks will work best to mean trees in the distance to you, others will symbolize rough grasses, while still others will be perfect for drawing a smooth expanse of water. Don't worry about doing it right, and *certainly* don't worry about doing it my way; if another mark feels right

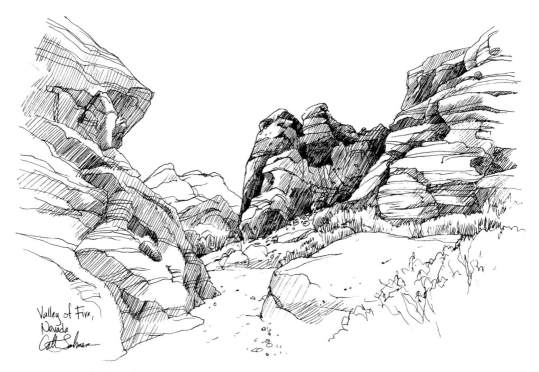

Valley of Fire. (Razor-tipped pen.)

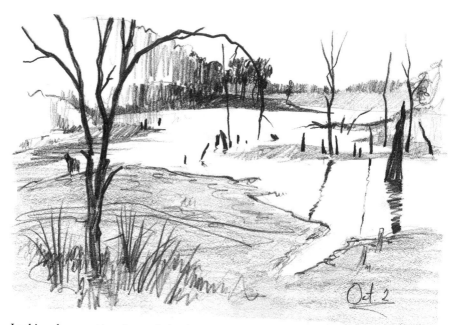

Looking for negative shapes helped me to correctly draw the shoreline of Rocky Hollow Lake in this simple, four-value sketch. (No. 2 pencil.)

to you, use it. There is no right and wrong to sketching landscape; there's only what works best for you, what satisfies you in a given instance.

If you are intimidated by the vastness of landscape—as we all are on occasion—if it seems simply too big or complicated to attempt, remember that it's all the same. Whatever you draw, whatever your subject—the process is the same. The techniques apply. Right-brain exercises work as well with landscape as with a single flower. Use a border to help contain or simplify. Look for relationships between the parts. Watch for angles and negative spaces. Use the rules of composition, or break them if the occasion warrants. Try out the varieties of value and the tricks of mood. Zero in on a section of landscape rather than trying the whole panorama. It's not as hard as it looks.

MATCH YOUR TOOLS TO THE LANDSCAPE

Choose tools or techniques carefully to express what you see—and what you feel. Try out your tools in different ways to see which stroke or line best expresses the scene. Let your mood have a hand in the decision; sometimes I feel contemplative and calm; at other times, my emotions are quite different. I match medium to mood, and landscape often affects my emotional climate.

Pen and ink can be used in a very linear manner, spare and elegant, and ink can be applied in solid or broken tones. You can achieve great detail or bold darks with ink, depending on how you choose to apply it. Let what you see suggest the technique.

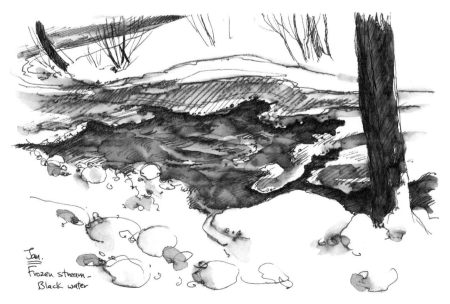

The inky water seemed to call for unusual treatment. I chose a nonpermanent fiber-tipped pen and wet the lines with clear water to capture that icy feeling.

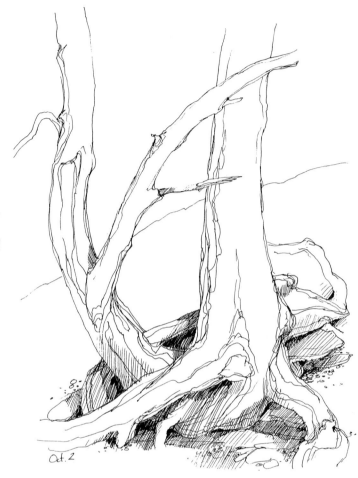

A black fiber-tipped pen can be quite effective to suggest fine detail. Another subject— one with stronger shadow patterns—might have worked better with a solid tone, but I was after a very linear effect.

Pencils can be used for their wonderfully varied line or as a way to capture some of the broad range of values before you. Used boldly, pencils can capture a simplified, almost abstract quality. Using a more delicate touch— especially if you have chosen a harder lead—you may be able to capture subtle nuances and as much detail as you could want.

Colored pencils seem to work especially well with landscape. With only a few colors and many of the same techniques or strokes I would use with graphite pencils, I can capture the basics of the scene in a satisfying way. When I am working on the spot, I appreciate the portability and convenience of colored pencils.

Watercolor is excellent for landscape sketching. I often use a mixed-media technique, here, and do my underdrawing in a dark, wax-based Prismacolor pencil that won't lift or sully under quick, fresh washes. For sketching purposes, I like the immediacy and simplicity of this technique.

At other times I want to do a study rather than a sketch. Then I can use more traditional techniques, layering washes and allowing each to dry thoroughly, adding some of the special effects explored in the last chapter.

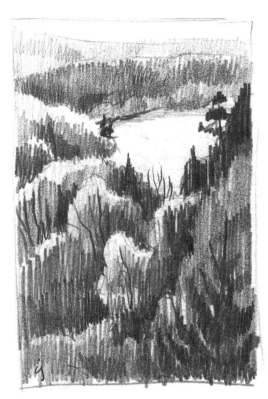

I used a mechanical pencil with HB lead for its wide range of values to suggest distance in this Ozark vista. A strong pressure on my lead was necessary to catch these bold value shifts. (Notice how the small sketch seems to have a sense of depth, thanks to overlapping forms and lighter, simpler areas of value in the background.)

Two watercolor tricks seem especially suited to sketching landscape. I often lift a wash quickly (while it's still fairly wet) with a paper towel or tissue to suggest dimension and form—within a line of trees or a rocky escarpment, perhaps. This technique hints at both depth and texture without overworking.

Spatter, also, is particularly suited to sketching. It's a quick technique that can stand in for a lot—it's symbolic. I spatter droplets of pigment from my stencil brush to capture the effects of rocky or sandy soil, distant foliage, wildflowers in a field—you name it. If I blot a few of these while they're still wet, I can get a great variation in tone that makes my sketch both more interesting and more accurate.

If you want, use a combination of tools and techniques to express your response to landscape. Purists may argue for one medium or another, unmixed and unsullied, for a show or exhibition, but for emotional response to landscape the point is just that—*your* response, and whatever it takes to symbolize that feeling. That's *your* choice. You're the only one who can know how the scene makes you feel.

SIMPLIFY, SIMPLIFY

Landscape sketching may not have been exactly what Henry David Thoreau had in mind when he offered his famous advice to "simplify, simplify," but it's a good way to approach the subject. Simplifying the elements of landscape is the not-so-well-kept secret of successful sketching in nature.

True, we need to get beyond symbolic thinking when it interferes with *seeing* what is before us. But when we try to deal with the complexity of landscape, symbols, and simplified forms may be the way to go.

One technique that helps me simplify is to work quickly. Then there's no *time* for overworking—or for too much intellectualizing, either. I just scribble down what I see, catching only the most important forms, elements, or values. Try working from the car as you ride down the road—with someone else driving, of course! As landscape flashes by, there is only time to capture the basics. Work small, here, to avoid frustration—thumbnail-size or just slightly larger.

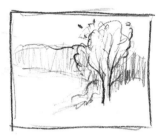 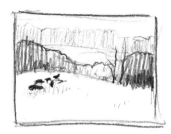 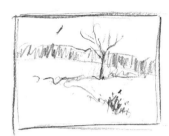

These three small landscape sketches were done quickly as we drove by at 55 mph— I didn't have time to overwork when reacting to this transient scenery. (Mechanical pencil with HB lead.)

Rocks, mountains, hills, water, distant trees, brush, weeds—all can be simplified when sketching landscape. Like the petroglyph makers of the American Southwest, we can use our own most expressive symbols to stand in for reality. There's no need to resort to a childlike cartoon of a tree, of course—but there's no way to capture every leaf and twig on paper, either. And no need to. (See Chapter 10 for more on trees.)

Look at some of the ways to suggest a distant forest in a landscape sketch; quick squiggles, zigzag lines, curved forms, shaded areas, all stand in for the real thing and get the idea across. Use whichever works best for you and best expresses the nature of the particular stand of trees you see. You may draw a forest of pines with a different sort of line from the one you might choose for an oak and hickory woods, for instance.

In a landscape sketch, hills can be simple lines; no need for detail or shading unless you just want to. It's their placement that's the key. If you observe carefully *before* touching pencil to paper, you can suggest one hill behind another as far back as you want to go. Arrange them to invite the viewer into your picture plane—or choose to sketch just that part of the view that accomplishes that end—and you've successfully used the principles of composition.

By using progressively lighter pressure on your pencil, narrower pen lines, or lighter colors (if you are working in other than black and white), you can suggest aerial perspective at the same time (as shown). Your landscapes seem to spring to life, no matter how simply you've drawn them.

Suggest water in the same way; analyze the basic movement and try to capture it in as few strokes as possible. This *is* a symbolic handling, but if it's right, like a Zen master's drawing, it will say it all.

If you need to, make a rough diagram of water currents or wave patterns. Blur your eyes to better see these overall patterns and to remove distracting details. It's often difficult to track that seemingly chaotic motion, let alone get it down on paper; a sketch of overall directional patterns helps.

Rocks come in as many shapes and textures as the landscape of which they are part. Environmental factors such as weather, leaching of water through soil, inland seas, and volcanic eruptions formed their wonderful variety; each cause creates a different effect. Large and small, rough and smooth, angular and rounded, striated or nearly featureless—look for ways to suggest the texture and form you see.

Your pencil can trace the fissures in a limestone bluff or produce smooth tones to suggest the undulating forms of the Southwest's slickrock canyons. Look for ways to suggest the frozen liquid forms of the volcanic rocks along the Atlantic seacoast, watching both for their overall shapes and for the convoluted, flowing textures within those forms—negative shapes and calligraphy might do it. If you like, blend graphite areas with a stump or tortillon (a rolled-paper blending tool), or your finger, or lift lights with a kneaded eraser for a wide range of effects. Your sketch can become almost photographic.

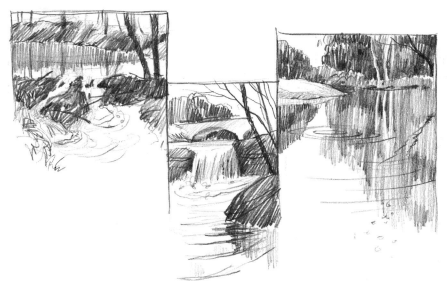

Water moves quickly as it falls over a precipice, mixing with oxygen to look snowy white; at other times it may move gently over a small obstruction or reflect, mirrorlike, the trees of the far shore when hardly a breeze stirs the air. A variety of strokes can be used to capture water in all its moods—consider whether curving lines, rapid, emphatic strokes, or smooth, straight lines best express what you see. (Mechanical pencil, HB lead.)

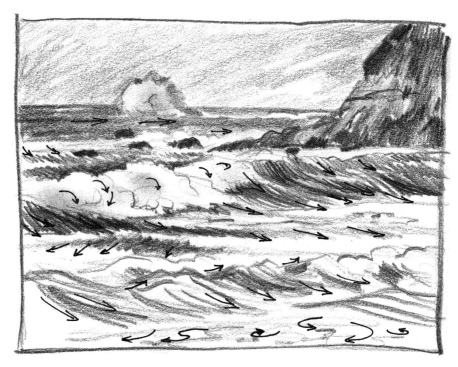

Diagram the flow to help you see what you're drawing. Keep it much simpler than this, if you wish—just enough to keep you aware of what's happening.

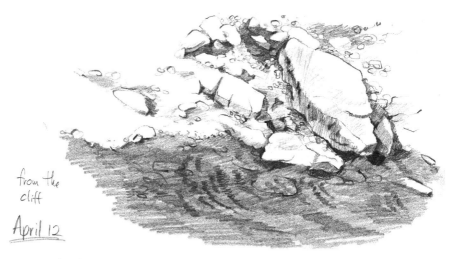

from the
cliff

April 12

A somewhat harder lead than my normal HB (F) worked well to capture the smooth gradations of rocks and water far below. Notice the variety of shapes, sizes, and planes when you sketch rocks—no two are just alike.

Combine the techniques you have explored for suggesting hills and rocks to portray mountains. Look for ways to express their particular texture; use that technique or medium that best captures the kind of mountains you see and your own response to them. The stark, stone façades of the Black Mountains might call for pen and ink or a more careful watercolor rendering, while California's steep, rounded hills might work best with a soft pencil rendering.

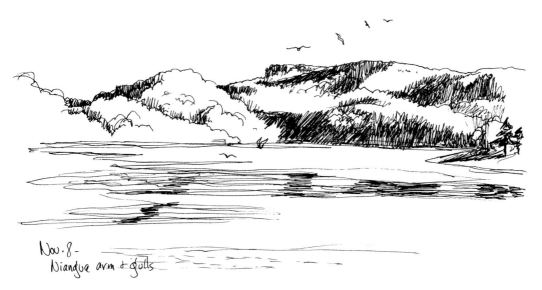

Missouri's Ozark Mountains are heavily wooded with oaks and hickories; here, I've drawn them in the early morning light using a fiber-tipped pen and quick, tight squiggles to suggest the leafy canopy.

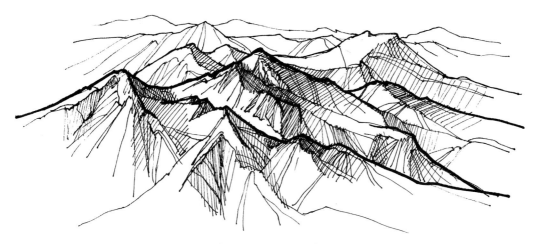

More rugged, younger mountains need attention to a different kind of detail. In this sketch, I've tried to capture the angularity of the Rocky Mountains and a sense of distance as the forms overlap and become simpler—using fiber-tipped pens of varying widths.

SOME HINTS ON COMPOSITION

Foregrounds may seem to present a problem, but there's no need for them to. This is a good place to interject detail, use a compositional arrow to lead the eye into the picture plane, or suggest a darker area closer to the viewer to give a sense of aerial perspective.

A road or path often begins in foreground and leads into the sketch; place it somewhat off center to keep it from being an uneasy element, and (generally speaking) let it lead gently rather than abruptly for more pleasing results. I often break this "rule," as you'll notice here and there—I *like* a path leading directly in and becoming smaller and smaller with distance; it's dramatic. I just don't place it dead center in my sketch. (See Chapter 3 for suggestions.)

Where I live, the foreground is often a comfortable combination of small rocks and rough grasses or weeds. I can suggest these in a few strokes, giving viewers a place to stand, as it were, while inviting them into the picture plane.

As you sketch landscape, you will begin to develop your own sense of composition. The rules can be used or broken. You may choose to place your subject at the juncture of the Golden Mean for a pleasing effect, as shown, or you may want to go for a more dramatic or direct approach.

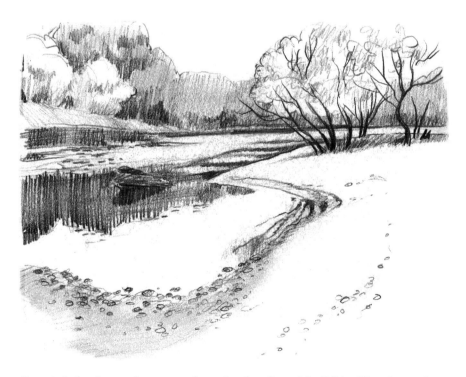

Repeated circular marks suggest the rocky shoreline of the White River in southern Missouri. In a watercolor sketch, spatter would have stood in for these pebbly squiggles. Notice, too, the sweeping S-curve that leads you into the picture and the varieties of moving and still water. (No. 2 pencil.)

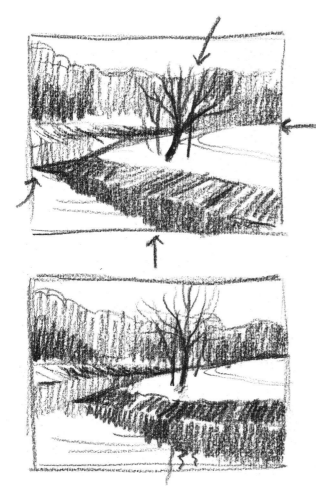

Move things around so they don't begin or end in awkward places. In my first sketch, arrows point to unfortunate placements or juxtapositions. Top, the tree just touches the rim of the hill; at left, the point of land touches the edge of the sketch, leading you out and away. At right, the curve of the hill is too close to the center of my picture and the same less-than-pleasing result appears in the reflection, foreground. See how much better the corrected version looks.

Watch where you place your horizon line. If you put it dead center where it bisects your page, the effect will be naive, childish—or worse, *boring*, something landscape never is. Raise or lower it somewhat (or dramatically) for best results.

Avoid juxtapositions in your sketches; if a tree top just meets the horizon line as you see it in nature, lower or raise it a bit. Lines that touch or meet distract the eye (as shown). Even if that's not how it looks in nature, we often seem to end lines or connect forms in just the wrong place. It's determined to happen; like Murphy's Law, if a line or form *can* end in just the wrong place to look really silly, it will. Being aware of that tendency can help you avoid the odd effects and juggle your sketch as needed.

SKETCHING THE INTIMATE LANDSCAPE

It's easiest, sometimes, if we approach only a small corner of the whole, as if we could dare acquaintance only on this small scale. It's more accessible, less daunting. Rather than try to depict a panoramic vista of the Grand Canyon with all its complex angles and value patterns, we can choose a slickrock side canyon. Instead of sketching the folded ranges of the Rockies, we can

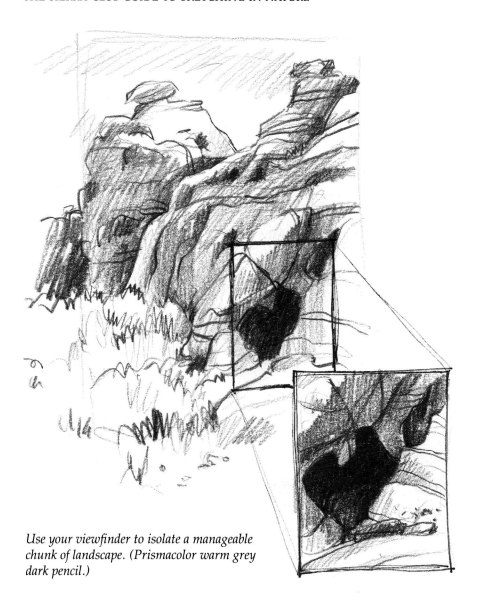

Use your viewfinder to isolate a manageable chunk of landscape. (Prismacolor warm grey dark pencil.)

zero in on a single, brave flower that sprouts from that rock and lives, somehow, in near-arctic tundra.

I call these small vistas "intimate landscapes," and thought the term was my own until I saw it in an Eliot Porter book from years past. The genius of nature photography had walked these woods before me; with apologies and gratitude, then, I borrow Porter's term. It fits.

Find a corner of Earth you respond to; use the viewfinder from Chapter 2 to zero in on a manageable bit of landscape, and move it around until you find a composition you like. Change and move elements within that intimate landscape as you wish. You'll seldom find a *perfect* composition, but don't be too quick to change it. Sometimes that very imperfection is what caught your eye in the first place. We're quirky people.

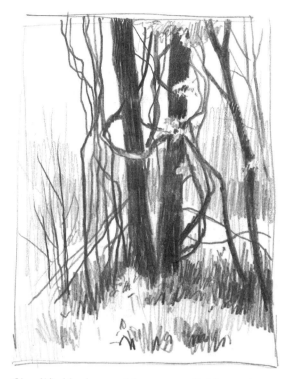

*Simplified background forms are a light gray to
keep them where they belong. (B pencil.)*

Use the principles of aerial perspective, even on a small scale; things in
the background can be simpler, lighter, or cooler in color to suggest distance
(as shown).

Focus on a single element as your center of interest, or explore an all-
over pattern; sometimes the thing itself—all of it—is what catches your eye,
not one element within the whole. (Think of the patchwork community of
plants on the forest floor, or a weathered wall of rock at close range.) Or
work in a more traditional way, leading the eye throughout the picture plane
(as shown).

THE LIVELY LANDSCAPE

Sometimes my sketch seems too empty, lonely—stark, somehow. There is
no sense of life. Many artists solve this by adding just a hint of life to the
scene—a few V-shapes in the sky to suggest birds in flight, perhaps. It's one
of my favorite devices; a planet without birds would seem an empty place
indeed.

But that's not the only way to introduce that spark of life. You can hint
at it, with a suggestion of an animal's tracks in the snow or beside a creek.
You can include a suggestion of *human* life by sketching a meandering stone
fence, a forgotten garden tool, a bright fishing lure caught in the branches
of a tree, a fence post.

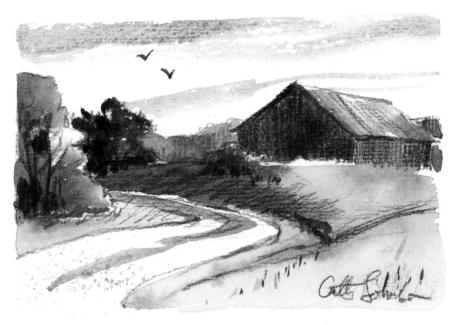

Two quick V's suggest birds in this watercolor sketch; the old equipment shed gives a sense of life, as well.

Or you can outright add a center of interest that is sentient. The eye goes immediately to life, no matter how simply it's depicted. My Alaskan sketch seems almost too simple, totally devoid of life if you cover the two grizzlies with your hand. Remove that mask, and your attention fastens on those big bears almost involuntarily. Pick up an animal or bird from another sketch, and use it to focus your landscape or give it drama—that's what I did here.

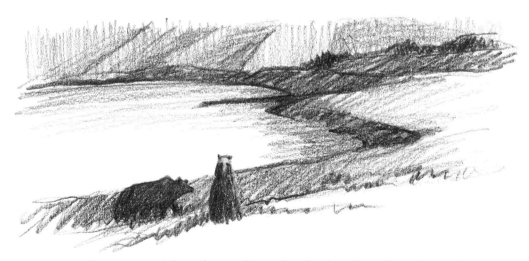

Your eyes go right to the grizzlies in this sketch; without them, it would be stark and unbalanced. (Berol Prismacolor.)

CLOUDS AND WEATHER

You may not have thought of them in just that way, but elements of weather are part of landscape, too. Sometimes the best part. There may be a dramatic storm brewing, casting deep shadows on the land. Curtains of rain alternately mask and reveal the horizon. There may be a driving snow, or piled-high clouds in a thousand forms that make you forget there's anything beneath them at all.

Sketch clouds from above them, if you fly, for a different perspective and a new understanding of winds and weather patterns. Notice that they now

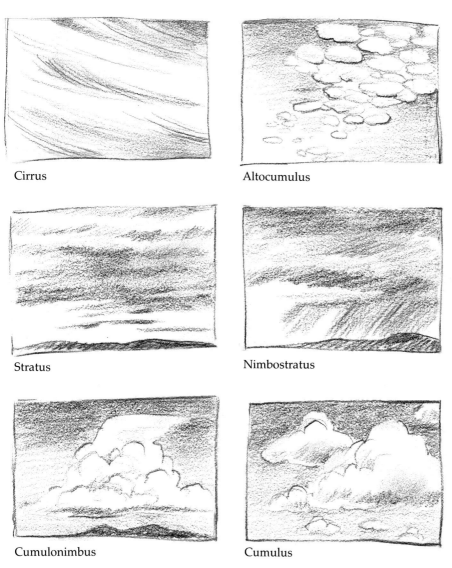

Cirrus

Altocumulus

Stratus

Nimbostratus

Cumulonimbus

Cumulus

This page of cloud studies helped me to realize the variety of forms and moods possible.

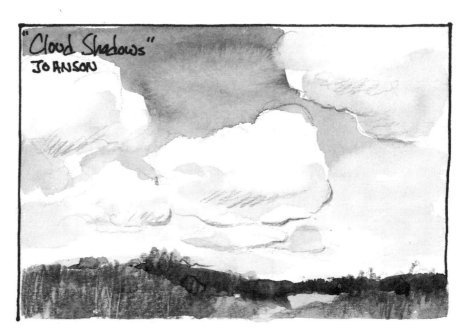

Here, puffy cumulus clouds cast shadows on the earth below. Notice that the horizon line is kept low to concentrate attention on the sky. (Watercolor sketch.)

follow a perspective more familiar on land, with closer clouds low in the picture plane and farther ones apparently higher; it's just opposite of what you see if you're underneath. As mentioned in Chapter 3, clouds follow the rules of perspective, no matter what their form, diminishing like hills in the distance. They can be dramatic compositional elements as well, evoking an emotional response.

The variety of forms is astounding. Cirrus clouds are as different from altocumulus as a wildflower is from a potato—in form, at least, if not in physical makeup. I like to sketch the types of clouds, noticing which may bring heavy weather and which promise a mild, sunny day. This information may come in handy later, when I want to include a dramatic element in a landscape that looks too calm and predictable.

When sketching landscape, it's best to let one area or another dominate. Concentrate on land and let the sky be secondary, or do a cloudscape and keep the land subordinate. Use your horizon line to accomplish this; a low horizon line focuses attention on the sky, where you want it. If you render the land with simplified forms or strokes, you can keep the attention where you want it, in the air.

LEARNING FROM LANDSCAPE

You may wish to go much farther than simply making a pretty picture. You can learn from landscape, or explore unfamiliar territory, getting to know a different piece of the Earth from your own. You may decide to annotate your drawings, track change, monitor pollution, or map the encroachment of civilization and its impact on the land, according to where your field of interest lies. Do as John Muir did, and mark the slow movement of a glacier in your field journal. Sketch the transition zones in a mountainous area or where salt marsh meets the sea, and note which creatures find a home or a migrational stopover there. Record the movement of river deltas or islands in flood. Sketch a lava flow—but with care.

Often, in my field journal, I use a small landscape sketch to give me a sense of place. This is quite simple, usually, just enough to remind me where I was and when. Then, other elements of landscape—the close-ups or details—may become the larger focus. Notes taken in the margin remind me of the nuts and bolts—identification of wildflowers or birds, season, time of day, and so forth, as noted in Chapter 4. But the tiny landscape is an indispensable part of the whole. I learn as much from it as from the more carefully drawn details.

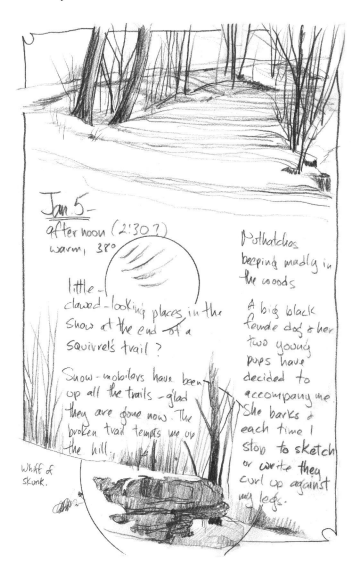

Landscape sketches are an important element in my field journals; they remind me where I was and what I found in that very specific habitat. I take notes directly on my sketch, as I have done here—they become a design element while providing information.

OTHER NOTES

Of course, my written notes may have other purposes as well. There are times when I simply need to be reminded of color nuances for later works. I write down what I see in the margins, along with any suggestions for change or emphasis. These written notes bring it back alive, even if I put the sketch away for ten years.

My notes may be musings, possibilities, suggestions for change. Just because I am out on a gray March day doesn't mean I can't draw something entirely different, in color or mood if not in subject. I can switch season entirely, or simply look for ways to emphasize what is there. I may choose to push the colors, "seeing" a cool blue or violet shadow or a warm sienna reflection where light bounces back into a dark area. When I work in black and white—which I most often do to keep my pack light and my supplies simple—I may need reminding that the distant hills were pale blue, the nearer trees were beginning to blush reddish with new sap, and the dead grasses that wave in the wind were as blonde as Monroe.

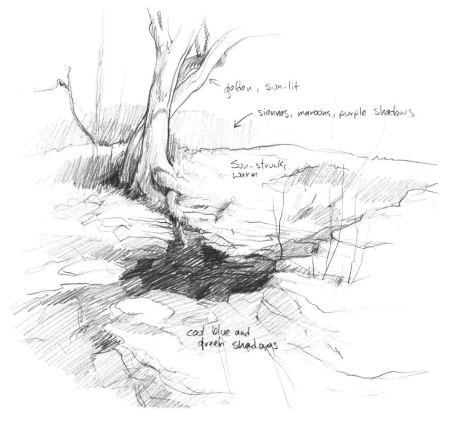

When working in black and white, it may help to make color notes directly on your sketch—either of what you see or of what colors you plan to use in the finished painting.

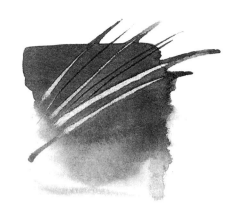

NINE

Plants and Flowers

Who can remain untouched by the beauty of wildflowers? They are almost universal in their appeal. I think I enjoy sketching these small bits of comeliness and grace more than any other subject. They are as varied as life itself; I'm never bored. Think of the tiny starlike flowers of the common garden chickweed, and compare its modest white delicacy with the showy beauty of bright orange butterfly weed—you'll begin to see what I mean by variety.

Where I live, wildflowers bloom from late February to the end of November. I can enjoy an intimate study of botany whenever I choose, exploring their varied habitat and capturing their ephemeral beauty on paper. Unlike the birds, mammals, and insects I am likely to find on my rambles, plants wait patiently to be sketched, never shy or frightened by my presence. It's almost as if the flowers made themselves accessible out of sheer goodwill.

Plant families are as interesting as Alex Haley's extended, intertwined relations in *Roots*. I love to track down the family tree of related species from clues as simple as the square stems of mint kin or as obscure as the relationship between wild rose and steeplebush.

And it's not over when the last flower withers. Weed seeds, spent flower heads, calyxes, and pods are fascinating to draw. There is a certain stark beauty in winter weeds. We are not distracted by sweet scents or candied colors as we may be in spring or summer; plans for survival have their own spare attraction. I can learn much from studying this more austere stage in the life cycle—how a plant reproduces itself, how its seeds are disseminated (in the air, by birds, and so on), what insects sublet its pods or galls.

Grasses, reeds, and other simple plants have a spiky, linear quality all their own. Their calligraphy is eloquent, their presence on our Earth essential. A sketch of the mixed plant community of a marsh or prairie may not contain a single flower, but is fascinating nonetheless.

In Missouri, there are a myriad flowering bushes to sketch. Bladdernut, sumac, elderberry—these are as interesting in shape, color, function, or ecological niche as any of the small flowers I find in the spring woods.

Wild edibles have pleasing shapes as well, and in sketching them I have learned their names and uses to add to my family's repertoire of wildings. We eat more interesting food now.

Bushes and shrubs often bear interesting flowers and fruit. Sometimes less showy than the wildflowers, they're worth looking for; the modest bladderpod flowers of spring become large, papery husks by autumn. Field journal page includes notes and progressions. (Mechanical pencil, B lead.)

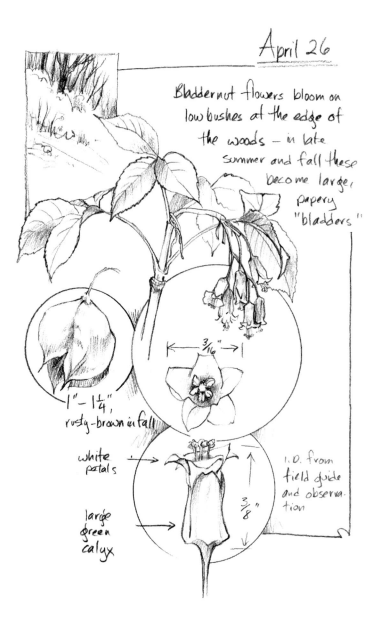

April 26

Bladdernut flowers bloom on low bushes at the edge of the woods — in late summer and fall these become large, papery "bladders"

1"–1¼", rusty-brown in fall

3/16"

white petals

large green calyx

3/8"

I.D. from field guide and observation

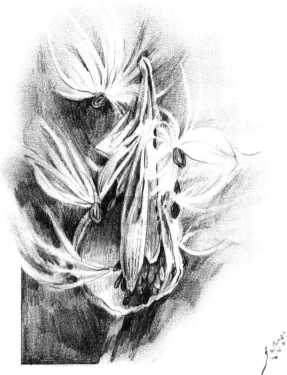

Pods and seeds can be as interesting a study as flowers. Here, I explored the silk-fine filaments of milkweed with a No. 2 graphite pencil. Smudging areas with my finger helped capture the softness of my subject.

I sat hidden in the reeds and grasses to watch the big predator fly over the swamp. Soon I was as fascinated by the angular shapes of the plants as by the hawk overhead. (No. 2 graphite pencil.)

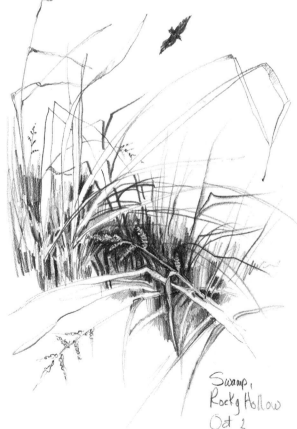

Swamp, Rocky Hollow Oct 2

Plants and flowers have always held a fascination for me. They are so diverse, even within a single species. And even among the simplest, most regular of flower shapes there is sweet variety. Petals are slightly different in size or shape, or one has been nibbled by an insect or withered in a too-strong sun; such imperfection suggests a vulnerability that stops me in my tracks. We share something slightly skewed—and precious.

DRAWING YOUR OWN BOTANICAL STUDIES

One of the most satisfying types of flower sketching is the botanical approach; I have at once the artist's pleasure of sketching and of making the plant's acquaintance.

I may sketch the plant pretty much as I see it, reproducing angle and growing habit as is, no matter how atypical, but I make sure that at least one flower or leaf is "diagnostic"; that is, fairly flat to the picture plane, with most of its details intact, so that it would be possible to make an identification of the plant from my sketch.

Rather than simply making a piece of art, a flower "portrait," if you will, a botanical can include the leaf, flower, seedpod, seed, and whatever other details you can discover. You may even wish to include what insects are observed in the act of pollination—or of eating the petals even as you watch.

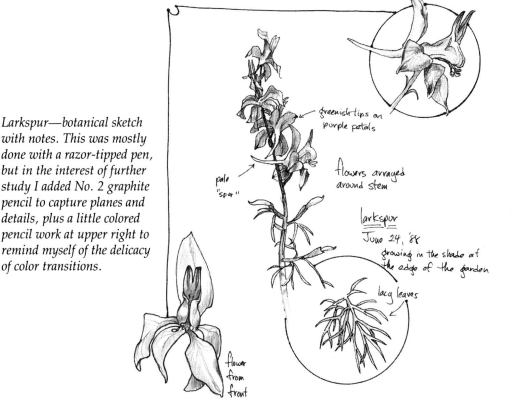

Larkspur—botanical sketch with notes. This was mostly done with a razor-tipped pen, but in the interest of further study I added No. 2 graphite pencil to capture planes and details, plus a little colored pencil work at upper right to remind myself of the delicacy of color transitions.

Notice if the flower grows singly on a stem or in a branched umbel, whether flowers bloom all at once or in sequence, or whether the stem is smooth or hairy, branched or straight, and try to capture what you see.

Observe how the leaves grow on the stem. Are they alternate or opposite? Are there an even or an uneven number? Are they all the same shape? How about leaf margins? Are they smooth, lobed, or toothed? Do the leaf veins march in a stately procession of lines down each side of the mid-rib or are they a seemingly random network of lines, like a sheet-web spider's snare?

Your sketches of these specifics will go a long way toward fixing the plant in your mind, whether you are making a detailed botanical study or a more conventional flower drawing. Often I show the details in close-up to aid in identification. Accurate observation will help you find the plant in a field guide or text. (Learning the names of the various parts can be of help, too. Some guides are organized by plant details or specific configurations.)

When I am doing a botanical sketch, I don't try to show background—the landscape the flower appears in, other plants, or flowers nearby, any of the things that might appear in a more conventional flower portrait. This is not a painting or drawing, per se, but a botanical, a study of a single plant and its habits.

LEARNING FROM FIELD SKETCHES

My botanical sketches are invaluable to me as a source of research and study. I can learn a great deal from the details I've included in my field journal. But as always, with field sketches, the written notes may be as important as the drawings.

I can learn the names of the various flower parts and their functions as I draw these details—sepals and calyxes to protect the developing bud; the stigma, style, and ovary of the flower's reproductive parts; the pollen-covered anthers on their stamen. If I write these names in the margin the first few times I sketch them, I will remember to look for them when I encounter other flowers. I will be able to find similarities or differences and perhaps glean clues as to the new flower's family or place in the ecosystem.

I can take notice of insect pollinators, or what spider is making home and employment of a flower's deceptively innocent petals. Something has chewed on that rose; what is it? An insect has made a nest in a curled leaf; a gall has formed around the eggs as if the leaf bubbled and swelled. A bird is eating the seeds. There is more to a wildflower than a pretty face and a sweet scent; our pleasure in them is incidental, a happy secondary to their primary purpose and position in the ecosystem. I want to decipher their mysteries; I ask myself as many questions as I answer, and enjoy the pursuit.

TRACKING PROGRESSIONS

When I sketch a botanical study of seeds and flowers and pods, I am tracking the progression of a flower's life cycle. Sketches such as this can help me understand the passage of time outside my own pell-mell life. Even

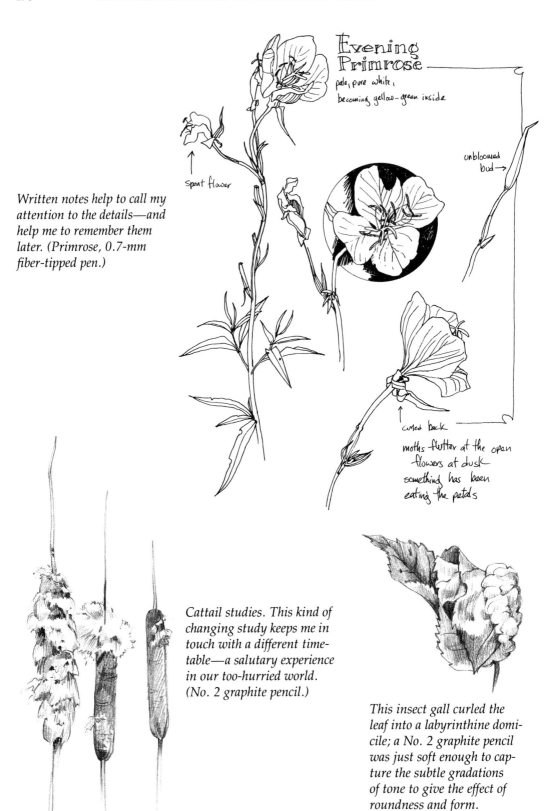

Evening Primrose — pale, pure white, becoming yellow-green inside

spent flower

unbloomed bud →

curled back

moths flutter at the open flowers at dusk something has been eating the petals

Written notes help to call my attention to the details—and help me to remember them later. (Primrose, 0.7-mm fiber-tipped pen.)

Cattail studies. This kind of changing study keeps me in touch with a different time-table—a salutary experience in our too-hurried world. (No. 2 graphite pencil.)

This insect gall curled the leaf into a labyrinthine domicile; a No. 2 graphite pencil was just soft enough to capture the subtle gradations of tone to give the effect of roundness and form.

small progressions—those that encompass only a part of the life cycle of a plant—give me greater understanding of something outside of myself. I sketch the firm, tight-knit spike of a cattail, then notice that a few days later that same spike has begun to come undone, to unravel at the seams and turn to a kind of pale brown fluff. It is as if it tries to escape—and so it does. A week or so later the fluff is looser yet, and blowing on the breeze. It's a different kind of clock from those I'm used to, but a better one, somehow.

FLOWER GEOMETRY

In sketching flowers, the most immediate—and accurate—way is to use a combination of right-brain techniques, especially if you are looking at something more complicated than a primrose. (I started to say "a daisy," but if you've looked closely at a daisy's disk floret you know it's anything but simple.) Look for negative shapes and the relationships between them. Sometimes drawing a border around a flower shape—even a light one I intend to erase later—helps me to see what I'm looking at. It's easier to find the angles of a curved flower if there is a straight line (or what passes for one) in the vicinity.

It may sound odd, but having that regular shape to measure against helps me to see the flower's or plant's *irregularity* more accurately. It's easy to fall into the trap of thinking a daisylike flower is perfectly round just because we've seen them drawn that way a hundred times. If I enclose my subject in a circular form—even an imaginary one—it helps me become aware of the great diversity of form within this basic overall shape.

To help yourself see, count petals, pistils, stamens, and so on. It's funny how often we assume a flower has an even number of petals, or that all wild

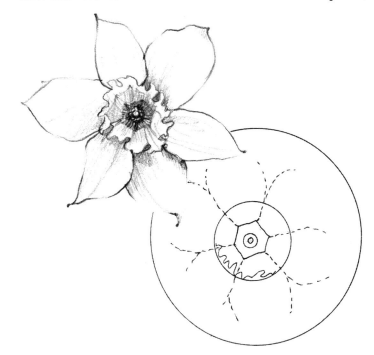

Flower forms often contain circles within circles—or their rough equivalent. Notice the relative shapes and sizes of these forms to more accurately draw your subject. Other geometry contains petals, pistils, stamens.

roses have exactly the *same* number of petals. They may, they may not. Such clear-eyed *noticing*, even to the point of counting petals, keeps your work from becoming mechanical and boring.

If I need further help in seeing, I might enclose the form in the nearest geometrical approximation of the shape. A daisy's head, of course, can be enclosed in a circle or an ellipse, depending on the angle. More complicated flowers might require several geometric shapes—a jonquil takes a circle or ellipse and a cone or tube shape, as does a jewelweed. Then use these geometrical "containers" as a gauge against which to measure the negative shapes and angles.

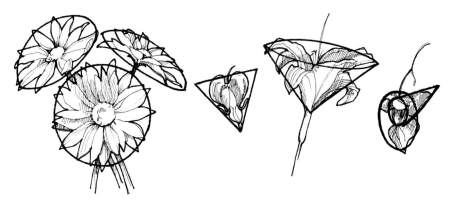

Geometric shapes imposed on natural ones (even if only in imagination) may help you to see them more clearly, then depict their angles correctly.

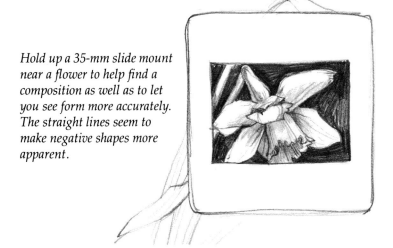

Hold up a 35-mm slide mount near a flower to help find a composition as well as to let you see form more accurately. The straight lines seem to make negative shapes more apparent.

If you don't want to draw unnecessary lines on your paper, just make dots at important turnings or angles. Suggest your oval in this way, or the cone shape—or imagine the geometric shape in place. No need to touch pencil to paper at all until you have the shape in your mind.

Your viewfinder, too, can help you to see what you're looking at, as well as aid you in finding a composition. My small 35-mm slide mount is just right for this kind of field work; most flowers visually fit the "window" with only a little manipulation as I move the cardboard closer to or farther from what I am drawing. (As you may have guessed, jonquils had just come into bloom as I wrote this.)

PERSPECTIVE OF THE FLOWERS

Even on such a small scale as this, the laws of perspective apply. Leaves that come toward the viewer look larger; if they come *directly* toward the eye, they may look foreshortened (as shown). If they turn away from the viewer, they may appear both foreshortened and smaller. In a bunch, the closer flowers will be larger and more distinct to the viewer—at least generally speaking—than those in the distance, even if that distance is only a matter of inches.

The human eye works much like a camera lens. If we focus on something close at hand, other things—even in the near distance—are less distinct. We see fewer details there because we aren't focused in on them. Take advantage of that fact as you sketch to suggest a sense of depth—and perspective—on the flat plane of your paper.

ATTENTION

The camera lens analogy also holds up if we talk of deliberate focus or attention, by the way. Like that lens, the eye can choose where to notice detail. You can direct the *viewer's* eye where you want it to go or indicate your own area of greatest interest (even if these sketches are only for yourself) by where you choose to place the greatest detail. A leaf may be closest to you in the picture plane, but if you're most concerned with a particularly lovely arrangement of petals—as in a violet, iris, or honeysuckle, for instance— why focus attention on a relatively uninteresting leaf simply because it's close by? You are the artist—focus where you like, and edit if you prefer.

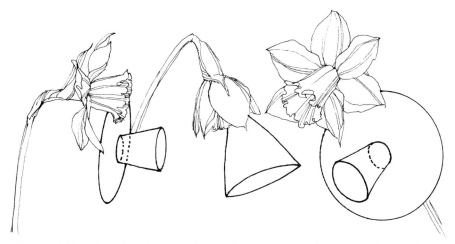

Flowers follow the rules of perspective, as does everything in nature. Again, simplified geometric forms may help you to see more accurately what is happening.

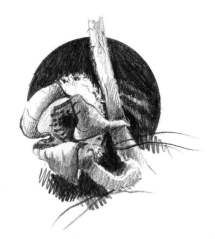

I zero in on my subject to find the most interesting detail. Here, it is the small, furry flower of wild ginger, like a tiny animal under the umbrella-like leaves. (Mechanical pencil, B lead.)

If time is a factor, edit *everything* else and sketch only the thing that caught your eye. You may never again get the chance to capture just that particular flower and its intricate details. Photographs, wonderful though they are, can be distorted or lose just the component you had hoped to preserve if your depth of field is just slightly off. Other, larger particularities such as leaves, stems, or even petals can be added later, if you wish, from a photograph or field guide.

FLOWERS IN LANDSCAPE

There are times when you may want to make the flowers you find a part of the larger picture, as indeed they are. No need to zero in on a single plant or individual flower. Sketch a landscape, and include the mixed flower community you find there. Your bright bits of life and beauty give a focal point to the broader picture.

Don't let detail trap you into overworking your sketch. Use only the amount you need to catch the feeling you're after. A gesture sketch might best capture the essence of that clump of flowers—it's amazing how much a few quick lines can express if you've gotten them in the right place.

If you really want to focus attention on the flowers you can use as much detail as you need—but value or color changes will often accomplish that focus without the need to overdraw.

You can suggest distant flowers in a landscape with a few quick squiggles—or, if you are working in watercolor, with a pastel spatter of opaque color. Try a loose ink sketch and use light-colored crayons to preserve some of your flower shapes. The wax repels the water in a wash, leaving a crisp, light spot. Single dots of white—or yellow, pink, blue, lavender, whatever—could stand in for a whole field of flowers for a rather pointillist effect.

PENCIL TECHNIQUES

When working in pencil, I use a varied line to sketch flowers and plants. The thick-and-thin lines help me capture the liveliness of my subject—but as you may have noticed, my "method" is more instinctive than planned. Use this technique more deliberately, if you like—heavier lines can hint at shadowed areas while thin lines stand in for those places the light strikes full on. Or use the bolder, darker lines to suggest those parts that are closest to you, the light lines to suggest a bit of distance, as discussed earlier in this book.

The varied pencil tones are wonderful for capturing form, depth, and value when sketching flowers and plants. I may not be able to draw actual color changes, but I can certainly use pencil pressure—value—to suggest *changes* in color. And if need be, I can switch to colored pencils for my primary medium or add a touch of color to a finished graphite sketch with colored pencils or watercolor.

PEN AND INK STUDIES

Pencil may be my favorite tool for sketching wildflowers, but elegant precision in an ink line captures a certain freshness of the subject. Whether I choose a fiber-tipped pen from the office supply store or a more expensive technical pen I prefer not to take out of the studio, the fine lines seem perfect. What I lose in the ability to suggest subtle gradations of tone I make up for in crisp detail, and I can always suggest shading with tiny dots. If I want a varied line (like the pencil line suggested a bit earlier), I can use a lighter pressure or a sketch pen or crow quill nib and liquid ink. These last don't

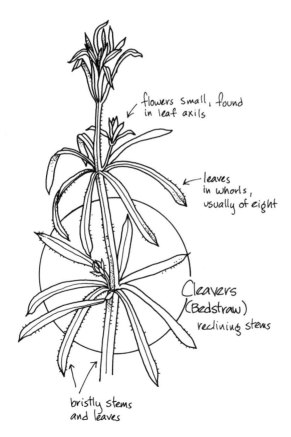

flowers small, found
in leaf axils

leaves
in whorls,
usually of eight

Cleavers
(Bedstraw)
reclining stems

bristly stems
and leaves

A pair of technical pens (0.25 and 0.35) captures crisp detail, whether in a sketch or work intended for photoreproduction. Using slightly differing nib sizes let me go bold where I needed to, while still allowing me to catch the finest details.

have the uniform, predictable lines of the fiber-tipped or technical pens; the effect can be quite lively.

Restated, repeated, or crosshatched lines can also give variety and interest to your flower sketches. Use these restatements to soften an area or contour, to suggest volume, or to give the impression of a bolder, heavier line without changing your sketching tool. Succulent plants such as cactus or purslane have thick leaves or pads like balloons filled with water; try restating lines to suggest their gentle contours.

Pen studies seem especially suited to field journal work. Details are sharp and written notes are easy to read, unlike my sometimes smudgy pencil hieroglyphs.

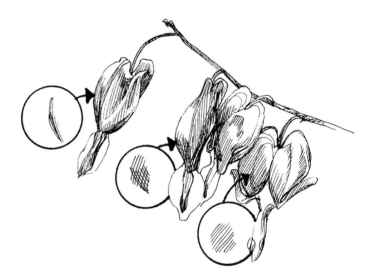

Restate pen and ink lines to capture form, depth, and value, left. Crosshatching (center) can make areas as dark as you wish, while simple, repeated lines (right) seem like luminous shadow areas. (Fiber-tipped pen.)

WATERCOLOR TECHNIQUES

Watercolor and wildflowers seem made for one another. Not only are the subtle colors of wildflowers more easily captured, but, used in a fairly controlled, dry-brush manner, watercolor can suggest the finest details. Try it wet-in-wet, as discussed in the chapter on watercolor, and details fade into the near distance. A combination of techniques can yield a startlingly real study.

When painting flowers, it's best to work from light to dark. It's easy to overwork or to go too bold too quickly and lose the delicacy of the subject. You can always add more color when your first washes have dried, but once your sketch has become garish it's tough to fix without making a muddy mess. And mud is anathema to painting wildflowers.

One of my favorite techniques is simply to sketch the flower or plant in pencil, using a fairly simple, direct approach with no shading or value changes. Then I lay in quick, light washes over that, letting the pencil drawing show through. It forms the backbone that I hang the colors on—I make no attempt to erase it.

WIDENING HORIZONS

Why stop with wildflowers and weeds? The plant world is full of shapes and colors to draw. I recently completed a series of mushroom studies and was awed by the configurations and functions of their various parts.

There are button mushrooms and shelf fungus, coral fungi and dead-men's fingers, witches' butter and stinkhorns. Mushrooms may have spore-bearing, sharp-edged gills, tubes, or teeth under that cap; they may have the familiar cap and stem, or they may be all cap, growing directly from their host. You may find them on rotted wood, live wood, or no wood at all. They may be parasitic or saprophytic, edible or poisonous. Mycology is a mysterious and fascinating study, and you can only enjoy it more through your sketches made on the spot. Like wildflower sketches, your quick field studies will help you identify what you've found and the more you take the time to *notice* about your subject the more useful your sketches will be.

Explore the varied forms of seaweed. Bladder wrack is graceful stuff, like hair growing on wave-smoothed rocks. There is a calligraphic quality to some of these ocean plants, while others are like sheets of brown paper perforated by a paper punch. They seem almost abstract, to one accustomed to the shapes of land plants.

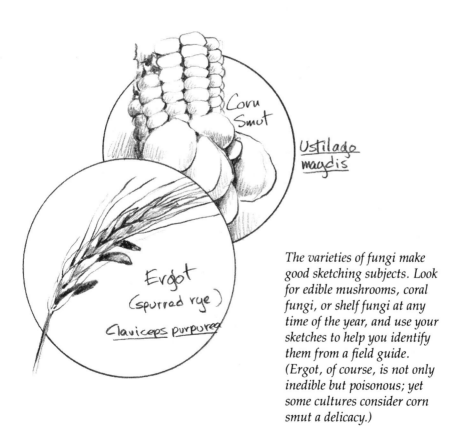

Corn Smut

Ustilago maydis

Ergot (spurred rye) Claviceps purpurea

The varieties of fungi make good sketching subjects. Look for edible mushrooms, coral fungi, or shelf fungi at any time of the year, and use your sketches to help you identify them from a field guide. (Ergot, of course, is not only inedible but poisonous; yet some cultures consider corn smut a delicacy.)

Mosses and lichens are fun to draw; one year I used my hand microscope with its fifty-power lens to draw the colorful lichen on an old concrete bridge near my home. I never would have realized the small beauty of this nearly invisible world if I hadn't stopped to sketch it. And the sketching led inevitably to questions that begged for answers. I learned more about lichens than I knew there *was* to know. Now I seem to find them everywhere. Reindeer moss (not a moss at all, but a pale, branched lichen that grows on bare Ozark soil), tiny cup lichen on the limbs of cedar trees, bright orange crusts on ancient gravestones—these tiny beauties are everywhere!

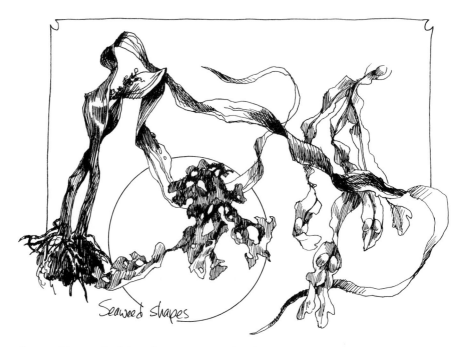

Seaweed is wonderful to draw; use varied techniques and strokes to capture its varied forms.

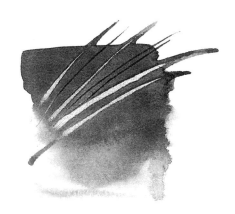

TEN

Trees

Trees, in most areas of the world at least, are an essential part of landscape—and of life itself. They make chlorophyll, use carbon dioxide, exhale oxygen back into the atmosphere on a monumental scale—without trees (and other green plants), Earth would be uninhabitable in short order.

These woods giants are environmental indicators; we read the passing of the seasons and the impact of weather and pollution as if interpreting an electrocardiogram. A long drought produces a blizzard of seeds and, when the tree is cut, visible evidence, in its narrowed rings, of growth stunted by lack of water. Wind marks the trees with invisible ink; we can see the direction of prevailing winds in their altered and responsive shape. Acid rain withers leaves, killing from the top down. From the clues offered by the trees, we can Sherlock our way to an understanding of our immediate environment.

A tree crowded in among others grows tall and slender, not branching at all until it "knows" it has a chance to grab for the light. One grown in a hostile environment where the necessaries of food and water are in short supply may be nature's own bonsai—a perfect, gnarled miniature of a full-sized tree of the same species. Where normal light and nutrients are available and the tree develops naturally, the family resemblance between it and its adaptable cousin may be only marginal.

Trees are endlessly varied in overall shape, branching, and leaf structure because of these factors—including the fundamental genetic stamp—as different as flowers in their lovely configurations. They possess a strength we can only envy; no wonder people attribute great power to them. Ancient Druids worshiped them; Native Americans say that they have spirits. One particular tree takes on the face of a jovial troll in my imagination, lifting his

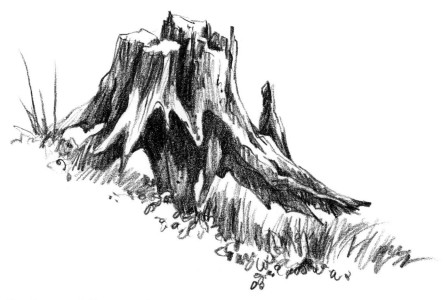

Pencil is especially appropriate to capture the subtleties of weathered wood.

glass in endless salute; it's a huge gall on an oak tree, and although I know what caused this strange face, it never fails to make me smile.

Trees have an odd emotional impact, a primitive hold on our imaginations. For an artist, this impact—of all trees, not just those bearing humanoid images—makes for a never-ending source of subject matter; for a naturalist, the source is one of learning, as well.

Habitat for thousands of birds and insects, their leaves and branches, hollowed trunks and tunneled roots are home for robins and raccoons, squirrels, badgers, tree frogs, and foxes. Butterflies and bees tumble at their open flowers or live among the leaves. No other plant family is so crucial to our shared existence—or so beautiful.

I love trees. I draw them over and over, exploring their immense and essential presence among us. They've captured my imagination in a way nothing else on Earth can.

SHAPES AND SIZES

As you sketch, notice the overall shape—this is a most *particular* tree, individual as a human face. In sketching the larger landscape, there is a place for symbolic handling—a repeated form to suggest the leaf canopy of a distant, forested hill, an angular, staccato line to stand in for bare winter trees. But when we focus on a single tree in a particular tree community, we are forced to pay attention to individuality. There *are* genetic factors at work, of course. Some trees are urn-shaped, like an elm; others conical, like a pine. Still others, like the crowded trees in my walnut grove, are tall and slender with limbs that branch in narrow V's. Others, like the sycamores by the creek, have a more open branch pattern and a generous, spreading crown. They toss their limbs in the wind like blown grass, but the oaks are gnarled and twisted and move hardly at all. Watch for these overall, species-specific

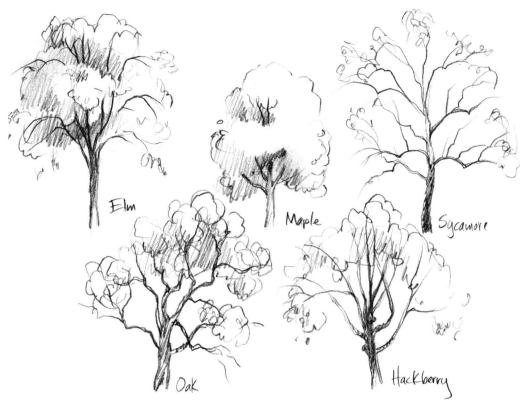

*Varying tree shapes and foliage patterns make for more interesting—and informa-
tive—sketches. (Mechanical pencil, HB lead.)*

shapes, but don't be bound by them if the tree you sketch doesn't follow the
textbook form. Environmental factors such as position in the forest, prevailing wind, damage (from wind or weather, human beings or other animals), available moisture—and sheer individuality—may have as much to
do with a particular tree's shape as its species.

The disparity of sizes may indicate that some trees are young and some
are mature—it may also reflect the variety of the woods community. There
may be tall trees such as the oaks and walnuts, but there may also be present
the smaller trees of the understory, the hawthorns and dogwoods and red-
buds—or whatever lower-growing trees are common in your area. Include
a mix of sizes and shapes in your sketch to add interest—and to reflect a
lively reality.

PERSPECTIVE

Use *perspective* as you sketch to give a sense of depth to your tree. Remember
to make distant trees smaller, simpler, lighter, and so forth. When sketching
an individual tree, perspective can help keep those branches where they
belong in the visual space you're recording.

Foreshortening the limbs that come toward you or reach backward
helps to suggest perspective, as does creating the illusion of space by over-

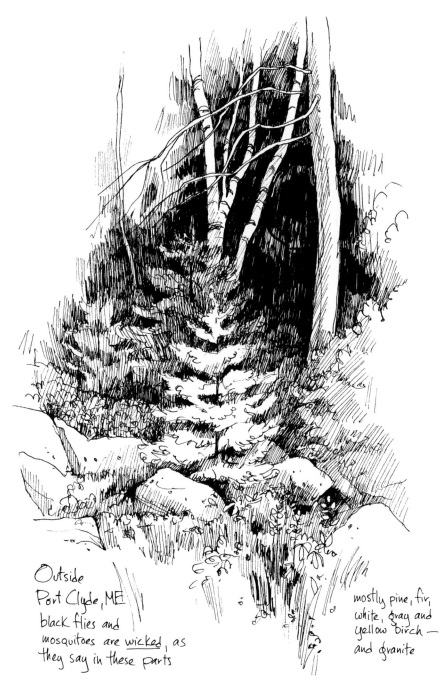

Outside
Port Clyde, ME
black flies and
mosquitoes are wicked, as
they say in these parts

mostly pine, fir,
white, gray and
yellow birch —
and granite

Most healthy forests are made up of small trees as well as large ones. Look for these variations to provide a sense of reality to your sketches. Here, young pines stand out at the edge of a forest of larger white birch and balsam fir. Where I live, the smaller trees such as redbud and dogwood may provide a variety of sizes and shapes. (0.7-mm fiber-tipped pen.)

lapping forms. Put one limb in front of the other, one tree in front of the other, to create this bit of visual magic.

Value helps capture the illusion of roundness and distance as well. (What is roundness, after all, but a kind of intimate distance in which one part of an object is closer to you while another turns away?) Using the gradations of light and dark will help you to show not only direction of light but this small depth that goes so far toward capturing elusive reality.

Distance may be suggested with value as you shade one area or another, showing that one form overlaps another in space. Cast shadows reinforce the illusion. Notice my pencil sketch of a dead tree; roundness, depth, and distance are all suggested with value—and with only a few shades, too. It's a simple sketch.

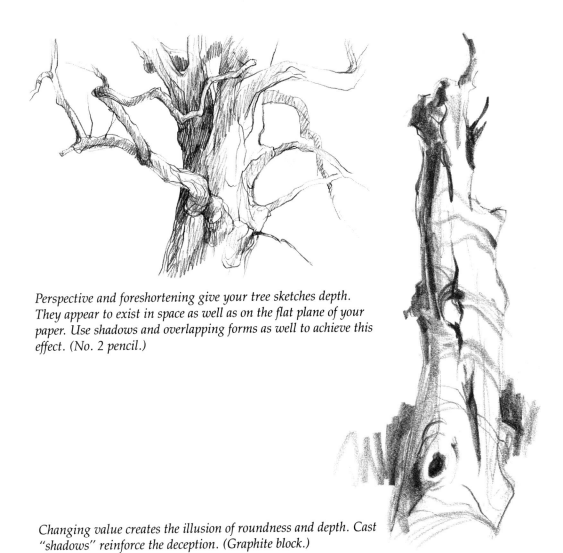

Perspective and foreshortening give your tree sketches depth. They appear to exist in space as well as on the flat plane of your paper. Use shadows and overlapping forms as well to achieve this effect. (No. 2 pencil.)

Changing value creates the illusion of roundness and depth. Cast "shadows" reinforce the deception. (Graphite block.)

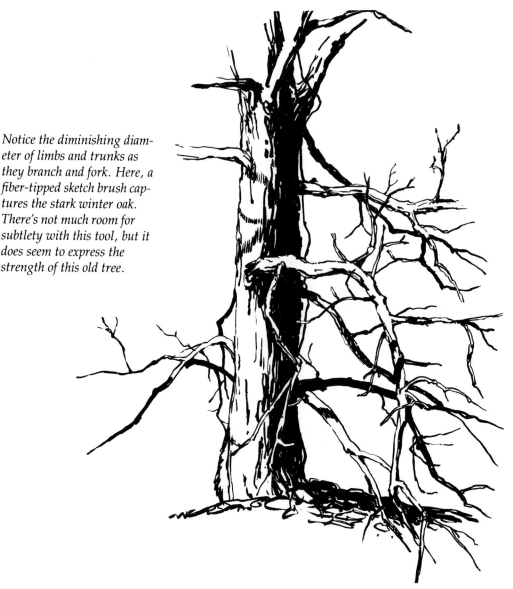

Notice the diminishing diameter of limbs and trunks as they branch and fork. Here, a fiber-tipped sketch brush captures the stark winter oak. There's not much room for subtlety with this tool, but it does seem to express the strength of this old tree.

FINDING THE SENSE OF TREES

Sketch trees with and without foliage to catch the sense of their shapes and to familiarize yourself with their basic forms. Get to know the *bones* of the tree to help you correctly define edges. Even when the tree is in full leaf, limb form, position, direction, and size all need to make sense (see sketch).

Notice, as you sketch, the branching habit of this particular tree—not only whether the tree has arced or angular limbs, narrow crotches or open-angled ones, but also how each successive branching reduces the overall volume of the trunk. Generally speaking, the main trunk or limb is proportionately diminished by the same volume as the smaller limb that grows from it. Paying attention to such details helps you to avoid common mistakes—you don't want to end up with a top-heavy tree that would blow down in the first good storm. I *have* seen a few trees that looked as if their initial branchings were larger than the main trunk—but as I circled the tree I usually found it was an optical illusion. Such trees are a curiosity, never the norm.

Vines use the larger trees as ladders to reach the light. Poison ivy, wild grape, bittersweet, Virginia creeper—these vines are sinuous and graceful, and enhance your sketches with a slow rhythm. Even in winter their snake-like, art nouveau lines are fun to draw. But look closely—sometimes it's hard to tell what is limb and what is vine. Watch for negative shapes to help you distinguish what's what—a limb will generally have a wider angle than a vine's snug fit, and an easily defined beginning and end.

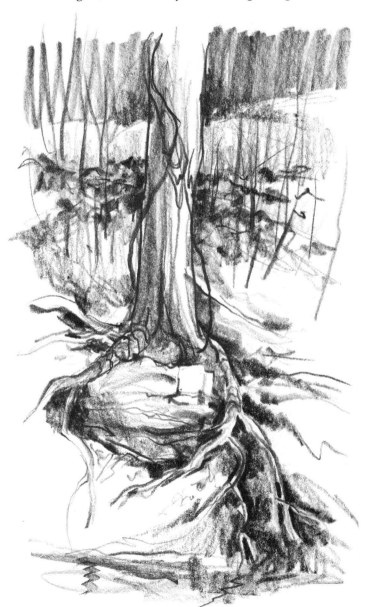

Vines may be as big as branches or as delicate and spidery as a drawn line. These add a bit of grace to a tough old tree as exposed roots clasp a limestone rock for support. (Flat sketching pencil.)

FOLIAGE

There are as many ways to indicate foliage as there are artists out there sketching—and moods to sketch in. When I am feeling bold and emphatic, I often use a quick zigzag squiggle of lines to stand in for leaf masses. I might alter their weight or angle to suggest shadowed areas, growth, or wind direction. Other times, simple, linear cloudlike shapes (shown) are sufficient, with only a suggestion of leaves at outer edges. In a more contemplative mood, I may draw tight, scalloped lines to stand in for the thousands of leaves that clothe a tree.

In pencil, the flat of the lead gives me a broad area of value for leaf masses. If I'm working in watercolor, a varied, tonal wash will get it, with perhaps a damp tissue lift here and there, and a bit of spatter when dry to give the feeling of individual leaves. See which technique works best for you, for your chosen medium, and for your mood—not to mention for the particular tree you're drawing. The chapter on landscape contains a few suggestions that can be adapted to this closer study.

Occasionally a sketch gets away from me and a tree tries to take over, filling the picture plane with a cloud of leaves. (Murphy's Law applies as well to sketching trees as to anything else. Better, sometimes.) If I first draw a light line around the tree shape's outermost branches I will stay within that shape. Other artists draw a quick arc at the top of the leaf or twig canopy to keep things from getting out of hand. If need be, I first indicate major branches and limbs to keep the logic in the form. Or I sketch leaf masses,

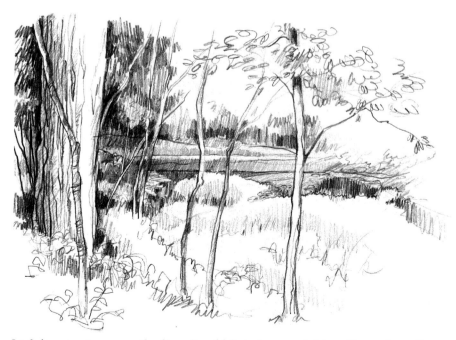

Look for ways to express the diversity of foliage in your sketches. Here, zigzag lines suggest distant tree forms while quick squiggles stand in for leaves on the small foreground tree. (No. 2 pencil.)

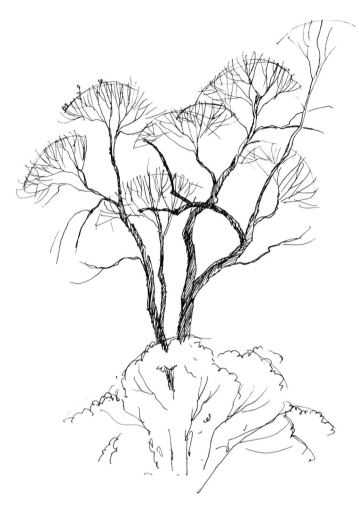

*Containing arcs help keep
these tree shapes honest; draw
them first in pencil, and erase
if you don't want them to be
part of your finished sketch.
(0.7-mm fiber-tipped pen.)*

letting shadowed areas suggest which are closest to the viewer and which are farthest away.

Remember that a fully leafed tree takes up three-dimensional space—it goes all the way around. It's easy to forget this when working on the flat plane of your paper, and to make trees that seem to be cotton balls espaliered on flattened branches—there are foliage puffs with holes between, and something just doesn't feel right. In reality, the same kind of perspective and foreshortening applies to the foliage of trees as worked to describe their bare limbs. Suggest these forms by allowing *some* windows to show through but others to only partly penetrate the leaf canopy, creating deep shadows with darker branch shapes within.

Add a few individual leaf shapes at the outer edges of these foliage masses and at the edge of the tree itself, and your sketch will look more natural.

Use value in foliage areas to help suggest season, as well. In the spring, when the leaves are new, keep them high key, as light as the sky—or lighter. Limbs stand out darkly against these delicately colored masses of leaves. Later, in full summer, the leaves are a rich medium value and limbs may

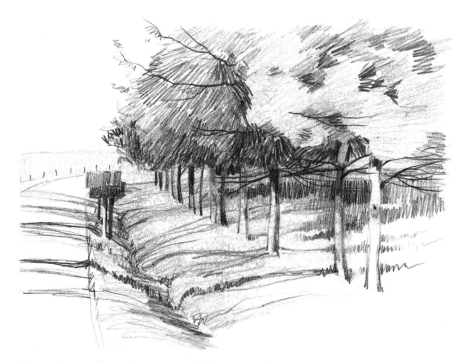

Strong linear effects give a sense of direction and movement to this small sketch. (No. 2 pencil.)

appear lighter by contrast. And nearly any time at all, the dark needles of the evergreen clan stand out somberly against the lighter green of deciduous trees.

Directional lines can give a sense of motion. If there's a brisk breeze, let your foliage lines follow like a weather vane. Here, a strong wind blew roadside pines till they were nearly a blur. I used repeated straight and diagonal lines to suggest that tumultuous motion, and it seems to have worked.

ROOTS

Tree roots may tell us more about the strength and tenacity of these forest giants than any other single aspect. Too bad these anchoring underground limbs are usually invisible. They hold the tree in place, but even more, they draw moisture and nutrients from the soil to keep the tree alive.

Near a creek that periodically floods or along a rocky outcropping, roots may be more visible. Their twisted, interlocking forms are wonderful to draw—treat them as you would limbs to capture their reality. Watch for perspective, roundness, value, and negative shapes. See how they, too, branch, becoming smaller and smaller like the capillaries in our own blood distribution system.

Some of my favorite sketches have been of uprooted trees or of roots that abandoned the anonymity of the soil to snake out over a rocky ledge. Their spiky angularity is dramatic; their exposed state is emotionally powerful.

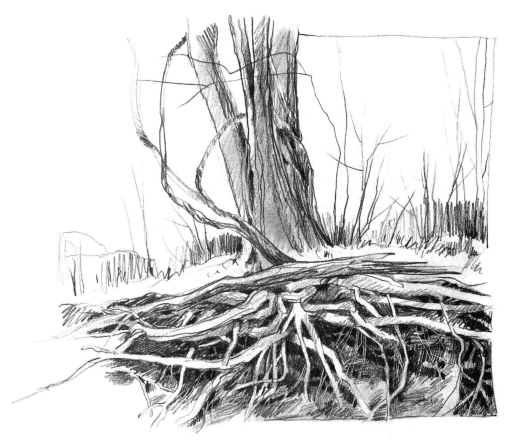

Here, the finer roots were incised deeply into my paper surface with a fingernail once I'd laid in the major root forms but before I added the negative shapes of dark shadows. The tiny roots stand out as white lines. Be careful not to actually cut the paper; use a blunt scribing tool. (No. 2 graphite pencil.)

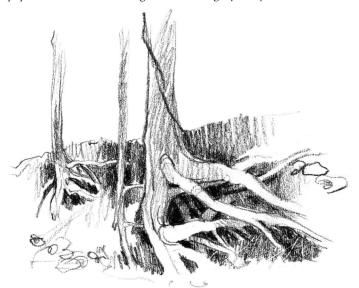

Value and negative shapes help to capture these trees clinging to the banks of my creek. (Berol Prismacolor pencil.)

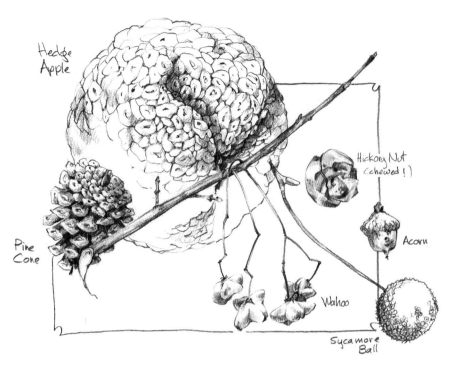

Cones and seed balls, nuts, and fruit found on a single afternoon. A fine-lead mechanical pencil allowed me to explore the varieties of detail without the need for frequent resharpening.

LEARNING FROM FIELD SKETCHES

Your field sketches are your best tools for learning about the trees you encounter. As always, written notes help to fix your findings in mind. Comparing what you've drawn to what you find in a field guide helps you see beyond illustrations and into the fabric of life. There's much more to a tree than its simple identification as a deciduous type or an evergreen conifer— or its specific identity within that larger classification.

Trees are not inert, unpopulated, or inviolate. They're part of the ecosystem. Your sketches take on a new sense of life when you reflect this truth. Show the woodpecker's drillings, the chickadee's nesting hole, the squirrel's leafy summer lounging platform. Sketch the bees that come and go from a honey hole. Draw the tooth marks of a beaver on a downed stump or the depredations of bagworms. Note what is coming and going. Notice which birds seem to prefer what trees—size, leaf cover, whatever—and see if you can discover why with your sketches.

Explore the varieties of fruits, nuts, or seeds in your area. It's a humbling experience to realize the wonderful diversity, with each tree designed to its specific niche.

Make leaf studies as a detail of your field sketches. Each tree's leaves have evolved through trial and error to meet individual needs. The elm's jagged-edged leaves discourage leaf-eating caterpillars (it's like climbing a long, jagged ladder), while the buckeye's huge, moccasin-shaped leaves grab all the light they can find in the crowded understory. Each oak family member has distinctive leaves that help identify it—they're like fingerprints. Each venation or vein pattern is uniquely interesting. Leaves may be as different as redbud's polished heart shapes and locust's tiny compound leaflets, but each has its specific logic.

Any good field guide to the trees will familiarize me with terms describing the various leaves (such as *simple*, *compound*, *pinnate*, and *palmate*) and their margins (such as *smooth*, *toothed*, *lobed*, and *wavy*). But the terms don't necessarily stick till I make them my own by sketching specific leaves. I like to hike until I find leaves that match those in the field guides, and sketch my *own* illustrations, labeling their parts and identifying the tree I've picked them from. Then, although my memory may be faulty, I know much more than I did before, and in an experiential way.

Collect leaves from your yard or a nearby park, and sketch them to acquaint yourself with the trees that grow in this specialized habitat. Compare your findings with those picked up in a mixed forest community. Look beside a stream after a flood to see what leaves have been deposited along the high-water mark; some may be exotic and unfamiliar to you. Try to identify them to find clues as to how far these travelers have come.

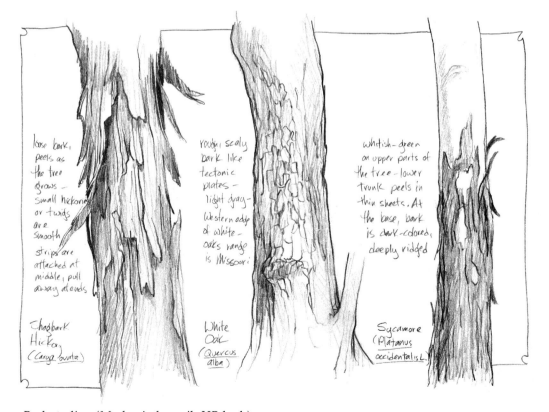

Bark studies. (Mechanical pencil, HB lead.)

BARK STUDIES

Bark is not generic; far from it. Each tree has developed the bark it needs, for protection and for growth. Make studies of these as you did the leaves, noting patterning, texture, color, thickness—anything that sets this bark apart from other, similar barks. Some are almost shredded-looking, like cedar, and others, like the American sycamore, peel off in huge plates to expose pale upper limbs. If you already know the tree, as you may from summertime leaves or fruit, then you'll simply become better acquainted. In winter, bark may be your best tool for identification. Cedar is quite different from sycamore, of course, but many oak family members have very subtle variations. Your field sketches will help you to pin them down.

If you are working in color, observe closely. Often people tend to portray tree trunks as a rich or dark brown. But look again: most are shades of gray, perhaps embellished with green algae or orange lichen. If it's rainy, the damp bark is almost black.

Look for ways to suggest bark texture in your more casual sketches, as well. Crosshatching or repeated zigzag lines may capture the roughness you see; careful areas of graduated tone may work best for trees with smoother bark.

I often use these zigzag lines to suggest both shadow and texture, then lay on a few darker lines to suggest individual bark configurations. These lines also help to explain direction of growth and volume. They can tell us how a limb grows from the trunk or if the trunk itself is straight, twisted, or curved.

Varied bark tones will give interest to these sketches; local color or value can be used for sparkle. Light and shadow affect the degree of texture you see as well as the degree of value. Look closely to see how you can use these shadows to express the rugged or smooth barks.

You can go as simple or as detailed as you like with your sketches. Here, three different drawing styles express the same subject, a single walnut tree. Let available sketching time and personal taste be your guide. (Mechanical pencil, HB lead.)

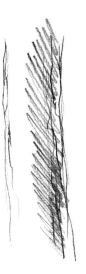
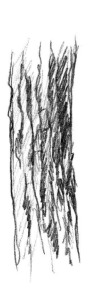
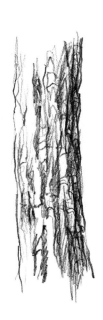

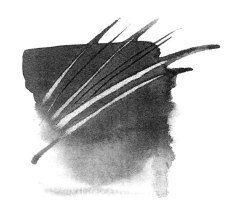

ELEVEN

Sketching in the Animal Kingdom

*B*EYOND THE MAGNIFICENCE of landscape, beyond the grace of flowers or the patient tenacity of trees, there is sentient life. It rivets our attention; we share something basic here. There is a moment of recognition. I never fail to freeze, to stop breathing for a second when I am surprised by another living being, whether it is a heron in the shallows or a white-tailed deer at the edge of the woods. If I'm lucky, I'll have my sketchbook in hand.

Sketching living creatures can be an artist's biggest challenge. Birds fly, insects skitter away, mammals turn to stone, wide-eyed, then run as if sprung from a trap. Life is in constant motion; unlike the flowers, a deer will not wait quietly while I explore every nuance of body configuration, ears, or the curve of a nostril. If I try to get close enough to see, or to circle for a different angle, the animal bounds away as if chased by the hounds of hell.

Wild creatures are shy of us and with good reason. They've learned that, generally speaking, anything with two legs and bold eyes is to be avoided if they value their lives—and pelts. The artist-naturalist pays the tab that a genetic memory of hunters has run up; we may go armed only with a sketchpad and pencil, or a camera, but a wild turkey or a bighorn sheep has no way of knowing that.

It is often easier to sketch birds than mammals; they tend to go on about their business without as much anxiety as the four-legged animals do, although in summer when the trees are fully leafed they may appear to be no more than dark, moving shadows overhead. Try a feeder near a window to provide an accessible source of "models"—you won't have the chance to sketch birds such as the large predators, but you can study avian body shapes from these available stand-ins. Use binoculars or a telescope to bring

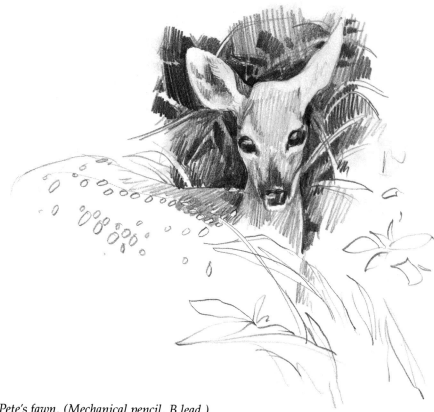

Pete's fawn. (Mechanical pencil, B lead.)

birds in close enough to see their field marks and appreciate their colors; a scope on a tripod allows you to sketch with your hands free.

No matter if you are drawing mayflies or marmots, the principles of sketching life are the same; one is no harder than another, nor more beautiful in its way.

CAREFUL OBSERVATION

To compensate for the propensity of animal life to *move*—after all, it takes longer to make the quickest sketch than it does to pull a trigger (or snap a shutter)—we hone our powers of observation to a flinty point. We learn to ask ourselves questions that will fix what we've seen in our minds: what is the animal doing? What is it feeding on? How large is it in relation to the family cat—or a cow? How large are its ears in relation to its head? How are its wings shaped—long and bent like scimitars or stubby and powerful? Are its eyes on the front of its skull, like ours, like the owls—or off to each side, like rabbits or deer? Is it camouflaged or boldly marked, and what is its basic color? Does it have stripes or spots or blotches? Where are they, and how large? What time of day is it? (This tells us something of which similar-looking creature might be about.) What is its basic stance? Can we guess at mood (alert, sleepy, angry, nervous)?

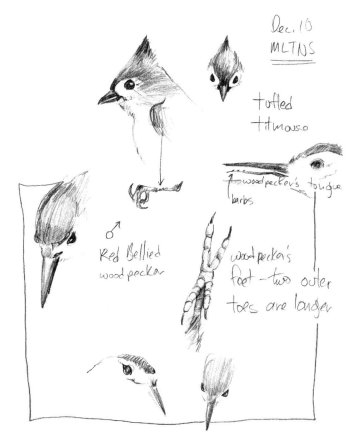

These birds were trapped in a mist net (very fine black net) for banding, allowing me the opportunity for detail sketches. The same birds visit my feeder, where I often sketch their varied forms. (Mechanical pencil, HB lead.)

All these questions may flash through our minds in seconds. Train yourself to notice—or to ask yourself comparable questions later—and you'll be amazed at how much you can recall. Make up your own memory jogs. You will be able to remember details you weren't aware that you noticed, with a bit of practice.

Questions like these not only help us to sketch in the details later, when we have the chance, but act as invaluable aids to identification. If I see a small-eared, chubby brown mammal about the size of a cat (give or take ten pounds), it could be one of several creatures—but if I've seen it in or near the water, that narrows the identification down somewhat. If it's seen at dusk or dawn, and has a small, ratlike tail, most likely it's a muskrat. If it is evening, you find felled trees nearby, and the creature you see is more the size of a small- to medium-sized dog—it's a beaver. (Of course, if it slaps its tail on the water in warning, the game is up. No further questions.)

On the other hand, if you surprise a rather similar creature in an old field or woods by day, it's a woodchuck. Your sketches, scribbled down in the instant before the creature disappeared, may not be enough identification: the questions you've asked yourself provide the answers, easily checked with a field guide or professional naturalist.

This kind of clear-eyed noticing can even save your life. Although I'd hardly recommend you pick up a snake of *any* sort if you don't know what it is, at least recognize the poisonous pit viper's broad head, hooded brows, and deep, heat-sensing pit between the eye and the nostril while you're asking yourself those questions. That one you don't want to touch, ever, not if it's still breathing. I *have* drawn a copperhead (one of the pit vipers common in Missouri) at close range, but it was one someone had unnecessarily killed with a rock. I had mixed feelings; regret for the loss of the snake and gratitude for the chance to study it closely.

GESTURE DRAWINGS

These quick 3- to 15-second drawings are tailor-made for sketching animals (see Chapter 3 for an overview of gesture sketches). They let you capture overall shape and stance in an instant, particularly useful for a moving sub-

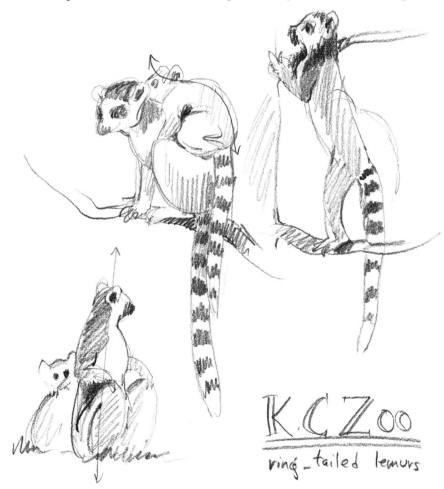

These quick gesture sketches were developed further when I had the chance to add a suggestion of form, value, and markings. Notice the curved line of the spine of the baby lemur on mother's back, and the upright stance of the adult at lower left. Seeing—or actually sketching in—these lines may help you to draw more accurately. (No. 2 pencil.)

ject. I can do three or four (or more) of these quick sketches if I am quiet and don't make the animal or bird feel threatened in any way.

If it helps to find the basic gesture, look for the position of the spine. Sketch it in as a graceful curved line, then hang your drawing on that.

Or be aware of the angle of stance. A straight line through the balance point will help you depict your subject accurately. I once did a quite complete painting of a red-tailed hawk that looked great to me—years later, I found that the bird's sharp-angled posture gave my painting away as the work of an inexperienced observer. The hawk would have fallen squarely on its hooked beak if it had maintained that position long.

BLOCKING IN FORMS

Once you have the gesture down, you may want to develop forms further by blocking in the shape in simplified, almost geometric forms. Often an animal's basic forms roughly conform to shapes that help you to see what you are looking at: a bean shape might work for the body, or an oval or circle. A tube can stand in for neck or legs. A triangle can contain the shape of a butterfly's wing. These shapes can be rendered quickly, then details and refinements added to bring your sketch to life. It needn't be a daunting prospect; a living subject is really no different from a landscape, if you just have the chance to sketch it in before it disappears.

Watch for overlapping shapes, as where the neck joins the torso. You don't want your drawing to look like the head was stuck to the body with a Popsicle stick, but as if it extends naturally from the spine—which it does.

Animal forms obey the rules of perspective, as does everything in nature. Notice that the far leg may seem shorter, the nearer ear larger. Look for these angles and relationships to give your sketches spatial veracity, but don't overemphasize. Just notice.

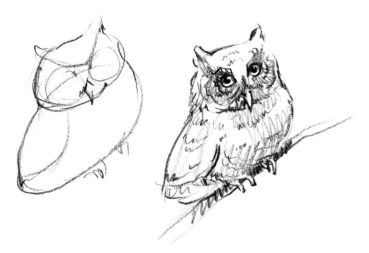

Simplifying overall shapes can make it easier to draw accurately. Notice that overlapping the shapes of the head and body makes for a natural-looking joining at the neck. (Prismacolor pencil.)

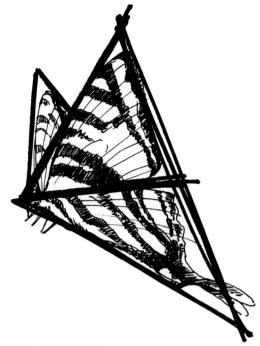

A triangle—or several of them—contains the shape of butterfly wings and helps define their perspective. (Razor-tipped pen.)

SKULLS AND BONES

If it helps you to draw more accurately, study the skeletal form of the animal you want to sketch. There are many good books on animal anatomy; my favorite reference is *Wild Animals of Missouri* (1981), by Charles W. Schwartz, published by the Missouri Department of Conservation. There are not only skulls and skeletons, but also details of fur and feet that help me to understand my subject better. (The book also contains information on habitat, breeding, feeding, and so on—I can't do without it. I only wish there were similar books—and as complete—available on birds, insects and spiders, reptiles, and all the other creatures that catch my eye.)

Such research is not always necessary, of course, when sketching. Some animals present such streamlined, simple shapes that there is no need to delve beneath the surface. But at times a coyote's hind leg seems awkwardly drawn; understanding how the bones fit together helps me to produce a believable drawing—and to capture action more accurately, as well.

I get as excited as a kid when I find a skull in the woods, evidence of some animal's habitation in my area. Sketching that skull, identifying it (usually with the help of Schwartz's book or my vet), studying vertebrae or pelvic bones I may have found nearby, speculating on the health of the animal and how it died, teaches me a lot about what creatures I share my locale with. I can draw these mute souvenirs at my leisure; they possess an austere beauty all their own. I feel like Georgia O'Keeffe as I do a detailed study of the deer skull I found down the creek from my cabin.

Road kills and other dead animals must be drawn soon after their demise if you plan to remain in the immediate vicinity for more than a few moments (unless, like the great horned owl, you have no sense of smell at all). Still, these animals give us an invaluable opportunity for close study.

I consider the death of a wild bird or a butterfly plastered to my car's grille a mixed blessing; I mourn the death but welcome the opportunity to draw at length. I may take the butterflies and moths home and keep their patterned wings under glass for reference; I make detailed sketches of mammals I have found, from every angle possible. How many people do you know who apply brakes with a screech and back up a quarter of a mile to pick up a recently killed quail to freeze for later drawing?

This young rabbit (shown) had had a run-in with my cat late one night outside my bedroom window. After trying to save the tiny, sentient bit of

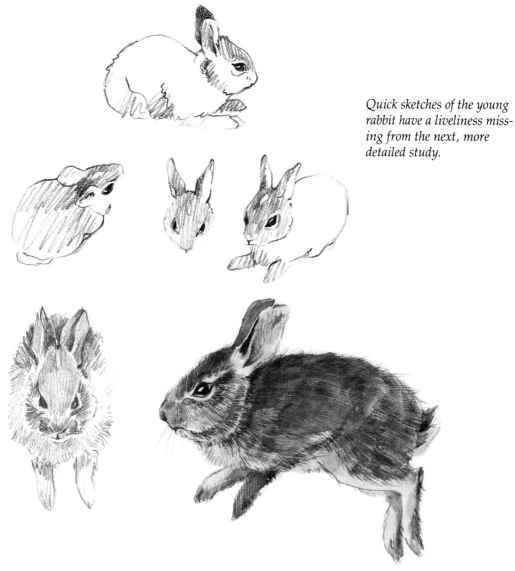

Quick sketches of the young rabbit have a liveliness missing from the next, more detailed study.

I was able to explore texture and form more carefully before burying this unfortunate youngster. Wild rabbits are so delicate they seldom survive the trauma of a run-in with a predator—or the well-intentioned nursing of a human. (See page 119.)

life for two days, I was saddened to find he had not made it through the third night. I had sketched him several times during the two days I nursed him; this final stillness let me do a detailed watercolor study of his pelt and body characteristics not possible with a frightened young animal.

If you can overcome a certain squeamishness, this kind of study is like finding a treasure—a sad one, perhaps.

MORE CONCENTRATED SKETCHES

If by chance the animal stays still longer (or if you are sketching long distance with the aid of binoculars or a telescope, so that you are not perceived as a threat), then there's time enough for more careful on-the-spot rendering, without the need to rapidly block in forms. In some wilderness areas, animals are not so wary of our presence—they haven't seen enough of us to learn fear. If there is time, watch for negative shapes to accurately render body or facial details. Try out contour drawing techniques. Do a memory drawing, letting the image soak into your brain (ask yourself those memory-jogging questions, if you need to); then if the animal moves away suddenly or changes position, you will remember what you saw.

VALUE AND FORM

Once the basic shape is in place, value—a simple range of lights and darks—can give volume and weight to your sketch. Use light and shadow to describe form. Suggest strong, direct sunlight with a broken line, if you like.

Watch where shadows fall, and note if they are *body shadows*, as are those where the form turns away from the light (under the belly, under the chin) or *cast shadows*, where the jawbone throws a shadow on the neck or

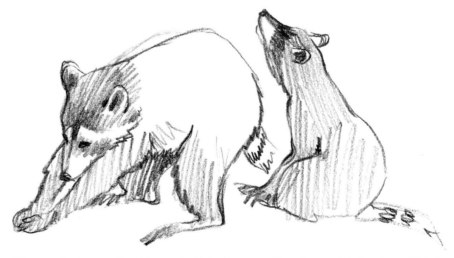

The use of value need not be so studied, of course. Even in a quick sketch, scribbled tones can suggest form, texture, and shadow. I felt no need to complete the tones within the larger sketch. (Prismacolor pencil.)

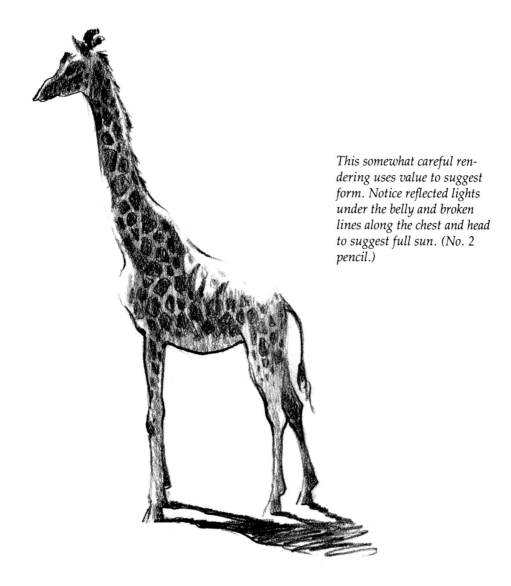

This somewhat careful rendering uses value to suggest form. Notice reflected lights under the belly and broken lines along the chest and head to suggest full sun. (No. 2 pencil.)

one leg shades another. Watch for reflected lights in the body shadows (not, usually, in cast shadows), and use these nuances to suggest volume. Let your shadow shapes follow the animal's form to emphasize roundness.

FIELD MARKS

Your quick sketches will be most useful for identification if you make note of field marks, those patterns or markings that set a red-headed woodpecker apart from a red-bellied one—or from a flicker. A few strokes of your pencil will be enough to tell you that the bird you saw far overhead was a turkey vulture, not a black vulture; the black vulture has white outer wing patches.

It's the same with insects and spiders; aside from overall shape and size—of which there is a wide variety—these field marks are essential for identification. A black spider without that almost spherical abdomen and distinctive red marking is not a black widow spider. The wonderful patterning and colors set one butterfly most definitely apart from another.

Make written notes by your sketches to help fix these marks in your mind, especially if you are not working in color—it's amazing how quickly you can forget what you've seen on a long day's hike. Notes and sketches bring it back alive.

Your sketches will be useful in comparing wing and beak sizes, leg length (or number, if you're drawing insects, millipedes, or spiders), or any other detail you may notice that sets one species or family member apart from any other. Similar species can often be differentiated by just such particulars. In the distance, especially in brush or at the edge of woods, it may be easiest to tell a deer from an elk by its antlers.

CAPTURING LIFE IN THE EYES

Often it's the eyes that best express life to us. They are ever-changing mirrors of mood and emotion. Eyes tell us a great deal about the animal: whether it is calm or anxious, angry or confrontational (and, in fact, whether it is alive at all). Catch that liveliness in your drawing and you've accomplished a great deal.

I often start a sketch with the eyes if I have the opportunity to do more than a quick gesture sketch and am able to work close up; if I don't get the sense of life here, I may as well start over.

Notice the shape of an animal's eyes. They are seldom perfectly round (even an owl's eye, viewed straight on) nor are they usually as elongated as our own. Does this particular creature have tilted eyes, or are they relatively straight from corner to corner? Are the irises light or almost as dark as the pupil?

Study an animal's eyes to see shape, position of highlights, and so on. Negative shapes can help you position eyes, as can an awareness of the shape of the skull and angle of the head. Notice how overall shape changes when the owl looks to the side or overhead in my sketches. (Mechanical pencil, HB lead.)

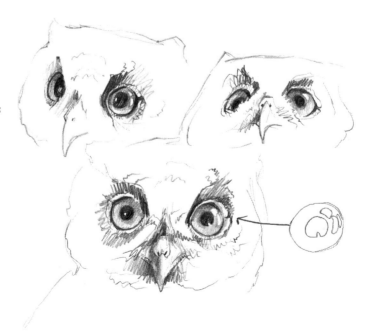

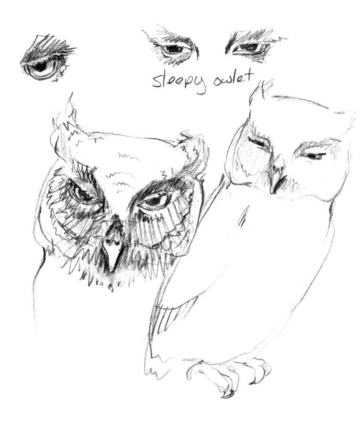

sleepy owlet

Sleepy owlet—note the change in eye shapes as it became drowsier. (Mechanical pencil, B lead.)

Eyes are affected by angle, by position, and by perspective. A creature looking to the side appears to have eyes of two different shapes and sizes. Draw what you *see*; never mind what you know. If they look different, draw them that way and you'll capture the sense of roundness—and of perspective—of the animal's skull.

Eyes that scan the sky overhead may appear flattened, due to the angle of the head. Again, they follow the rules of perspective and position. Make a line following that basic curve, if you need to, to capture correct alignment.

Notice the position of the eyes on the head. How near the center line are they, both vertically and horizontally? A youngster's eyes, like a child's, will often be lower on the face, with proportionately more forehead or brow. The eyes generally take up more space in the young (they really *are* bigger in proportion to skull size, though not so exaggeratedly as greeting cards sometimes suggest), and they have a softer expression. The demarcation between pupil and iris may not be so pronounced as in the adult.

The highlight in the eye is often what gives that spark of life. It can suggest a great deal more, if you wish. The orb or eyeball is round, in most species; let the highlight follow this shape, however subtly, and the effect is quite different from a simple dot of white. In cartoons, these highlights are often drawn as an odd windowpane shape—fine if your animal is indoors by a window, which is hardly likely! The highlight, by the way, *can* be a simple white dot, if it reflects the round sun or other single light source. Careful observation is again the key.

Draw around the highlight to preserve the white, add it later with opaque white paint, or scratch it out with the tip of a sharp blade; you'll be surprised at the lively eyes that suddenly look back at you from the page.

RENDERING FUR

Mammals have pelts of all descriptions—long-haired and blowy, short and sleek, and everything in between. Observation and logic are your best keys for capturing that be-furred effect.

A very short-haired, shiny animal might best be drawn with areas of tone to express the shine with no attempt at rendering individual hairs at all—or with perhaps a few sketched in at shoulder or rump to stand in for the rest. If you are working quickly, as I was when I sketched this young raccoon, a few quick squiggles will do it. This approach works well with any animal with longer fur.

If you prefer a more contemplative approach, layer your strokes in pen and ink or pencil, watching for direction of growth patterns, natural breaks at bridge of nose and at the chest, and so on. Wet fur or hair is always darker and may clump together in points (as shown).

More pressure on your drawing tool, a softer or darker lead if you are using colored pencils, or a heavier application of strokes gives you darker areas to suggest fur patterning or shadow areas. But in a quick sketch, as many of those done from life will be, it isn't necessary to worry much about actual coloring or individual patterns. The important thing is catching the liveliness of the animal, the position or shape. Careful studies of color or pattern are more suited to drawings or paintings than to sketches.

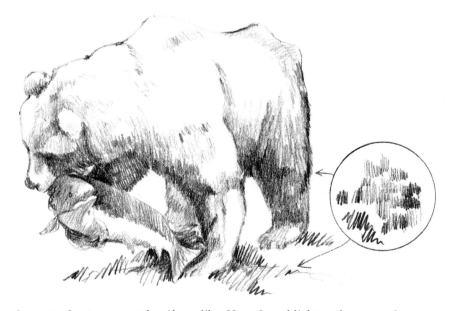

Layer strokes to suggest fur, if you like. Here, I used lighter, shorter strokes to suggest the bear's pelt, then rougher, heavier ones for the grass beneath. (2B pencil.)

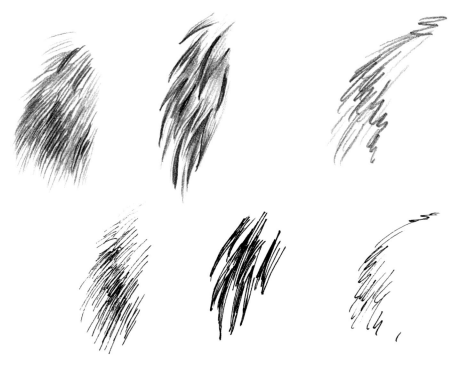

In these samples I've used pencil in the top three and rolling-ball pen in the lower. Left side shows repeated strokes to stand in for dry fur, while heavier, clumped, V-shaped strokes in the center suggest wet fur. At right in each medium, a quicker, simpler squiggle would still look like rough fur—this is a sketch, after all, not a photographic rendering.

CATCHING THE SHINE

Wet or moist skin, glossy scales, or a seashell washed by the tide have the same highlights as an animal's eye. There are strong contrasts of light and dark where surfaces are wet, moist, or shiny.

Watch for where the light strikes, along natural contours or rises; these lights and darks can help define form. Preserve the white of your paper, or regain it later by scratching or adding opaque white to suggest this wet glow.

Dry surfaces, like a weathered shell far from the sea, have lost that shine. Values are closer to one another; a range of subtle grays is more likely than sharp demarcations of dark and light—at least if you want to depict that dryness. Be aware of surface characteristics to help your sketches take on reality.

FILL A PAGE WITH SKETCHES

If you have the opportunity, fill an entire sketchbook page (or several) with quick drawings of the animals you see, catching them from the front and back and side, standing up, lying down, flexing wings, swimming. (I often practice in this way while watching nature shows on the public television channel; it keeps my hand-eye coordination in fighting trim.)

These sketchbook pages are invaluable for later studies or paintings; although they may be little more than gesture sketches, more than likely I will have caught the truth of the animal *for myself* in a way I can't do by looking at someone else's still photograph. This allows me to get to know my subject on a much more intimate level than is possible from a single sketch, drawing, or reference photo. I begin to catch the sense of how an animal moves through its various activities—and, if I am lucky, a bit about how the animals in a herd or family group relate to one another.

DETAIL SKETCHES

Let's face it—animals in cages are not the same as those living free, or even the same as those in a beautifully photographed nature special. We've lost some innate truth about that animal's life when we see it only behind bars.

But there is one big advantage to sketching at a zoo or nature center where animals may be kept in cages, or even as taxidermy mounts. We have the chance to study details closely. Take this opportunity every chance you get; it's irreplaceable.

I occasionally have a young animal or bird for a few hours between the time it leaves the local nature center and the time it can be released in the

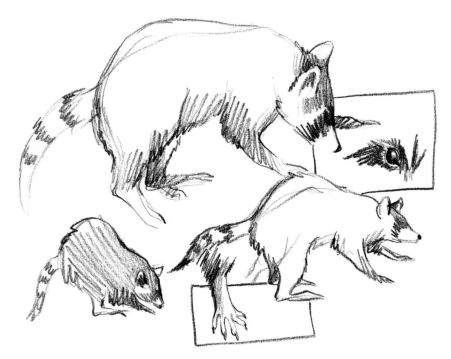

A young raccoon kept until it could be released at dusk provided the opportunity to sketch details of eyes and feet as well as body configurations and pose. Notice that when the animal moved or when I drew a line incorrectly, I simply restated in the right place. (Prismacolor pencil.)

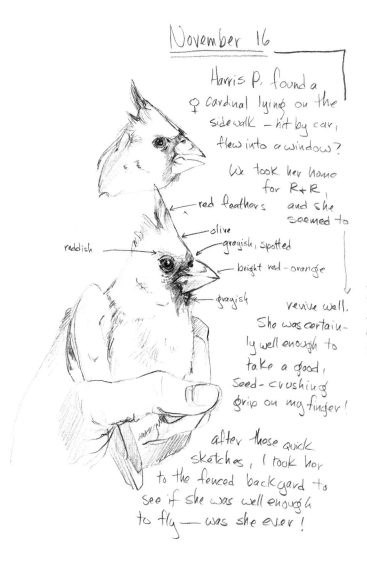

November 16

Harris P. found a
♀ cardinal lying on the
sidewalk — hit by car,
flew into a window?

We took her home
for R+R,
red feathers   and she
                        seemed to

olive
reddish   grayish, spotted
               bright red-orange

grayish   revive well.
              She was certain-
              ly well enough to
              take a good,
              seed-crushing
              grip on my finger!

after those quick
sketches, I took her
to the fenced backyard to
see if she was well enough
to fly — was she ever!

A cardinal stunned by impact with a window was a perfect subject. I was able to observe details ordinarily missed. (Mechanical pencil, B lead.)

wild. As mentioned earlier, my veterinarians at the Excelsior Springs Animal Clinic know of my interest and call me in when they have an injured creature I might like to sketch. In this way, I have been able to draw the close-up details of a white-tailed deer and fawn, a young raccoon, a great blue heron, a bobcat, a red-tailed hawk, and many other creatures too shy (or too smart) to allow me close in the wild. It's been a wonderful experience, and one I'd recommend to anyone interested in sketching animals. Let your local nature center, veterinarian, state conservation official, or taxidermist know you'd be interested in any sketching opportunity; you'll be gratified at the response.

One word of caution—make sure the taxidermist is a talented one and that mounts are reasonably fresh. You need accuracy you can count on. (That—and an untrained eye—was the problem with my hawk painting.) Old, dusty mounts may have lost their shape; make sure the ones you sketch are truly useful to you.

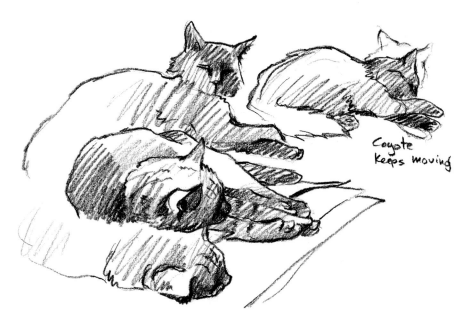

Pets can stand in for other, less accessible animals to help you keep in practice and understand overall shapes. (Prismacolor pencil.)

STAND-IN MODELS

You may not always be lucky enough to see an animal in the wild, although birds and insects are fairly ubiquitous. Mammals are shyer and often nocturnal. Keep your sketching abilities in practice by sketching your pets; a domestic tabby is not that different from a bobcat, after all, and dog forms are much like wolves. I'm not sure I could tell a close-up of a dog's nose from that of a coyote. Fish in an aquarium make fine subjects, and their basic shapes are very like their wild counterparts.

My cats are among my favorite subjects; they're hams, and seem to enjoy my appreciation of their loveliness and unique charms.

LIFE IN LANDSCAPE

No need to focus exclusively on a bird, mammal, or insect as your primary subject. Not everything needs to be a close-up. Include it in the larger landscape, as a focal point or just to add a touch of life to your sketch. As I've noted, I often use the suggestion of birds in the sky—simple V-shapes—to bring a sketch to life. Quick dots and dashes can suggest bees at a bee tree. A deer shape in the distance gives a sense of mystery to landscape.

Far off or in the middle distance as well, birds in flight are a powerful tool to change a flat sketch into a magically dimensional one. It's not as difficult as it might seem. Watch the stance of the bird, the angle of its flight trajectory, as well as the angle and shape of wings and body. Drawn accurately, your sketch will even suggest species or locale: a turkey vulture holds its wings in a shallow dihedral, geese fly in V's, shorebirds are as distinctive in flight as at rest—if they ever rest!

These additions can make the difference between your sketch itself having life or seeming oddly deserted. A sketch of the Maine seashore without its contingent of gulls and cormorants would look strange indeed.

MAKING COMPARISONS

Your sketches can be important adjuncts to learning if you use them in that way. Making comparisons between species, behavior patterns, size, shape, and so forth can teach you a great deal about the varieties of nature and how it works.

You may be interested in the effects of drought on animal life; your sketches of normal and drought-stressed animals can teach you a great deal. Even rural and urban or suburban comparisons can give rise to questions: Why are the deer that live in the nearby state park so fat and sleek, while those that frequent my local, small-town park are thin and have dull coats? How do behavior patterns differ between shorebirds and crows, for instance, and why do peregrine falcons have such a difficult time in the wild but seem to be doing just fine, thank you, in downtown Kansas City? These amateur comparisons can help me find answers from someone who knows.

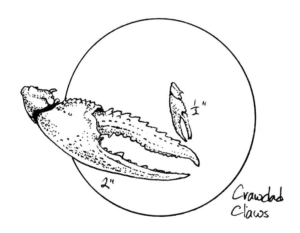

Use your sketches to make comparisons in size, shape, configuration—here, I learned the wide range possible in crawfish claws. (Razor-tipped pen.)

SIGNS OF LIFE

You may be about on a day when not an animal is to be seen (though a day without insects or birds is hard to imagine). You may like the sense of tracking, of a Sherlock-Holmes-like deduction that comes from reading the clues. You can learn a great deal about your area by sketching the signs of life you find: bird nests, insect tunnelings, galls and cocoons and chrysalises, mammal tracks, and so on. Learn to differentiate fox from dog tracks, and you'll know a great deal more about what's happening in your neighborhood.

Get to know the distinctive handlike marks of a raccoon, and you'll realize they are just as curious about us as we are about them. When I built my cabin in the woods, my piles of lumber were marked each morning by the trail of a curious raccoon and her babies. The deer seemed quite interested in what we were doing, as well. I never *saw* them, but each morning I'd find fresh tracks at the edge of the woods.

A sketchbook record of these signs can be just as interesting as drawings of the animals themselves; perhaps in some cases, more so. I can take the time to really explore the tracks of a deer—the size tells me whether this is an adult or a fawn (usually together, of course); the depth tells me how heavy the animal may be—a big buck's prints can sink into the earth farther; the shape tells me if the animals are walking or running.

Don't be disappointed if you see no animals when you go to sketch; just look deeper for whatever you can find. I found a single feather left like a calling card, telling me that a barred owl youngster visits my clearing when I'm not there.

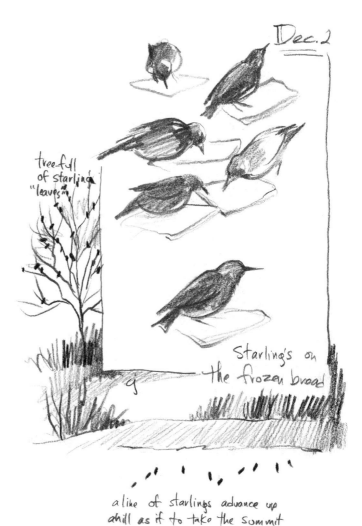

Bird shapes close up and at a distance make this sketch lively and informative. (Sketch pencil, B lead.)

Dec. 2

tree-full of starling "leaves"

Starling's on the frozen broad

a line of starlings advance up ahill as if to take the summit from an enemy!

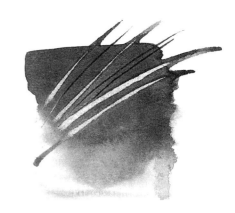

TWELVE

Sketching as a
Means to an End

*A*S WE'VE DISCOVERED by this stage of the game, sketching need have no more purpose than the doing itself—the pleasure of it. It's discovery and exploration in one, both means and end. But it *can* become a means to a specific end, whether that end is simply learning about the things you see or a more involved preparation for a larger or more detailed work, a drawing, illustration, or painting.

For example, you can pass time with a sketchpad; there's no need to let yourself be bored, ever. On a recent long wait at O'Hare Airport, I sketched my fellow passengers-to-be and it seemed only minutes before they told us to board the plane. (It was not, believe me.)

Calm your anxieties the same way. I'm not an old hand at jet travel, and it still seems quite aerodynamically impossible to me. I tend to white-knuckle a bit, but the naturalist in me discovers the incredible clouds beneath our wings and soon I've passed an hour or so with my sketchbook, understanding, finally, why something that is made up of minuscule bits of water vapor can agitate our plane in midair like bubbles in a saucepan. In my concentration on drawing, I've forgotten to be afraid of the agitation.

Sketching can record your experiences in a very personal and satisfying way; to me, more satisfying than the rolls and rolls of film I expose. On a recent trip to Maine, I shot seven rolls of snaps and filled half a hardbound sketchbook. Although there are many *more* images on film (over two hundred) and they are necessarily more varied, the thirty-nine sketches get to me. I remember the scents of balsam fir and seaweed as I sketched, and the hoarse, barking cries of great black-backed gulls. I recall the difficulty—all too clearly—of sketching at the edge of the woods while swatting constantly at blackflies and mosquitoes. I see the subtleties of fog's invasive curtain off the ocean in my mind's eye and hear the foghorns.

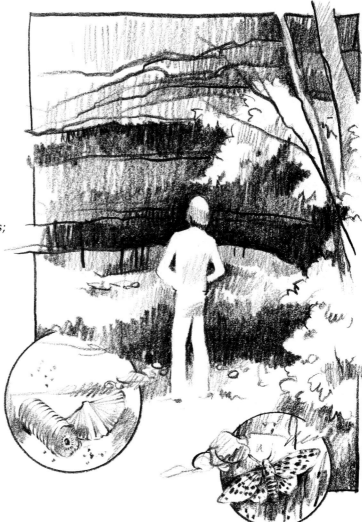

Sketchbook page with details; Ha Ha Tonka State Park, Missouri. (Prismacolor pencil.)

As a working artist-naturalist and professional illustrator, I know that my sketchbooks are as necessary to me as a trap is to a lobsterman or a camera to a photographer. I've got to have them. The details I record and the landscapes I sketch may turn up five years later in an illustration or painting or simply contribute to my understanding of a subject so that my work rings true. To anyone who paints wildlife or landscape, I can't recommend highly enough the practice of regular sketching.

Sketching can be an invaluable adjunct to study—whether formal and directed, in pursuit, perhaps, of a biology degree, or casual and self-directed for the sheer pleasure of learning. My sketched observations may find their way into my writing, never reaching the visual stage—in print—at all. Sketching can be a way to compare notes with the experts or the field guides and to discover if your findings are correct. A field sketchbook is a necessity if you plan to study at the college level; degree of artistic talent is beside the point. It can sharpen your powers of observation, letting you make your *own* comparisons.

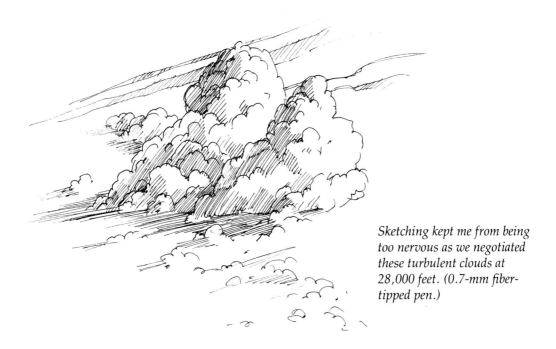

Sketching kept me from being too nervous as we negotiated these turbulent clouds at 28,000 feet. (0.7-mm fiber-tipped pen.)

THE NATURALIST'S DISCIPLINE

Whether you are a professional naturalist with a duty to the public or the scientific community or simply a dedicated amateur like myself, sketching can increase your experiential knowledge. When I sketch every day, I become more deeply acquainted with the natural rhythms, the ebbs and flows and growth and dyings of the world around me. I can keep my finger on the pulse of my tiny bit of Earth, monitoring its robust health or the stress of a long drought. I explore my own territory or get inside a new one, using the tip of my pen as a compass point to guide me.

Make no mistake, sketching *is* a discipline. It may not be easy to take time away from family and obligations—but set aside that time for yourself. It's important, for your own well-being as well as for the possibility of discovery. It's not always pleasant to sketch in the Midwest when the thermometer reads 100 degrees and counting upward and the humidity threatens to curl my paper under my hand. And the desert Southwest requires special precautions for survival if you plan to sketch in summer, so such precautions also become part of the discipline. It takes a bit of emotional distance to draw a road-killed quail or a particularly fierce-looking black widow spider, though in doing so you lose a bit of that squeamishness and a fair chunk of fear. (When I began drawing spiders, I was deathly afraid of them; as I forced myself to continue the study I found one day to my surprise that fear had become fascination without my noticing.)

As mentioned in Chapter 5, you may want to take specialized tools to aid in more accurate observation—binoculars, hand lens, and the like. But the discipline of doing, itself, is the most important tool. You may not be in the mood to produce a masterpiece; you may not have time to spend a half-hour to an hour on a habitat sketch supplemented with detail studies. Rather than letting yourself off with the excuse that you don't have time, instead do two or three quick gesture sketches, a memory drawing, or a modified contour sketch—but do it *often*. Your sketches need not be works of art. Composition, value range, or perspective don't even have to come into play. Just scribble down what you see and make written notes as supplements; you'll find the simplest sketch is sufficient for learning.

These sketches will allow you to delve more deeply into the published information available and let you ask more intelligent questions of the experts in the field. A life spent largely inland hadn't prepared me to wonder particularly how gulls extracted the meat from the neatly enclosed crabs and shellfish they feed on by the sea in Maine. The few gulls that find their way up the Missouri River to the lakes in my neck of the geographical woods seem mostly fish catchers by necessity, though we do have our share of freshwater mussels and crayfish, the inland relative of oceangoing arthropods like the lobster. Sketches of gulls dropping shellfish on the rocks near the lighthouse—and on the macadam road on the pier—reminded me of what I'd read years before, and I poked around in the remains of the gulls' dinner both literally and figuratively as I drew.

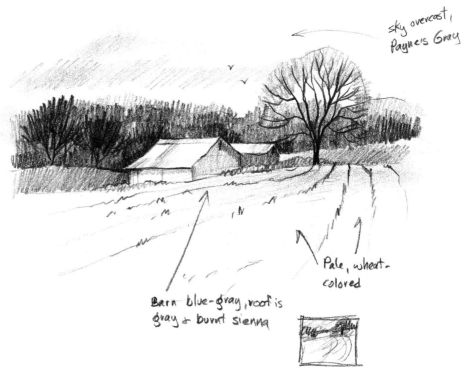

There are enough details present in this sketch—with notes—that I could do a satisfactory painting from it. The subject possessed strong value patterns, good compositional lines, and subtle colors; I responded emotionally to the scene as well as intellectually (these were our own barns when we lived on the farm); all the elements were there. Note the tiny thumbnail sketch in the lower right that helped me decide. ("Woodless" drawing pencil, HB.)

USING YOUR SKETCHES TO PLAN
A FINISHED WORK

Sketches may be used as studies for a larger work, a planning step that allows you to explore composition, subject, format, or mood quickly, without investing too much time. When I am planning a half-sheet watercolor (15 × 22 inches), I may do two or three quick thumbnail sketches to explore placement, value patterns, or whether a vertical or horizontal format would be more effective. A whole page of planning sketches can give me enough information for a half-dozen paintings—or only one.

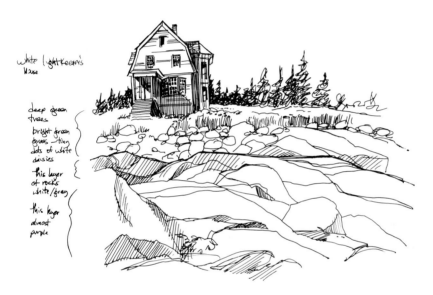

I knew I'd be working on the resulting painting later in the workshop and indoors; color notes let me remember clearly what it was that drew me to the sunny, summer scene. (See color section for finished painting.)

Capture salient features for later works. Try to be aware of what makes your subject unique, and zero in on that, either by letting that area of your sketch be most detailed or by doing larger detail studies on the same page for easy reference. In Maine, I began a painting of a tide pool a few hours past low tide. By the time I was ready to tighten up and render final details, the tide was rising inexorably. To my page of thumbnail and value sketches, I added a few barnacle studies and a sketch of the blue mussel that provided my center of interest, and finished the painting ensconced above the high-water line. In less than thirty minutes, my tide pool was under water.

This same kind of detail sketching can be helpful if you are visiting a new area you're unlikely to return to—at least before you complete your painting. Detailed sketches of wildflowers or rock formations can figure in later works, ready whenever you are.

ATMOSPHERIC ASIDES

Written notes can be helpful in completing a painting, to capture mood and color scheme in addition to the kind of notations most often used on field sketches (date, time, and so on). Here, I might note temperature and weather notes (cool, foggy? hot and blue with humidity?) or mention the birds I hear as I sketch. I may note my own mood—it could be homesick or peaceful, or simply a quiet openness to the experience. I might attempt to describe the fog with words as well as pictures. Later, these asides help me recapture mood and respond emotionally—once again—to my subject. It's a mental trick that helps me access inner "files." Even something so intangible as a scent noted in the margin can help me to feel the original excitement and produce a painting with more depth and feeling.

Oddly, these atmospheric notes that never appear at all in the finished works may be what keep them from being mere illustrations. They trigger feeling that lets me convey something intangible in my work. They're keys to memory.

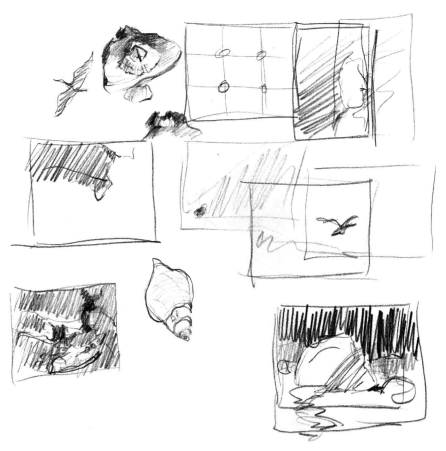

This is a page of explorations—a couple of thumbnail value sketches, a few quick gesture sketches, a memory sketch of a seashell (dog whelk?), and detail studies of barnacles. It's as interesting to me as if it contained a finished sketch. The barnacle details ended up in a painting later that day. (Mechanical pencil, HB lead.)

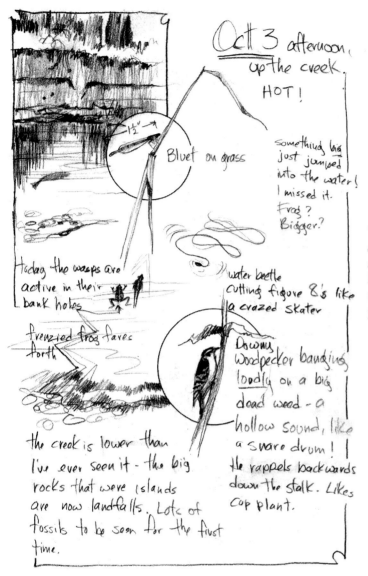

Oct 3 afternoon, up the creek. HOT!

1½"

Bluet on grass

something big just jumped into the water! I missed it. Frog? Bigger?

Today the wasps are active in their bank holes

water beetle cutting figure 8's like a crazed skater

frenzied frog fares forth

Downy woodpecker banging loodly on a big dead weed - a hollow sound, like a snare drum! He rappels backwards down the stalk. Likes Cup plant.

the creek is lower than I've ever seen it - the big rocks that were islands are now landfalls. Lots of fossils to be seen for the first time.

This field journal page has almost as many words as sketches. It brings the day back as clearly as if it were this morning. (Mechanical pencil, B lead.)

PUTTING IT ALL TOGETHER (WORKING FROM A NUMBER OF SKETCHES)

We don't always find just what we want to paint—or sketch, for that matter. You may come on the perfect habitat for a large landscape painting but at the juncture in time when *you* occupy it that habitat is as deserted as a small-town street at midnight. You wish there were a heron stalking the shallows or a moose up to its elbows in a still lake. You want to indicate the rocks and shells at the waterline, or suggest human habitation on a deserted stretch of coastline for scale—or for a sense of human recognition. A well-stocked sketchbook is a gold mine of details to add into such a scene. Here you may find a detail to add to a too-bare foreground, or a bit of additional information about the wildflowers you've only suggested.

Don't be afraid to mine those sketches for the elements you need—just check your additions for accuracy, especially if you are working for reproduction or if your work will be seen by wildlife enthusiasts. These people know what they're about; they can spot a mistake from a mile away, so before you play around with what you saw, do a little checking first, especially if you're on unfamiliar ground. Herons *do* frequent salt marshes, just not on the day I was there, so I was safe in including it in a painting of a marsh in Maine. But you wouldn't see a western jay on the Atlantic seacoast, for instance, no matter how much you admire that rich brilliant blue or how well it would complement your color scheme. A nocturnal animal wouldn't be calmly going about its business in broad daylight; that's where your written notes as to time of day or locale can help to keep you honest—and accurate.

TRANSFERRING YOUR SKETCH TO THE LARGER FORMAT

If you've settled on the basics of subject, format, and composition and produced a sketch you like, next you need to transfer the forms to your paper or canvas. But it's so easy to lose the spontaneity—or even the accuracy—of your sketch when it comes time to enlarge it for painting.

If you can work by eye, just redrawing your subject in larger format, do so. But if it seems difficult, there are a number of possible alternatives.

The classic grid technique can be most useful when shapes are crucial. Just divide your paper into nine sections (as shown) by drawing two lines vertically and two horizontally. (You can, of course, draw as many as you like if you want total accuracy; a one-inch or half-inch grid can be very useful.) If you don't want to draw these lines directly on your sketch, tape a piece of tracing paper over your drawing and make the grid lines on that.

Then make lines in the same proportions on your larger canvas or paper. Keep them quite light, in pencil or charcoal so they can be erased. Finally, simply draw what you see in each small box on your sketch into the corresponding space on your final working surface. Breaking it down in this way seems to help both the right and the left sides of the brain to deal with the complexities and subtleties of the process.

A more twentieth-century solution is to use an opaque projector—but it also requires equipment you may not have. A small opaque projector of the type most of us might own can take only a 6-inch original; larger images must be projected a section at a time, matching the edges as you go. The images tend to go in and out of focus as the device warms up (it houses an electric light bulb)—not usually a major problem in painting from nature (especially on the landscape scale), but the dickens if you're doing something that requires accurate perspective and tiny detail.

An art school, advertising agency, or large studio might have a lucidograph—a "Lucy" as it's called in commercial art. This is nothing more than an opaque projector on a truly grand scale; it can take larger images and tends to distort less. Try to rent time on one if you need such accuracy, or

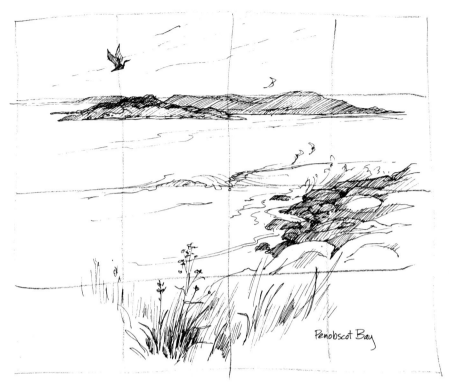

The grid method works well to transfer a sketch to the larger format. I would draw a rough approximation of these same grid lines on my watercolor paper, lightly, so they are easy to erase from the completed work, then sketch in the shapes as I saw them in each small rectangle. It's much easier, sometimes, to redraw several smaller segments than to try to recreate the angles or relationships of a larger area. (Sketch, 0.7-mm fiber-tipped pen with pencil grid lines.)

get permission to use one from a school. These large projectors may cost several thousand dollars, a bit much unless you are a professional illustrator.

Whether you're working with a Lucy or a more modest opaque projector, the room must be fairly dark for best results. You may find this a distraction; it can be hard on the eyes after a time, as well.

Tracing paper sketching can be a happy method; enlarge by grid or by eye, or do your original sketch on tracing paper. Erase (easy to do on this surface), or layer with fresh sheets until the image is accurate at the size you want. Use Saral or graphite paper between your tracing paper sketch and your finished working surface, and transfer your image to the final sheet. If you don't have access to graphite paper for transferring, remember the old school method and rub a soft pencil over the back of your tracing paper sketch. Flip it back over, tape to your finished sheet, and redraw over the lines; the image will appear on your working surface.

An even simpler transfer method, if you don't mind your image being reversed, is to turn the tracing paper sketch over, tape it in place so it won't shift about, and draw directly over your original lines. If you've used a fairly soft lead, they'll reproduce clearly enough to work from, a mirror image of your original.

Finally, if my sketch is just the size I plan to use in the finished piece, I may simply use a light box—or my studio window—to transfer it to a finished surface. Tape clean paper *over* your sketch and lay it over the opaque glass of a light table. A window works just as well, in the daytime, at least, although your hands may get tired of working in the upright position. Draw the major lines as you see them for an accurate image. Several sketches or individual elements can be combined in this way.

The only drawback to this method is that it requires sketching on paper that will be translucent when light shines through it—no matboard scraps here—and that can be easily manipulated. My hardbound sketchbooks do make this method difficult, but usually not impossible, with some sleight of hand. I can hold up a single page to the light and sketch over my second sheet lightly, or my husband offers a second pair of hands to hold the book up against the light for a few minutes.

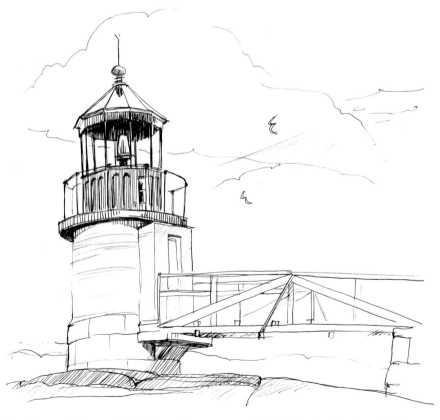

I used a variation on the lightbox theme to transfer this sketch of the Marshall Point Light to Denril, a surface very accepting of a number of mediums. I hated to tear the original from my sketchbook—and I didn't want to take the chance of getting those planes wrong—and so I didn't. I used translucent Denril directly over my hardbound sketchbook page and traced over it with a black ballpoint pen.

CREATIVE CROPPING

Your sketches may contain several latent compositions, allowing you more than one finished work for the same time and energy expended. Keep open to the possibilities. Use a viewfinder here, too, this time on your sketchbook page, to find areas to develop further. You may have enough information for a painting in a bit of distant landscape; a foreground may deserve further development. An interesting arrangement of lights, halftones, and darks can be enlarged to fill the picture plane.

Look at it from the other end, as well. You may have finished a painting that just misses the mark. Maybe you tried to do too much in one painting, or some areas are exciting and vivid while others just fall flat. Most artists find they like one area of a painting better than another, or that the foreground, say, just seems to present a problem. It may be boring, or too busy. Who is to say that a painting must be a full-sheet watercolor or a standard canvas size? Zero in on the areas that excite you, and cut away the rest with a sharp knife or a straight edge and scissors.

Use that viewfinder, again, to help you isolate the area—or areas—you like. Or cut two generous L's from matboard and move them around to find the spot you want to save. Remember, there may be more than one. Creative cropping can give you two or three wonderful, small works from one large failure. Develop them further if you like, or leave them as is. Mat, frame, and you're finished.

KEEPING A TRAVEL SKETCHBOOK

Your sketchbook can become a trip journal, one of my favorite uses. A hard-bound book format is especially useful, since it lets me maintain a consecutive continuity throughout, and keeps my memories safe in a permanent form. My Maine sketchbook contains fellow passengers, daily discoveries, detail studies, landscapes (and, yes, lighthouses), birds, shells, tide pools, written notes and musings, plus sketches of the stormy skies and towering clouds we flew back through. Other sketchbooks chronicle a trip to Nevada's deserts or a simple camping trip to the state park near my home.

Don't feel your travels must be exotic and far away to merit recording in journal form. Remember Massachusetts's most famous naturalist, Henry David Thoreau, who said, "I have traveled much in Concord." Well, I've traveled much in Missouri, specifically Clay and Ray counties, and feel they deserve a permanent record as much as Nevada's Valley of Fire. The experience itself allows me to appreciate home ground and to see that there is much to discover about the familiar.

Even a slightly different outlook opens my eyes to new sketching subjects. Drawing from my canoe allows me to explore habitat difficult to reach by land, making me privy to the feeding of a young green heron by its harried parent and letting me explore the muskrat's territory—from the muskrat's point of view. The silence of my canoe is wonderful for letting me get close enough to sketch without alarming the birds and animals I see.

If you choose to work from a boat or canoe, just remember to keep supplies simple, and waterproof if possible. A graphite or wax-based Prisma-

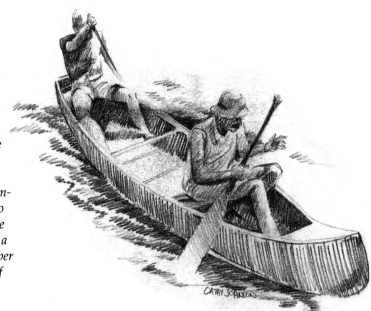

It was my turn next in the old canoe; I love to sketch from the water for a new viewpoint—birds and mammals seem more inclined to ignore me there, letting me get much closer in. Using a No. 2 pencil on typing paper freed me from the worry of losing—or dousing—my hardbound book.

color pencil, a permanent felt- or fiber-tipped pen would keep your work from being a total loss if spattered by a wave or dribbled on by an errant paddle—not to mention a full-scale dunking. This is a good place for expendable equipment; I'd never take my hardbound trip journal in the canoe, which is too easy to capsize. A small ringbound sketchbook works fine, and sketches can be transferred or taped in place in the larger book like keepsakes if you prefer.

While moving in the water, it may be best to keep supplies in a Zip-lock plastic bag or other waterproof container, then work only when you stop—especially if you're the prime mover. My husband often paddles slowly (without splashing) so I can continue to sketch—a great arrangement!

PERSONAL NOTES

A travel journal, like a field sketchbook, can be both written and drawn. Keep your observations and experiences noted in the margins or on facing pages, if you like, to bring it back alive. Keep souvenirs—small leaves or wildflowers (if these are not endangered), a spray of balsam fir, a napkin or placemat map from a roadside diner, even your baggage stub, tucked into the book. One traveler I know keeps all her "official papers" (in China, you need a ticket to sit on public benches; she passed up a needed rest to hang onto her souvenir), bits of memorabilia, notes, art, and photos in a single book, the most evocative work I've seen. I feel as though I'd gone with her on her world-wide adventures.

Your own travel sketchbooks can have the same effect and, as you muse over them, it will be almost as if you were there again in person. It comes back that clearly. A trip to the Galapagos may be a once-in-a-lifetime experience, but the memories can last forever.

WHERE TO BUY ART SUPPLIES

Most art supply stores carry the basic supplies for working on the spot. If they don't have a special section of travel supplies, keep your eyes open for things that will work for you—a small watercolor box or palette, a pencil box to keep your individual pencils in, a set of colored pencils, small or hardbound sketchbooks, and so on.

Office supply stores can be a good source for many of your needs—pencils, both wood and mechanical; pens; erasers; pencil boxes; and occasionally even colored pencil sets; inexpensive watercolors; and sketchbooks. (The inexpensive watercolor sets are fine for getting started, but graduate to better quality as soon as possible.)

But, aside from these obvious sources, where can you find supplies for sketching outdoors? Hobby and craft stores often carry the basics—sketchbooks, pencils, a minimum supply of paints and brushes.

Stationery stores or departments often have their own versions of what we used to call "empty books"—hardbound journal-style books with blank pages. Some of these are quite useless for sketching, with paper much too slick or thin, but others have satisfyingly heavy paper with a nice tooth for a number of mediums.

If you find you like a flat sketching pencil but are seldom near an art supply store, try a hardware store or lumberyard; often you can get a variety of hard pencils there.

Check with camping-supply stores or army surplus stores for water containers—my old canteen-and-cup arrangement came from one of these. Newer army surplus models are green plastic—probably lighter to carry—and have a snap-on cap.

These are the places to look for daypacks, as well. One with lots of pockets is wonderful for field work, with places to keep almost anything you need—with the exception of a folding stool or easel. Mine has room for a large watercolor palette and block, sketchbooks, water container, a thermos and lunch, plus a foam pad for sitting (eliminating the need for a folding stool quite nicely). Outside pockets carry small binoculars, a hand lens, and other incidental tools safely away from the art supplies—which do tend to get messy at times. Some daypacks even have slots for your favorite pens or pencils; talk about organized! Most are waterproof, an important consideration for field work.

If you are unable to find what you want near your home, consider mail order. These are some of the best sources I've found for sketching supplies:

—Daniel Smith, Inc., 4130 First Avenue South, Seattle, WA 98134, is, bar none, the finest source for the outdoor artist to my knowledge. Look in the large catalog for pack chairs, folding easels, traveling and field-style watercolor boxes, folding travel brushes (they carry a nice selection of their own folding brushes in both Kolinsky sable and synthetic blends), canvas brush carriers, watercolor blocks from size 5″×7″ to 18″×24″, pastels, colored pencil sets as well as individual pencils, a sketcher's brush pen, folding stools—you want it? They've got it. Add that to the fact that they're a pleasure to work with, have a customer-service department with encyclopedic knowledge, and fill orders with the care of a brain surgeon at work, and you'll see why I deal with Dan.

—On the East Coast, check with New York Central Art Supply, 62 Third Avenue, New York, NY 10003. Discount prices and eighty years of experience plus a wide selection of specialty items recommend this company to the outdoor artist.

—Dick Blick, P.O. Box 1267, Galesburg, IL 61401, has a very complete catalog of supplies; order from the location nearest you for quickest delivery. (Locations are listed on the back of the catalog, which is sent from the main office, above.)

—Pearl, C. C., 308 Canal Street, New York, NY 10013, advertises itself as the world's largest art and graphic discount center; I've talked to people who've ordered from them and were quite happy with the selection and service. They *do* advertise the small Cotman watercolor field box for some $30 less than list—definitely worth looking into.

—When you order from Utrecht, 33 Thirty-fifth Street, Brooklyn, NY 11232, you're ordering direct from a manufacturer and savings on colors, canvas, and so on can be impressive. Utrecht also carries other manufacturers' products. My cousin has dealt with them for years, and happily. The catalog is free.

—Recreational Equipment Inc., P.O. Box 88125, Seattle, WA 88125, has a catalog of camping and outdoor gear of use to the outdoor artist: look here for daypacks, field notebooks, folding stools, and canteens and other water carriers. Some of the latter are superior to artists' supplies in that they are very lightweight and leak-proof.

(Check with other camping-supply catalogs for a variety of usable items.)

WORKSHOPS AND
SKETCHING OPPORTUNITIES

T HERE ARE ALL TOO few of these available to the artist seriously interested in sketching rather than one of the more formal disciplines like
watercolor or oil, but many *do* include some field sketching as a part of the
curriculum. (Mine do, at any rate.)

To find an area of the country, a workshop, or a teacher that interests
you, look in the March workshop issue of *The Artist's Magazine*, 1507 Dana
Avenue, Cincinnati, OH 45207, (513) 531-2222 (or check your newsstand or
art supply store). I found a few there that looked promising, and that was
just among the larger ads. Look also in *The American Artist*, 1515 Broadway,
New York, NY 10036, for workshop information.

Check with your local college or university; there may be a summer or
evening program or a workshop on sketching or drawing.

Nature sanctuaries sometimes sponsor field sketching workshops or
seminars; the Martha Lafite Thompson Nature Sanctuary in Liberty, MO,
has several a year. Some national parks offer workshops in sketching, too.

Art museums sometimes sponsor workshops; call to find out, or express your interest—they may look into the possibility just for you.

Check nature and outdoor magazines for workshop possibilities: *Au-
dubon*, *National Wildlife*, *Outside*, *Sierra*, *Walking*, *Wilderness*, and so on, for
information on nature travel tours and photography workshops. Although
my luck in discovering workshops intended for field sketching in these
sources was poor, a tour or photo workshop will take you where you want
to go. Do your own work when you get there, or supplement with photos.

Or contact:

—Clare Walker Leslie, naturalist/artist and author of *Nature Drawing: A
Tool for Learning*, among others. 76 Garfield Street, Cambridge, MA
02138.

—Maine Coast Art Workshops, P.O. Box 236, Port Clyde, ME 04855. Contact Merle Donovan. This is beautiful sketching country; I recommend it highly. A number of artists provide workshops through the June-to-October season.

—Roger Tory Peterson Institute, 311 Curtis St., Jamestown, NY 14701. Phone (716) 665-2473. Various techniques for sketching in nature are covered in these workshops, which are given around the country.

—Jessica Zemsky and Jack Hines, P.O. Box 1043, Big Timber, MT 59011. Jessica and Jack have been doing workshops at a remote mountain lodge for twenty-one years. They emphasize sketching and drawing as well as working from nature. In addition to their own teaching stints, Jessica and Jack bring in a variety of other well-known artists, like Robert Bateman, Nita Engles, and Guy Cohleach.

Check with your local artists' association for workshops and sketching opportunities close to home. Galleries, as well as the art departments of schools and colleges, should have a contact name for you.

BIBLIOGRAPHY

*I*T MAY BE difficult to find a workshop that will offer outdoor sketching opportunities, but there are a number of helpful magazines, such as *The Artist's Magazine* and *American Artist*, as well as many excellent books on the market that can guide your individual studies, whether your interest lies strictly in field sketching, wildlife painting, or working from nature in general.

Books come and go; some that are available now may not be by the time you read this. Check with your local library, or look at national or state parks stores; you may be surprised to find something very special.

Some of the most useful books are from the masters; they're not instructional, per se, but they *are* inspirational. Look for Rembrandt, Michelangelo, Winslow Homer, Asher Durand, and Andrew Wyeth; their sketches are some of the finest around.

Here are some of my favorites:

Adams, Norman, and Joe Singer. *Drawing Animals*. New York: Watson Guptill, 1979. This older book is an oldie but goodie and well worth finding.

Dodson, Bert. *Keys to Drawing*. Cincinnati: North Light Books, 1985. This book is not about drawing from nature per se, but the information it offers on drawing is superb. Beautifully designed.

Edwards, Betty. *Drawing on the Right Side of the Brain*. Los Angeles: J. P. Tarcher, 1979. The revised and expanded version, 1989, includes a color section. This is the bible for learning how to see like an artist.

Gayton, Richard. *Artist Outdoors*. Englewood Cliffs, NJ: Prentice-Hall, 1987. The U.S. West is the locale for this lovely book. Fine landscape drawings.

Gurney, James, and Thomas Kinkade. *The Artist's Guide to Sketching*. New York: Watson Guptill, 1982. This is one of my favorite books on sketching everything you can name—urban as well as wild.

Hinchmann, Hannah. *A Life in Hand: Creating the Illuminated Journal*. Salt Lake City: Peregrine Smith Books, 1991. A wonderful and inspiring little book that comes in a slipcase with its own sketch journal for you to work in.

Johnson, Cathy. *Drawing and Painting from Nature*. New York: Design Press, 1989. Covers painting, drawing, old masters and new.

———. *Painting Nature's Details in Watercolor*. Cincinnati: North Light Books, 1987. A watercolor-oriented study of nature.

———. *Sketching and Drawing*. Cincinnati: North Light Books, First Steps Series, 1995. Step-by-step instructions cover the basics in a sketchbook format.

———. *Watercolor*. Cincinnati: North Light Books, First Steps Series, 1995. Another step-by-step informational book covers the basics from supplies to easy techniques.

Leslie, Clare Walker. *The Art of Field Sketching*. Dubuque, IA: Kendall/Hunt, 1995. A wonderful introduction to the subject; includes the work of professional naturalists, illustrators, and students.

———. *Nature Drawing: A Tool for Learning*. Dubuque, IA: Kendall/Hunt, 1995. This book truly is what the title promises. Enjoy it.

Mohrhardt, David. *How to Paint Songbirds, How to Paint Shorebirds*. Harrisburg, PA: Stackpole Books, 1989. Step-by-step offerings in gouache and acrylic, sketching, reference drawings.

Sims, Graeme. *Painting and Drawing Animals*. New York: Watson Guptill, 1983. There is more drawing than painting here, and the technique is fresh and interesting.

Noninstructional books can also be quite useful; look at the sketches in field guides and nature anthologies. Look for books on specific areas or ecosystems and for naturalist/artists' published sketchbooks (Keith Brockie, Janet Marsh, Clare Walker Leslie, Marjorie Blamey, and Glen Loates come to mind).

But for sheer inspiration and an intimate look into what field sketching can be, I recommend any of Ann Zwinger's books, richly illustrated with her wonderful pencil drawings.